PENGUIN BOOKS

A QUESTION OF ECONOMICS

Peter Donaldson was born in Manchester in 1934 but left shortly afterwards for Kent, where he went to Gillingham Grammar School and won an open scholarship to Balliol. He read politics, philosophy and economics, and graduated from Oxford in 1956. He then taught very briefly in a secondary modern school and for two years in a college of technology before taking up a university appointment at Leeds. He was a lecturer in the department of economics at Leicester University from 1959 to 1962, when he also did a good deal of work for the Leicester and Nottingham University adult education departments and for the Workers' Educational Association.

At the end of 1962, he was one of the first British university teachers to be seconded to key positions in underdeveloped countries under the scheme for Commonwealth Educational Cooperation. He was appointed, for two years, as Visiting Reader in Economics at the Osmania University, Hyderabad, and subsequently extended his stay in India to four years.

From 1967 to 1991 he taught at Ruskin College, Oxford. Over the years he has also done a considerable amount of broadcasting, including two series for radio, two for BBC television and one for ITV. His many books include *Worlds Apart*, *10 × Economics*, *Economics of the Real World* and, with John Farquhar, *Understanding the British Economy*, all of which are published in Penguin.

A QUESTION OF ECONOMICS

Peter Donaldson

Supplementary material by Roy Moore

Penguin Books
in association with Channel Four Television Company Limited
and Yorkshire Television Limited

PENGUIN BOOKS

Published by the Penguin Group
Penguin Books Ltd, 27 Wrights Lane, London W8 5TZ, England
Penguin Books USA Inc., 375 Hudson Street, New York, New York 10014, USA
Penguin Books Australia Ltd, Ringwood, Victoria, Australia
Penguin Books Canada Ltd, 10 Alcorn Avenue, Toronto, Ontario, Canada M4V 3B2
Penguin Books (NZ) Ltd, 182–190 Wairau Road, Auckland 10, New Zealand

Penguin Books Ltd, Registered Offices: Harmondsworth, Middlesex, England

First published in Pelican Books 1984
Reprinted in Penguin Books 1990
10 9 8 7 6 5 4 3

Reproduced, printed and bound in Great Britain by
BPCC Hazell Books
Aylesbury, Bucks, England
Member of BPCC Ltd.

Typeset in Linotron Times by
Roland Phototypesetting Ltd
Bury St Edmunds, Suffolk

Illustrated by Raymond Turvey

Contents

Preface

A Question of Economics is for those who have no previous knowledge of economics but are bemused by the typical presentation of economic news and information in the newspapers and on television and radio, to the point at which they feel they should improve their understanding of matters that so profoundly affect us all. It is for those who wonder just what *is* the FT Index, what it *means* when it is announced that 'the pound had another bad day' – or who are more deeply concerned about mass unemployment, the future of the social services, our long-run economic and social prospects. It is for those who rightly sense that there is a deep rift between economists which has to be understood if we are to make a rational economic choice between the political alternatives on offer.

What I have done is to take twenty key economic issues of today and to present them as clearly as I can without simplifying them out of recognition. Each chapter takes one of the questions that form part of current controversy and explains the basic economic principles involved and the value considerations that underlie the analysis, with the text supplemented by additional illustrative material where appropriate.

How did we lapse from full employment and can we ever re-achieve it? What happened to the prosperity promised by North Sea oil? What are monetarism and Keynesianism and do they work? Is Britain now more competitive? What caused the world recession and how have others coped? These are the broad issues dealt with in the first half of the book.

The second ten chapters draw out the economic and value implications of increased reliance on 'market forces' – the provision of private health care, privatization of industries, incentives and income distribution. They also look at major power groups like big business, the City and the unions, and ask questions about the role of the individual in the economy.

I have reluctantly limited the scope of the book to aspects of the economic debate as it is taking place in the UK of the mid eighties. Wider considerations – of alternative approaches to economics, the operation of economic systems very different from our own, and the grotesque inequalities that continue to divide the nations of the world –

7

are neglected here simply because a view of our own immediate problems absorbs all the space available.

I am deeply grateful for the work of my friend and colleague, Roy Moore, in not only providing all the supplementary material but also in earlier drafting; I am only sorry that his commitments prevented the even fuller involvement that we had originally envisaged. My thanks are also due to Chris Jelley, Head of Education at Yorkshire Television, for his help in the early planning stage, and to Adrian Perry, Vice-Principal of Shirecliffe College, Sheffield, for his general encouragement and particular contribution to Chapter 9. Finally, there are Sheila, and Sally, Adam and Amanda – who would be embarrassed to appear on the flyleaf but to whom this, like all my work, is implicitly dedicated.

The book is associated with a twenty-part television series made by Yorkshire Television for Channel 4. It follows the order and broad programme content of the series although it is designed to have an independent existence of its own.

For those who wish to study the subject in more depth the National Extension College has published a self-study text based on the book. The text may be studied independently or as part of an NEC correspondence course. Students who enrol on the course and successfully complete the recommended course-work will be eligible for a B Tec Record of Success, which is one part of the B Tec Certificate in Business Administration.

Details of the NEC material are available free on request from:
National Extension College,
18, Brooklands Avenue,
Cambridge, CB2 2HN

1

Can We Afford the Dole?

● *Do you regard the unemployed as work-shy? Too pampered by state benefits to bother to look for work? Perhaps if today's young people took proper advantage of better education in more relevant subjects, they might have a better chance of getting jobs?*
OR
● *Do you sympathize with the unemployed as casualties of economic policies and industrial change? Are you edgy about the extent to which these consequences are concentrated upon particular groups of people in our population? And in particular concerned at the huge rises in young people's unemployment and in longer-term unemployment? Mustn't there be something seriously wrong somewhere?*

This opening chapter looks at the nature and scale of the UK's rising unemployment, and what it is costing to support it.

The winter of 1971 was a watershed, with unemployment in the UK creeping above the 3 per cent mark for the first time during the postwar period: three quarters of a million people out of work. Some of these showed up in the statistics only because they were in the process of moving from one job to another – what economists call 'frictional unemployment'. Some were 'unemployable' because of physical or other disabilities. (The lowest annual unemployment ever recorded was just over 1 per cent, in 1955.)

But that left 3–400,000 wanting work, capable of work and unable to find it. This was a number far in excess of the jobs waiting to be filled – most of which were anyway in areas or needing skills which didn't match those of the unemployed.

It was a matter of considerable concern. There was a widespread view that unemployment was approaching a politically unacceptable level. The prospect of it rising still further, to above a million, was barely thinkable.

But at least it was a far cry from the *mass* unemployment that had blighted the interwar years. No one contemplated the possibility of that

The Rising UK Unemployment Rate (expressed as a percentage)

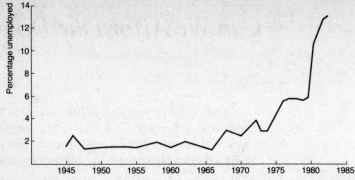

Note:
- Until the late sixties the UK's rate of unemployment hardly exceeded 1½ per cent.
- In 1971 it reached 3 per cent for the first time since the war.
- By the late seventies it was settled at around 6 per cent.
- In the eighties it has been around 12 per cent.

Source: *Abstract of Labour Statistics*, Ministry of Labour and Department of Employment.

ever recurring. The suggestion that in little over a decade the number out of work might be well over three million and rising would have been dismissed as inconceivable. Democratic society would never again tolerate such a trauma. Certainly no government would be able to survive the mischance or mismanagement that led to such a disaster. Indeed, we would be on the verge of social and political breakdown.

Attitudes to unemploy- ment

And yet in the mid-eighties, instead of anger there is almost apathetic acceptance of unemployment, resignation rather than outrage. The existence of millions out of work poses no overt threat to the government of the day. Whatever happened to the revolution?

There are many causes of this seemingly indifferent attitude of the electorate:

- The widespread view that mass unemployment is due to forces which it is not possible for governments to control.
- The number of those remaining in work who continue to become better off and who do not feel that their own job security is threatened.
- The belief that unemployment is the necessary price to be paid for achieving competitive efficiency and low inflation.

These are matters to which we shall return at length in subsequent chapters. But first we look at the surprisingly prevalent myths suggesting that the problem is greatly exaggerated by the substantial proportion who are simply work-shy and therefore unemployed of their own volition.

Jobs and vacancies

Most crudely, this view is supported by reference to the number of jobs seen advertised in the newspapers or by anecdotal accounts of the difficulty in finding someone to mend the garden gate. Plenty of work for those who really want it and are prepared to seek it out.

How Do We Share Our Unemployment?

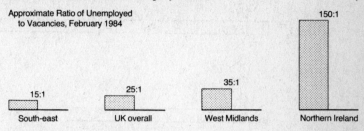

Approximate Ratio of Unemployed to Vacancies, February 1984

15:1 South-east
25:1 UK overall
35:1 West Midlands
150:1 Northern Ireland

Source: Department of Employment.

The truth is very different. In 1984, the national ratio of registered unemployed to registered job vacancies was no less than twenty-five to one. In some parts of the country, it was massively greater – in Northern Ireland, for example, with one vacancy for every 150 jobless. Regional disparities like this have always existed. But today, even in the most prosperous areas like London and the south-east, unemployment dwarfs the employment opportunities. Once a regional problem from which certain parts of the country were largely immune, unemployment has now become a national disaster – although certain sections of the community are still particularly badly hit.

Occupational Hazards

Estimated rates of unemployment

White collar   6%

Manual   20%

Source: Estimated from Department of Employment data, March 1982.

Work-shy?

Another version of the myth that the army of the unemployed is largely made up of volunteers points to the cushioning effects of the welfare state in reducing the will to work. However, the facts hardly support the bar-room fantasy that the unemployed luxuriate on the

11

Average Earnings (Weekly), April 1983

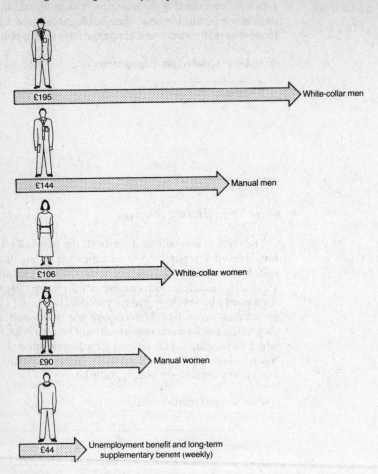

£195   White-collar men

£144   Manual men

£106   White-collar women

£90   Manual women

£44   Unemployment benefit and long-term supplementary benefit (weekly)

Source: Department of Employment New Earnings Survey and Department of Health and Social Security.

'social', worrying mainly about where to park their cars while collecting their state hand-outs.

Certainly the level of poverty endured by the unemployed of today is not that of the 1930s. They are better off than they would have been then, as indeed are those who are in work. But:

• It is estimated that the average family is likely to receive only 30–50 per cent of its work income when unemployed.

• The basic unemployment benefit for a family with two children is only

£44 a week compared with average male earnings of £160 a week.
● Unemployment benefit only lasts for one year. Thereafter, the unemployed must rely on supplementary benefit but this is payable at a short-term rate which is 20 per cent lower than the long-term rate available to other beneficiaries.
● The gap between the average income of the unemployed and average earnings has widened in recent years.
● Supplementary benefit is not generous. Indeed, social researchers frequently apply a definition of the 'poverty line' in the UK as supplementary benefit *plus* 40 per cent.

Surely only a small minority of those without jobs have such an extreme aversion to work that they willingly accept such penal consequences of unemployment?

Poverty trap

This is not to deny that there are those who find themselves caught in the so-called 'poverty trap'. A small proportion of the total unemployed are on *relatively* high supplementary benefits, generally because of the number of their dependent children. For these the purely monetary incentive to work may be quite low. That is because accepting a low-paid job may involve tax and other deductions such as national insurance contributions which together mean that their additional take-home pay is negligible.

However, there are three points to note even about this group:
● Many of them may none the less prefer to work for their income rather than receive it in the form of state doles.
● The problem of the poverty trap stems partly from the tax structure, but also from the existence of low pay, which itself falls within the general definition of poverty.
● When jobs are simply not available, how many people are actually work-shy is an academic question.

In this respect the recommendation from some economists and politicians for 'solving' the problem by reducing the level of benefits paid to the unemployed is callous or irrelevant. Either it *would* increase the number of jobs available – but at wage rates below the poverty line. Or it would not, so that those remaining unemployed would merely find their present living standard further depressed.

But the fact that many of those *in* employment earn incomes only little higher than those on the dole must be one of the factors explaining why those in work are perhaps less passionately sympathetic about the plight of the unemployed than might be expected. The problems of unemployment and of low pay are overlapping.

Financial cost of unemployment

The penalties attached to being without work are severe. But it is those in work who actually have to foot the bill. Keeping more than three million people in unproductive misery is very expensive indeed.

Thus on average it costs each person in this country who has a job no less than £700 a year, about £14 a week, to pay for unemployment.

Estimates suggest that the total financial costs of unemployment are currently running at some £17,000 million a year – more than half the amount that we pay in income tax. It is more than the revenue that government receives from the North Sea at the time of its peak exploitation, the oil and gas that were once heralded as ushering in an era of unprecedented prosperity for us all.

There are two main categories in the financial costs of unemployment:
● There is additional *spending* by government in unemployment benefit, supplementary benefit and redundancy money.
● And there is the *loss of revenue* – the income tax, national insurance contributions and taxes on goods and services – that the unemployed would have paid had they been in work and earning higher incomes.

Apart from these direct costs there are others to take into account which are important, even though we can't attach a precise money value to some of them.
● There is evidence that unemployment leads to undesirable and costly social effects like stress and nutritionally related deterioration in the health of the unemployed and their families, drug addiction and an increase in certain types of crime.
● There is the nearly £2,000 million a year recently being spent on a variety of work experience and youth training schemes. Some of these may be purely cosmetic while others have considerable intrinsic merits. But to the extent that they do not in themselves create additional job opportunities they must be regarded as a further burden on the taxpayer arising from unemployment.

Long-term Unemployment: Proportion of Total Unemployed by Duration

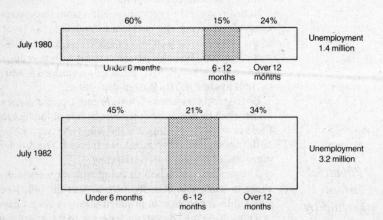

Source: Department of Employment.

14

The economist's approach

In addition to calculating and arguing about the financial bill for unemployment, economists also have their own distinctive way of looking at the 'costs' involved. This stems from their general view that a central problem common to all economies is that there are only limited resources available from which to meet a wide range of competing demands.

These resources, often called 'factors of production', consist of:
- *land* – including not just agricultural and building land itself but also other natural endowments like mineral deposits, climate and fertility;
- *labour* – the total quantity and quality of human skills, knowledge and enterprise;
- *capital* – a country's accumulated stock of factories, machines, docks, roads, schools and hospitals which directly or indirectly contribute towards future production in the economy.

It is possible to add to these resources (or to deplete them) but only at a relatively modest rate in relation to the total. They are therefore relatively fixed in supply.

But the calls that we would like to make on them are to all intents and purposes unlimited. Disapproving though some critics of our consumer society may be, the great majority of people would like to buy *more* clothes, washing-machines, video recorders, holidays and the like. There is a pressing need for improvements in the health service and education, sewage and other public amenities. Our stock of housing badly requires increasing and improving. British industry is due for wholesale modernization.

The upshot is that resources are *scarce* in relation to the potential demands that might be made upon them. Thus *if* they were all fully employed, then it would only be possible to increase production of a particular sort by reducing the output of something else. Awkward economic choices would arise. More housing or more factories? More missiles or better hospitals?

Opportunity cost

It is on this basis that the economist measures the cost of producing something: in terms of the sacrifice of alternative production that it entails. This is known as *opportunity cost*. Cost, in other words, calculated by the output opportunities that have to be forgone as a result.

But does the concept of opportunity cost still apply when resources, far from being scarce, are lying idly unemployed – where we could have both more houses *and* more factories, more missiles *and* better hospitals? It certainly does, because unemployment has an opportunity cost in itself, the lost output of all sorts that might otherwise have been produced if resources had been fully utilized.

This is very difficult to measure and all that can be offered here are guesses as to the order of magnitude that might be involved. One such estimate was made by the Manpower Services Commission in 1981 and indicated that for every 100,000 extra unemployed over a base of

700,000 there would be an opportunity cost of £590 million forgone output. On this basis the true economic cost of three and half million out of work would be some £14 billion.

Cutting off the Chancellor's Nose to Spite His Face

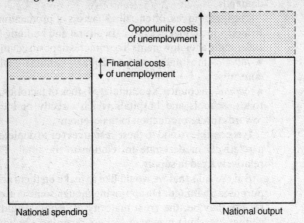

Opportunity costs of unemployment

Financial costs of unemployment

National spending

National output

The *financial costs* of unemployment, representing government payments to the unemployed and loss of potential government tax revenue from them, are serious enough . . .

. . . but the *opportunity costs* of unemployment representing national output forgone by failure to use available labour resources, are greater still, especially on a cumulative basis over the years.

The figure is very similar to that of the financial costs of unemployment, but that is coincidental and the two must be clearly distinguished:
• financial costs are transfers of income from the employed to the unemployed which give them purchasing power over part of *existing output*;
• the economic cost shows the value of production *over and above* existing output levels which has been lost as a result of unemployment.

Loss of potential output

There is some overlapping of the two totals because the financial costs include the tax payments that workers would have made if they had been employed. But beyond that, economic cost measures output which could have been produced, was not produced, and has been lost for ever. So far we have done the sums only for a single year. Adding the totals together over a period of time, say 1979–84, we get a grand loss in potential output of the order of £60 billion. That is nearly one-third of all that we produced in 1984 – or four times what we spend annually on the NHS or defence.

Even this may be an underestimate of the opportunity cost inflicted by years of mounting unemployment. Since 1979 the economy has frequently stagnated or declined. If, as well as achieving full employment, it had continued to grow at some 2½ per cent per annum, then national output would, astonishingly, now be half as much again as its present level. (It can be argued that this was not possible because of the slowdown in *world* economic expansion during these years. But one of the main factors in the world recession was the rise in oil prices from which Britain should have been relatively immune as a result of the fortuitous exploitation of its own reserves at this time – as we shall discuss in Chapter 8.)

Costs of closures

The notion of opportunity cost can also be applied to cases where fresh unemployment is threatened. Take for example a steel plant or coal-mine which is clearly incurring financial losses. Should that be the end of the matter, a clear criterion for closure and a consequent increase in unemployment? The economist is interested in the uses to which the resources involved might otherwise be put. If the plant is highly specialized and specific to the industry and if no alternative openings are available for workers losing their jobs, then the conclusion may well be that the *economic* cost of maintaining present production is practically zero. Closure may simply reduce output without bringing about a more efficient redeployment of resources.

Costs of expansion?

To look at the question the other way round, is it not true that the opportunity cost of *increasing* employment is also negligible? Getting people back to work leads to a double pay-off:
● a reduction in the present tax burden of maintaining the unemployed;
● availability of goods and services that we shall not otherwise produce.
Surely it is better for people to be paid for producing something than for producing nothing?

Or are there hidden opportunity costs in such expansionism as well? Might it be that if employment were stimulated this would lead, for example, to unacceptable inflation or to balance-of-payments difficulties of such an order that unemployment would naturally re-emerge? Would they therefore not be 'real jobs' that were created? Is there some sense in which we can't *afford* to boost the economy?

Certainly there are economists who argue along these lines and this has been the rhetoric of recent governments. It is a debate that will occupy many subsequent chapters.

Unemployment, some will claim, has been a necessary evil. It is an inevitable adjustment to the excesses of postwar economic policy that led to soaring inflation and a loss of competitiveness. Unemployment is the painful price that has to be paid to bring inflation under control and to create a leaner, fitter economy capable of competing in world markets.

For the moment all that we can conclude is that the price has been an

17

extraordinarily high one – and to suggest that an economy in which there are millions who are unwillingly, unhappily unemployed is one in which something has gone radically wrong.

How Many Unemployed?

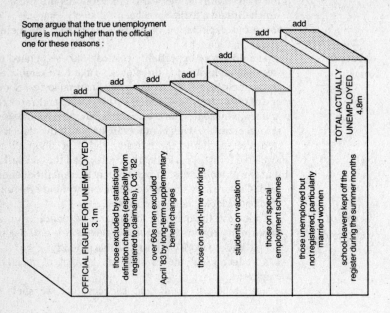

Some argue that the true unemployment figure is much higher than the official one for these reasons :

add — add — add — add — add — add — add

OFFICIAL FIGURE FOR UNEMPLOYED 3.1m

those excluded by statistical definition changes (especially from registered to claimants), Oct. '82

over 60s men excluded April '83 by long-term supplementary benefit changes

those on short-time working

students on vacation

those on special employment schemes

those unemployed but not registered, particularly married women

school-leavers kept off the register during the summer months

TOTAL ACTUALLY UNEMPLOYED 4.8m

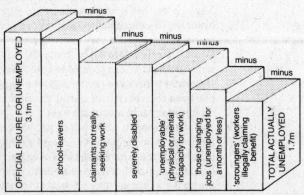

Others offer examples of categories, counted in the unemployed total, whose inclusion is questionable and therefore inflates the true figure:

minus — minus — minus — minus — minus — minus

OFFICIAL FIGURE FOR UNEMPLOYED 3.1m

school-leavers

claimants not really seeking work

severely disabled

'unemployable' (physical or mental incapacity for work)

those changing jobs (unemployed for a month or less)

'scroungers' (workers illegally claiming benefit)

TOTAL ACTUALLY UNEMPLOYED 1.7m

Source: Inspired by David Lipsey, *Sunday Times*, 6 November 1983.

2

Is Britain Going Bust?

'Britain's balance of trade in manufacturing goods deteriorated sharply in the first three months of the year, although this was offset by a record surplus in oil trade, according to official figures out yesterday.'

Economics news such as this regularly appears in newspapers and on television screens, underlining how the UK, once the 'workshop of the world', now buys more manufactures from abroad than it sells. The chances of your consumer durables, such as car, TV, video, etc., being imports have never been greater.

But it is not only manufactured goods which affect the UK's foreign trade and finance. If your last holiday was spent abroad, or if the occupational pension fund to which you contribute has been increasing its investment overseas, you will be contributing also to the balance of payments under other headings.

There are thus many ways in which we affect, and are affected by, our balance of payments. This chapter looks at these, including the scale of the deterioration which has been concealed by our North Sea oil.

For better or for worse?

What we are told is happening to the economy and what we see with our own eyes are sometimes difficult to reconcile. The shops and showrooms seem as bulging and bustling as ever. New car registrations, sale and hire of video recorders, installations of fitted kitchens, foreign holiday bookings – all are at odds with the picture of economic woe painted by so many of our economic commentators.

The facts of the matter are painstakingly compiled by the government statisticians:

● taking a long view, we have on average become some two and a half times better off during the postwar period;

● average industrial earnings by 1984 had reached some £7,500 p.a. – that's £150 a week;

● even in the years 1979–83, average take-home pay (after allowing for inflation) rose by about 5 per cent.

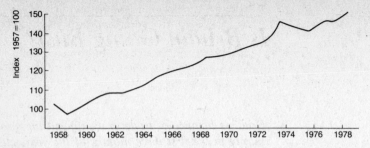

UK Standard of Living: Real Income per Head (1975 prices)

Source: OECD and NEDO.

But for millions of people these facts, too, are an unrecognizable portrayal of their actual economic condition. Whether *you* feel better off, whether indeed you really are better off, depends on a great variety of factors. The main one is if you are one of the 13 per cent unemployed or of the 87 per cent who still have a job. But your prosperity will also be affected by where you happen to live, your age, colour and sex, size of family and the industry or occupation which you work in. The figures just quoted are averages, not generalizations, and they conceal at least as much as they tell us.

The mystery remains of how, as a nation, if not for all its members, we have managed to maintain and even increase our affluence during these recent difficult years – with one factory closure after another, massive loss of ground to our foreign competitors *and* the huge burden of mass unemployment. If we were to call in a firm of accountants to scrutinize the books, what might they have to say about the present state of UK Ltd?

UK Ltd

They might point first to the vast assets of the company – its natural resources, labour force and capital stock. Over a long period of time these have been expanded, improved and combined more efficiently to generate ever-increasing levels of output. The UK performance in this respect might be criticized on many counts – the consultants might list the inadequate training and attitudes of labour, weaknesses in management, and insufficient investment in new capital as being among the factors holding UK economic growth at rates below that of its rivals. But until the past decade the economy, after 1945, did more or less consistently achieve a 2½–3 per cent annual rise in output, a historically unprecedented growth rate.

During recent years the record has been altogether less satisfactory. And in assessing the present and future viability of UK Ltd, there are two interrelated items in the company accounts that call for most particular attention. The first is the windfall gain enjoyed by the UK as a

20

result of North Sea oil and gas since the mid-seventies. And the second is the state of UK trading and other transactions with the rest of the world.

North Sea: benefits and uses

These are interrelated because the benefits of the North Sea bonanza are seen in two main ways:
- in providing government with an immensely lucrative source of tax revenues – by 1984, £11 billion, some 13 per cent of the total;
- in saving us having to earn the huge amounts of foreign currency that would otherwise have been needed to pay for imported fuels.

During the mid-seventies there was considerable debate about how the once-and-for-all benefits from the North Sea could be maximized. For example, should the revenues be used to cut other taxes while maintaining government spending at its present level, or to finance additional public expenditure? But the main focus of the debate was how (and not *whether*) the windfall could be used to strengthen the economy in readiness for when the oil ran dry rather than simply fritter it away in greater immediate consumption. There were those who argued that this could best be done by putting money into people's pockets – and relying on them to undertake the necessary investment. And there were those who thought such funds would be better directed through government agencies.

TODAY'S SPENDING OR TOMORROW'S INCOME?

This distinction between consumption and investment is a key one in economics.
- **Consumption** means spending in order to satisfy immediate, or *current*, wants such as food, clothing and fuel.
- **Investment** means spending in order to create or maintain the ability to produce goods and services for a *future* flow of output. Such spending is also known as *capital* expenditure. It may be on *fixed* assets, such as buildings, plant, equipment and machinery, or on stocks of materials.

(Investment in economics thus has a different meaning to its everyday use as a description of buying shares or saving with a building society, etc.)

Both consumption and investment can be undertaken by either the private or the public sector. Consumption can be by private individuals on cars, videos, etc., or by public spending on various services such as health and education. Similarly, investment can be by private businessmen in plant and equipment, or take the form of capital expenditure on hospitals, motorways, etc., by government departments, local authorities and nationalized industries.

21

There was general agreement within the 'great debate' of the seventies that investment rather than consumption should be benefited by the UK's North Sea oil. Argument continued, however, over whether the investment should be publicly controlled or left to the private sector of individual consumers and private businessmen.

In diagrammatic summary:

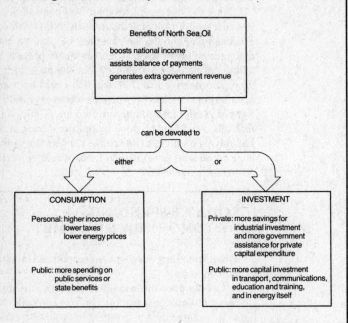

Although everyone seemed agreed that the right-hand box should take priority for the application of the benefits of North Sea oil, its proceeds have in fact been devoted exclusively to the financing of additional unemployment in the lower half of the left-hand box.

The outcome can have satisfied neither school of thinking. The era of self-sufficiency in oil has coincided with a deep recession, the causes of which we shall be examining in later chapters. The main effect of that recession has been mass unemployment – involving, as we have seen, a huge financial cost. Oil revenues have been used to meet that cost without the increases in taxation that would otherwise have been necessary. In other words, oil has been mainly used to allow us to maintain and, indeed, even increase our levels of consumption.

What is more, a substantial proportion of this consumption has been of foreign rather than UK goods and services – paid for from foreign currency that would have been needed for imported fuels if the North Sea had not been exploited. For the details we must look at the UK *balance of payments*: that is, the record of all our transactions with the rest of the world.

Balance of payments

This is an area in which it is difficult for the non-economist to get excited. Partly this is the result of ignorance about what the accounts actually mean; for example, does a 'surplus' in our dealings with foreigners represent earnings that mean a hospital due for closure can be kept open after all? Partly it is because the balance of payments seems an abstraction remote from our everyday lives. But in fact it has the most serious implications – for jobs and for our standard of living.

The main component in a country's balance of payments is the account of all the trade it does with other nations in goods or merchandise – so-called 'visible' imports and exports. This *balance of trade* is that generally referred to by newscasters when they gravely intone last month's 'trade figures' (often made even more meaningless by a comment from the Economics Correspondent suggesting they are 'distorted by exceptional factors').

Why trade?

Trading with other countries is simply specializing internationally in the same way that we do internally. It enables us to obtain commodities that we could not produce ourselves because we lack the natural resources. And, more importantly, it makes it possible to obtain goods more cheaply. Specializing in those goods that we can produce most efficiently and exporting them is a cheaper way of getting hold of other goods than by making them ourselves.

In the latter part of the nineteenth century the pattern of specialization was very simple. Britain's imports consisted almost entirely of food and raw materials. These were converted into manufactures sufficient not only to meet home demands but also for export. But even in this heyday of British industrial supremacy, exports of manufactured goods were not enough to pay for the required level of imports. There was always an 'adverse balance of trade'. This 'trade gap' was to remain a persistent feature of the UK balance of payments for many years. In the interwar period, for example, exports of manufactures earned sufficient to pay for only some two thirds of our visible imports.

The trade gap

Changes in the balance of trade

During the postwar years, massive changes have taken place in Britain's balance of trade. If the early seventies figures are compared with the previous ones there are three striking differences to be seen:
● The trade gap had dramatically narrowed. During the period since the war, merchandise exports had come to pay for on average more than 90 per cent of visible imports – and sometimes even footed the whole bill. This important structural change had begun with the sustained 'export drive' of the immediate postwar years.

24

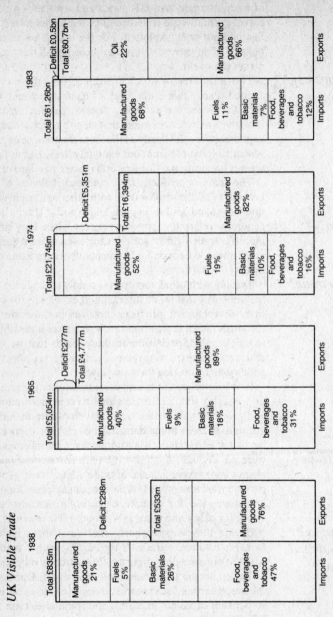

UK Visible Trade

1938

Total £835m — Deficit £298m — Total £533m

Imports
- Manufactured goods 21%
- Fuels 5%
- Basic materials 26%
- Food, beverages and tobacco 47%

Exports
- Manufactured goods 76%

1965

Total £5,054m — Deficit £277m — Total £4,777m

Imports
- Manufactured goods 40%
- Fuels 9%
- Basic materials 18%
- Food, beverages and tobacco 31%

Exports
- Manufactured goods 89%

1974

Total £21,745m — Deficit £5,351m — Total £16,394m

Imports
- Manufactured goods 52%
- Fuels 19%
- Basic materials 10%
- Food, beverages and tobacco 16%

Exports
- Manufactured goods 82%

1983

Total £61.26bn — Deficit £0.5bn — Total £60.7bn

Imports
- Manufactured goods 68%
- Fuels 11%
- Basic materials 7%
- Food, beverages and tobacco 12%

Exports
- Oil 22%
- Manufactured goods 66%

Source: Monthly Digest of Statistics, UK Balance of Payments 1970,
UK Balance of Payments 1983, British Business, 6 April 1984

• The pattern of trade had become a good deal more complex. A large and increasing proportion of imports now took the form of finished or semi-finished manufactures. The division of labour between countries had become much more sophisticated, with the leading nations exchanging increasing quantities of industrial goods between themselves.

• Britain had now become heavily dependent on imported oil to fuel its industrial expansion – amounting in 1974 to some 19 per cent of its total visible import bill.

In the eighties the picture at first sight looks highly cheering, particularly in two respects.

• The trade gap has virtually disappeared – with visible exports frequently even earning a substantial *surplus* over spending on visible imports.

• Britain has become a net exporter of oil. Instead of being a major drain on foreign exchange earnings it is now positively contributing towards them.

The importance of this turnaround on the oil account can be judged by estimates that in 1983 the North Sea benefited the visible trade balance to the tune of some £13.5 billion. Put another way, that means that without it there would have been a trade *deficit* in 1983 of about £13 billion. But since we did strike lucky in the North Sea, why speculate about the state of the balance of trade without our own oil? There are two good reasons for doing so. First, North Sea supplies are currently reaching their peak and will thereafter begin to diminish. And second, the other elements in the visible trade balance have been changing very unfavourably.

The non-oil account

What has happened in recent years is that the deficit on *non-oil* items in the balance of trade has sharply widened from £2 billion in 1974 to £7.5 billion in 1983. And within the non-oil account, the absolutely crucial figure to note is that for imported manufactures and semi-manufactures – industrial goods of the kind on which Britain's past prosperity has been built; these have been rising much faster than exports of manufactures until, in 1983, they actually overtook them.

For the first time since the industrial revolution we are now importing more manufactures than we are exporting. It is a momentous fact. For well over a century we have relied on manufactured exports not only to pay for imports of manufactures but also to make a major contribution towards the bill for our supplies of food and basic materials. We are now for the first time in the position that the manufacturing sector actually *adds* to this bill – in 1983 by over £2 billion.

Invisibles

It is not possible though to draw any conclusion at this stage because there are other elements in the balance of payments yet to be taken into account. Thanks to oil, the trade balance has been in surplus despite the deficit on manufactures whereas, as we have seen, there has always traditionally been an adverse trade gap. This in the past has been more

From Workshop to Oilwell
UK Visible Trade Balances

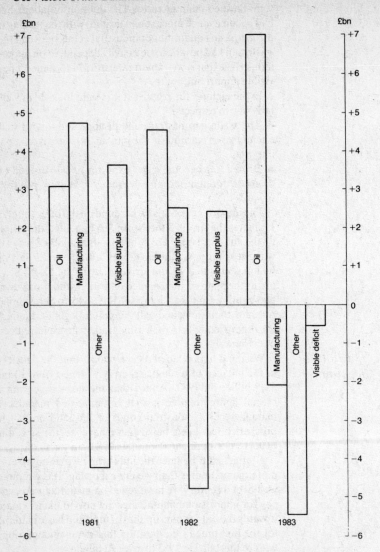

Source: *Bank of England Quarterly Bulletin*, vol. 24, no. 1, March 1984.

or less filled by a surplus of so-called invisible exports over invisible imports. (Together total visible and invisible trade comprise the 'balance of payments on current account'.)

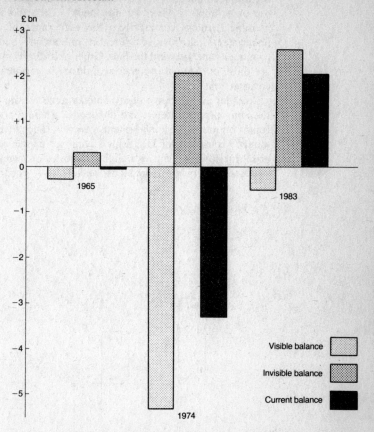

Source: *UK Balance of Payments*, 1970, 1982; *Economic Trends*, no. 365, March 1984.

'Invisibles' stem from transactions with other countries that do not involve the transfer of tangible goods but which none the less lead to current payments and receipts in just the same way.

Thus invisible exports are any such items that give rise to payments by foreigners to UK residents. For example, French holiday-makers in Britain will be spending the pounds that they have bought with their francs – on hotel bills, food, travel. This has exactly the same effect on the balance of payments as if we had exported to France an equivalent value of goods.

The main type of invisible trade is in the provision of services of which tourism is just one example. Others are the payments that result from the use of shipping or civil aviation (invisible exports when foreigners use ours, imports when we use theirs). Then there are substantial invisible earnings coming from the wide range of commercial and financial services provided by the 'City of London' – banking, insurance, commodity markets and the like. Other particularly important services are those of the civil engineering industry in consultancy on overseas construction.

Another major source of invisible earnings for the UK comes from the item 'profits, interest and dividends'. These represent the annual return on past British investments overseas. Such investments may be 'direct', consisting of UK firms having set up subsidiaries abroad – acquiring foreign plant or building factories or owning land. Or UK residents may own foreign stocks and shares – 'portfolio' investment.

UK Invisible Trade, 1983

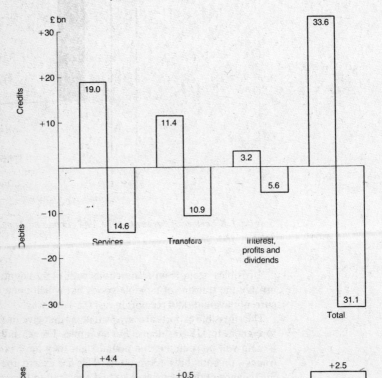

Source: *Economic Trends*, no. 365, March 1984.

UK Inward and Outward Investment, 1983 (£bn)

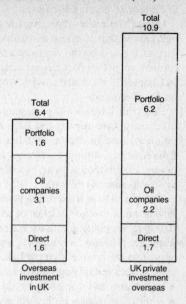

Source: *Economic Trends*, no. 365, March 1984.

The flow back from these assets accounts for about a third of our net invisible earnings.

Altogether invisible earnings have recently been of the order of some £30 billion a year. That is roughly half what we get by selling manufactures abroad – about a third of our total export receipts. However, the *net* contribution that invisibles make towards the balance of payments is only about £2 billion a year because invisible imports are also very substantial.

A key question is whether the invisible surplus can in the future be expanded to compensate for the deteriorating balance on manufactures which is at present being concealed by the benefits of North Sea oil. Part of the answer lies in what is happening in the third and final element in the balance of payments – the capital account.

Capital movements
The capital account lists those financial flows between countries caused not by the need to pay for goods and services but to set up production elsewhere or to buy foreign financial assets which, as we have seen, subsequently lead to a return flow of invisible exports.

The outflow of such capital from the UK was regulated for most of the postwar period by the British government. Since 1979, however, these exchange controls have been ended. The result has been a very large movement of funds overseas. By 1982 direct investment had risen from

29

£30 billion to nearly £50 billion, and portfolio financial investment from £12 billion to nearly £38 billion.

One of the main arguments for encouraging large-scale investment overseas is that it offers a sensible use for the balance of payments surplus created by the North Sea because it will generate a stream of future foreign currency income at a time when oil is beginning to dry up. In Chapter 15 we shall be asking whether this has been at the expense of home investment.

But, from a balance of payments standpoint, the gains from overseas investment have anyway to a large extent been offset by the substantial *inflow* of foreign capital that has simultaneously been taking place. Consequently, although earnings from UK investment abroad run at nearly £5½ billion a year, we also pay out in profits, interest and dividends some £4 billion.

The balance of payments problem

Those who have lived throughout the postwar decades will remember how often in the past balance of payments weakness has so often been the signal for political calls for restraint and general belt-tightening. But ironically it is now, when North Sea output makes the overall account appear so favourable, that the balance of payments in fact contains the most serious underlying weakness:

● an adverse and worsening balance on trade in manufactures;
● a positive balance on invisibles – but quite inadequate to meet the non-oil deficit;
● oil earnings due shortly to begin their decline.

In this sense, we are now living on borrowed time. The average family is consuming some £1,000 a year of imported goods and services that is only being paid for out of oil earnings. And spending on imports would be much higher still were it not for the fact there are more than three million unemployed.

When the oil runs out

What happens as the oil runs out? The optimistic view is that the gap will be filled by the growth of new high-technology manufactures, the sale of know-how and higher invisible earnings. But there is little evidence as yet to suggest that these will suffice (Britain's share of world invisibles trade is in fact declining at a time when that of others like France and the US is increasing).

This is a matter that we shall return to in Chapter 6. But we have already seen enough to suggest that in the record of our transactions with the rest of the world there are clear signs of economic weakness that have so far been masked only by North Sea oil.

In fact, there is no chance that Britain will actually go bust. But there *is* a real possibility that our future living standards and jobs will be threatened by the need to balance our international books. Tucked away in the complex accounts of the balance of payments, we find the second major symptom, along with mass unemployment, that all is far from well with the British economy.

3

Have We Forgotten the Thirties?

Comparisons are often drawn between today's unemployment and the unemployment of the twenties and thirties. Are you inclined to regard today's problems as
- *much less serious than between the wars?*
- *about as bad?*
- *considerably worse?*

   More generally, do you regard unemployment as
- *the result of economic forces outside government control, including workers pricing themselves out of jobs, which only the free working of market forces can resolve?*

   OR
- *the consequence of an inadequate level of demand for goods and services, for which governments could and should take responsibility?*

   This chapter looks at similarities and differences between the unemployment of the thirties and the eighties, and at contrasting government policy responses, in seeking an answer to the question, 'But haven't we been here before?'

- Unemployment over three million.
- Manufacturing output down by more than 15 per cent.
- Loss of foreign competitiveness.
- Decline of traditional industries.

The thirties and the eighties

   The thirties or the eighties? Since the beginning of industrial time economies have been plagued by the periodic fluctuations of the 'trade cycle' – regularly alternating booms and slumps in employment and output. But after the disaster of the thirties it seemed that these had been ironed out to a considerable extent. What has happened in the late seventies and early eighties shows that the economics of recession cannot after all be consigned to the history books.

   In one vital respect the eighties are not as bad as the thirties. The

31

decline has been from a much higher initial level of output and affluence so that the degree of absolute poverty and hardship experienced by the hardest hit victims of the recession is not comparable to that suffered fifty years earlier.

But there are other ways in which the new Great Depression is proving worse than the previous one. For example, unemployment in 1984 was continuing to rise while at a similar stage in the thirties it had begun to fall rapidly; long-term unemployment, of those out of work for more than a year, is substantially greater this time. Investment, particularly in the public sector, has fallen much more sharply in the eighties than in the thirties, and interest rates remain at much higher levels.

There is, on the other hand, a striking parallel between then and now in the diagnosis and prescription offered. What is being said and done now is quite remarkably like what was being said and done then. Someone who had hibernated for half a century might well think that economic thinking had meanwhile remained quite static. Nothing could be further from the truth, because the intervening years had in fact seen a major revolution in the way most economists and governments thought and acted about economic problems. But that, in turn, has been followed by a counter-revolution: a re-assertion of old ideas.

We must trace these extraordinary changes in economic fashion to explain the present lack of consensus amongst economists. About the major issues that confront us – like unemployment, inflation, the role of government and economic growth – there is a deep division of views which must be baffling to the non-economist trying to understand current economic issues.

The old orthodoxy

There was an embarrassing intellectual problem for the economist analysing the growing unemployment of the late twenties and early thirties: in theory it should not have happened. The century and a half after the first great economist, Adam Smith, had seen the evolution of a body of classical economic analysis at the heart of which was a belief in the self-correcting nature of an unregulated economy. *Laisser-faire*, leaving the economy free from government meddling with market forces, would achieve the most efficient use of resources – and full employment.

Wages and unemployment

Unemployment means that the supply of labour (the number of workers offering themselves for hire) is greater than the demand for labour (the number that enterprises are willing to employ). It's as if there is a 'glut' of labour. For classical economists this was as easily explained as a glut of strawberries or any other commodity coming on to the market. Any stall-holder nearing the end of a day's trading with remaining stocks of strawberries knows the answer – lower the price until sufficient new buyers come in to 'clear the market'.

Similarly with labour. Unemployment could only occur if the price of labour, the wage being demanded, was too high. Lower the wage rate and any temporary excess of labour would be employed. If in the real world unemployment persisted it must therefore be due to 'imperfections' in the market preventing wages from falling. It was not difficult to find the culprits:

Imperfections
- governments setting fixed payments – to their employees and to those receiving state pensions, unemployment and other benefits;
- trade unions – fighting to increase or at least maintain their members' living standards. But such resistance, according to the classical economists, only benefited those in work at the expense of others, who consequently lost their jobs.

HAVEN'T WE BEEN HERE BEFORE?

The Macmillan Committee on Finance and Industry was set up in 1929 and reported in 1931. Its deliberations provide interesting parallels with current arguments. The case for cutting unemployment benefit to provide more incentive to work is one example. Here is how it was dealt with by Professor Henry Clay of Manchester University.

23 July 1930

CLAY: . . . the Unemployment Insurance scheme . . . it is alleged, by making it possible to live without finding work, reduces the incentive to find work, and so slows down the rate at which workers transfer themselves from declining industries to new occupations. The scheme may have some slight influence in this direction; but jobs are not created merely by seeking them. . . . I think the provision of unemployment relief does lessen the activity of people seeking work; . . . where there have been expanding trades capable of absorbing labour specialized to one of the depressed industries there has been an enormous movement – for example, from shipbuilding; still better from general engineering. The whole group of trades employing mechanics was very much inflated by the war and was the group in which unemployment was most serious. By 1925 the men in those industries had got out of them, they had gone to Coventry and Birmingham, to the motor industry, and had found other outlets. That was the result not of any action on the part of the government or anybody else, but of the workers in those industries. They did not stay on the Tyne and the Clyde drawing unemployment pay, they heard there were jobs in Coventry and Birmingham and they went and got them . . .
MACMILLAN: It was the want of work, not of the will to work?
CLAY: On the whole.

Government and unemployment

The implication of this argument was that unemployment was only the fault of governments to the extent that they themselves impeded pay cuts. In the twenties and thirties they acted accordingly. They reduced the salaries of their own employees like teachers and civil servants, and they cut unemployment benefits which might otherwise have set an artificially high floor to the wage rates of those in work. Beyond that it was up to employers in the private sector to get wages down to a level at which employment and output would pick up.

Above all, government should avoid getting in the way of economic recovery generated by private enterprise. The famous 'Treasury View' of the time held that any attempt by government to *create* jobs – by, for example, public works spending on roads or railways – was doomed to failure. Such expenditure simply drained resources and finance away from private-sector producers, whose spending would fall by a similar amount. Government should therefore

- keep its spending as low as possible to encourage private investment;
- balance the budget – limit public expenditure to what could be financed from taxation – and not be tempted into additional borrowing which would only reduce private outlays.

Altogether then the old orthodoxy was a powerful endorsement of *laisser-faire*. It pointed to the impotence and undesirability of government intervention in an economy that would be basically self-righting if left to its own devices.

The Keynesian attack

But reality suggested otherwise. And a fundamental attack on classical theory was evolving which was completed when John Maynard Keynes finally ended his 'long struggle of escape' from 'habitual modes of thought and expression' with the publication in 1936 of his *General Theory of Employment, Interest and Money*.

Keynes and others had for many years before been questioning the validity of the classical theory. The policies based upon it seemed to him perverse – making the situation worse rather than better. Take, for example, the Treasury View that releasing resources from the public sector (by, for instance, a 10 per cent cut in the dole in 1931) would stimulate private investment. As Keynes wrote at that time:

> What are we releasing resources for today? To stand at street corners and draw the dole. When we already have a large amount of unemployment and unused resources of every description, economy is only useful from the national point of view in so far as it diminishes our consumption of imported goods. For the rest, its fruits are entirely wasted in unemployment, business losses and reduced savings. *

More generally, Keynes saw no reason for assuming that in an unregulated market economy full employment would be the natural outcome. Unemployment was much more likely, because of a failure of total spending in the economy to match total output at a level that would ensure all resources being used.

Total spending, or *demand*, comes from four main sources:
- *consumption* – chiefly by households on food, clothes, domestic appliances and the like;
- *investment* – private and public enterprises buying new plant and machinery, stocks of raw materials, etc.;
- *government* – on programmes like defence, health, education, roads, social security;
- *exports* – representing the part of our output that is bought abroad (offset to the extent that we in turn buy imported goods and services).

Too little demand

The basic Keynesian proposition was this: in an unregulated economy there is no reason why the multitude of spending decisions from these four sources should add up to the total just needed to buy all the output that the economy can produce with full employment. If they don't, then there is a *deflationary gap*, a shortfall in demand. Part of output will remain unsold, producers will cut back accordingly and unemployment will occur.

In particular, a discrepancy between spending and production plans is likely to result from the fact that saving and investment are to some extent undertaken by different groups with different motives. For the classical economists, thrift was to be encouraged because it led to investment. Keynes disagreed. *Attempts* to increase saving would lead to lower consumption. Firms would find themselves selling less than they had anticipated and reduce their production, laying off workers in the process. There would be lower incomes out of which *less* rather than more would actually be saved. For Keynes, saving in times of depression was a vice rather than a virtue. For him it was investment, through raising incomes, that led to higher saving rather than the other way round.

* J. M. Keynes, *Essays in Persuasion*, Macmillan, 1931.

Too Little Spending

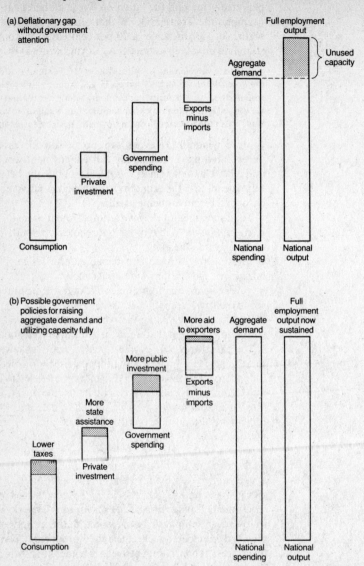

(a) Deflationary gap without government attention

Consumption
Private investment
Government spending
Exports minus imports
Aggregate demand
Full employment output
Unused capacity
National spending
National output

(b) Possible government policies for raising aggregate demand and utilizing capacity fully

Consumption
Lower taxes
Private investment
More state assistance
Government spending
More public investment
Exports minus imports
More aid to exporters
Aggregate demand
Full employment output now sustained
National spending
National output

What caused unemployment was lack of demand, insufficient spending. The factories and equipment were there, idle or under-used. Workers were desperate for jobs. Firms were losing money. All that was missing was the purchasing power which, ironically, would be created if only firms were to re-employ workers and to pay them incomes. The trouble was that it would not benefit any *one* firm to do so because its workers would only spend a tiny proportion of their incomes on the things they themselves produced. What was needed was for all firms to expand employment simultaneously. But there was no mechanism for bringing this about.

Demand management

The answer, according to Keynes, could only lie in government intervention. This would have to be of a nature and scale never previously attempted. What it had to do was to *manage* the level of demand. Thus if spending was insufficient to buy full employment output, it was up to government to step in and increase it, thereby plugging the deflationary gap and preventing unemployment.

This it could do in one of two broad ways:

● It could stimulate private sector spending on consumption and investment by tax cuts, lower interest rates or inducements like grants towards new investment.

● It could directly increase its own spending by raising welfare benefits or undertaking public works programmes like railway electrification. This would involve deficit financing – spending in excess of its tax revenues – a deliberately unbalanced budget based on borrowing either from the banks or from savings that would otherwise lie idle.

Such an injection of demand, argued Keynes, would have a 'multiplier' effect over and above the initial increase. A construction project, for example, would bring building workers back into employment and raise their incomes above what they had been getting on the dole. A large proportion of this increase they would then spend, thereby expanding demand for other goods and services. This would lead to more orders and more employment in the industries supplying them – and as fresh workers were taken on they in turn would spend more and bring about yet another round of increased employment, incomes and spending . . .

The Keynesian Revolution

The implications of the 'Keynesian Revolution' as it became known were hard for economists and politicians of the time to stomach. It was an attack on:

● traditional *economic theory* accepted and taught by leading economists for generations past;

● the principles of *sound finance* embodied in the notion that it was the duty of governments to balance their budgets;

● the *political* belief in *laisser-faire – that governments should not interfere with the free workings of the market economy.*

It was this last breach with conventional wisdom that was most fundamental. Keynesian theory suggested that an unregulated capitalist economy would *not* lead to an acceptable outcome. Market failure implied the need for substantial and continuous intervention by the state in the workings of the economy. If we wanted full employment, then it could only be achieved if government assumed *responsibility* for managing the level of total demand in the appropriate fashion. This was the way, not to overthrow capitalism, but to save it.

Keynesian ideas came too late to alter the attitudes of policy-makers in the interwar years. But by the postwar period they served as the basis for demand-management policy not only in the UK but also in most of the other industrial nations. And it seemed to work – with the decades up to the seventies seeing unprecedently high levels of sustained employment and steadily growing prosperity.

But despite this, the phase of Keynesian consensus was to prove relatively short-lived. Its fall from grace was even more rapid than its

---

THE CHANCELLOR'S FOUR PRINCIPLES, 1979

(1) **Incentives**. 'We need to strengthen incentives, by allowing people to keep more of what they earn, so that hard work, talent and ability are properly rewarded';

(2) **Freedom of choice**. 'We need to enlarge freedom of choice for the individual by reducing the role of the state';

(3) **Public Sector Borrowing Requirement**. 'We need to reduce the burden of financing the public sector, so as to leave room for commerce and industry to prosper';

(4) **Pay and inflation**. 'We need to ensure, so far as possible, that those who take part in collective bargaining understand the consequences of their actions.'

The four main points of the new strategy, as stated by the Chancellor in his Budget speech, are set out above. They represent a complete change of attitude towards the way in which our economy works, and are intended to remove the constraints imposed by the tax system and by the unduly large role previously played by government – releasing initiative and enterprise.

For these new policies to succeed, control of inflation is essential. The government's part will be to establish sound money through firm monetary discipline, and fiscal policies consistent with it, including strict control over public expenditure. The public sector will be as subject to this control as the private. Previously public spending has tended to determine the raising of finance; in future the reverse will be the case. A start has now been made on bringing public expenditure down. Forecasts suggest that the economy is unlikely to grow in the period immediately ahead. The Chancellor said that this could not be taken to mean that this Budget is unduly contractionary; an easier fiscal stance would only fuel inflation, leading in the end to less growth and employment.

Treasury Economic Progress Report, June 1979, on Sir Geoffrey Howe's first Budget.

initial acceptance. During the sixties and seventies there was mounting criticism of demand management from both the left and the right of the political spectrum. In the event it was the latter who won the day.

The new orthodoxy

What replaced Keynesianism was not a new radical breakthrough in economic thinking and policy. Astonishingly it was a restoration of the old orthodoxy:

● questioning whether managing demand could really create more jobs – or instead simply caused inflation and worsened long-run employment prospects;

● insisting that it was dangerous and irresponsible for governments to spend more than they received in taxes;

● re-asserting the importance of market forces through 'rolling back the public sector'.

The political rhetoric, the economic theory and the economic policies of today have a familiar ring because they are essentially those of the thirties. Once again, unemployment has ceased to be the responsibility of government because unemployment is said to be caused by too high wages – over which government has relatively little control. Once again, public spending must be held back in order to release resources for

---

WAGE CUTS IN THE 1980s

Half a century on, Professor Patrick Minford of Liverpool University revives the arguments for cuts in benefits and wages:

My estimates suggest that at rates of pay only 10 per cent below existing market rates, unemployment would effectively disappear. In other words, 2¼ million more jobs exist at rates of pay up to 10 per cent below the rates workers will not now willingly accept. These jobs are not taken . . . because they are too low-paid relative to benefits . . .

. . . This is lunacy. The community has a right to expect people to work if they can . . . Therefore my principle will be to create inducements for the unemployed to take the jobs that potentially exist at lower wages . . .

. . . We propose to put a ceiling on benefits receivable as a fraction of previous work income (net of tax, work expenses, etc.). That ceiling would be set at 70 per cent, so providing in general *at least* a 30 per cent incentive to work. In the longer term I would go further and make unemployment insurance a private matter, to be taken out at personal expense in the market, subject to some minimum cover the state would insist upon. The date for this substantial change in regime is set at 1990, since it is a particularly radical departure, requiring considerable further public education.

'State Expenditure: A Study in Waste', supplement to *Economic Affairs*, April–June 1984.

productive use by the 'wealth-creating' private sector. And once again, the aim is to reduce the role of the state in the economy in the belief that the operation of the free market will do the job better.

Today there is therefore a deep division amongst economists. On every major question there are two broad views and many variants of each. In subsequent chapters we shall try to explain both sides of the debate. The reader will not be provided with clear-cut answers but at least be put in a better position to form his or her own view.

4
What's Happened to Inflation?

What do you *think causes inflation?*
● *When industry's costs, particularly wages through trade union pressure, rise faster than production, prices will inevitably be* pushed *upwards.*
● *When demand in the economy, especially consumer spending, runs higher than the economy's capacity to produce, prices will inevitably be* pulled *upwards.*
● *When the money supply – the availability of credit through the banking system – increases, this will inevitably be* reflected *in the level of prices.*
   Dealing with inflation will clearly be influenced by the choice of explanation. This chapter also looks at the price *to be paid for the reduction in inflation. How much of a fall in output or a rise in unemployment are you prepared to accept as the price for enjoying a lower rate of inflation? What price inflation?*

Who'd be a Chancellor? It's difficult to think of many over the years whom we have grown to love. Dalton, Cripps, Butler, Gaitskell, Home, Healey, Howe, Lawson. Altogether sixteen of them since 1945, mostly remembered, if at all, for the medicine they handed out rather than for their generosity or their masterly economic policies.

But spare them a thought. Imagine for a moment that it is *you* at Number 11 – with all the expertise of the Treasury at your disposal and the Governor of the Bank of England only a phone call away.

The year happens to be 1965. But with regard to one of the many problems you face it might have been any of the previous twenty-one years. None of your predecessors has managed to halt *inflation* – a rise in the general price level, last year at the rate of about 2 per cent. Inflation is worrying for many reasons:

Why worry about inflation?

● it is unpopular with the voters;
● it is unfair to fixed-income groups;
● it often hits hardest at the lower paid who spend a greater proportion of their incomes on items like food and fuel, the price of which frequently rises faster than the average;

Demand-pull

● it makes it more difficult to compete abroad if British inflation is greater than in other countries.

Before you can do anything about it you must be sure of its cause. So you call in one of your Economic Advisors. He confirms what you suspected – that inflation is the result of living beyond our means. 'An excess of aggregate demand' is how he puts it.

Demand-Pull

Demand-pull inflation is the consequence of an inflationary gap. This is the opposite of the diagram on p. 36

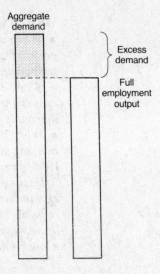

Aggregate demand

Excess demand

Full employment output

What this means is a mis-match between spending and production plans like that which we described in Chapter 3. But this time it is a case of the uncoordinated spending of households, firms, government and foreigners adding up to *more* than the value of full employment output at current prices. We have an *inflationary* rather than a deflationary gap. Something has to give, and that something is prices.

The various groups of spenders are in effect forced into bidding resources away from each other. For example, there is no reason why a firm should not set up business in an area where there is already full employment. But it can only do so by attracting labour and land away from their present uses – through offering a higher price. Generalize this throughout the economy and you have what the Economic Advisor calls *demand-pull* inflation. The answer is to dampen down demand.

● Raise taxes.
● Increase interest rates.
● Make public-spending cuts.

Not a politically attractive package. And can you be sure that you have successfully identified the basic cause of inflation? To check it out, you consult with another of your Economic Advisors. As you feared, he is highly sceptical of everything that has been put to you so far.

Cost-push

Inflation, according to him, is not caused by excess demand pulling up prices. It is due to the upward pressure of the various costs that go to make up prices. The most obvious is wages. One of the results of your success in maintaining full employment is the increased bargaining strength of trade unions. They can demand wage rises above what is justified by increased output per worker – and employers accede because it is the consumer who will pay through higher prices.

Cost-Push

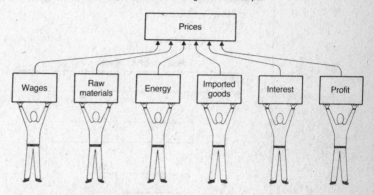

'Cost-push' inflation, by contrast, is the result of production costs rising faster than output

Higher cost of imported raw materials may also at times play an important part in pushing up prices. Or firms may raise prices to cover the expense of new investment or to widen their profit margins. And governments, too, may contribute towards inflation by increasing taxes, which firms then try to pass on to the consumer.

Inflation, he concludes, is caused by *cost-push*. And the answer must lie in the problematic area of devising an acceptable and workable prices and incomes policy.

What should you do in face of such conflicting advice? The process of inflation is clearly via a wage–price spiral, but what causes what? Is it too much spending, with wages and other incomes rising simply to compensate for higher prices? Or are trade unions and other cost pressures the original villains of the piece?

Phillips curve

Perhaps one way of killing two birds with one stone would be to let unemployment rise by just a *little*. That would both cut demand *and* make the unions think twice about pushing for exorbitant wage increases. (Didn't you read somewhere about the 'Phillips curve' suggesting there was a historical connection between unemployment and inflation? Apparently, higher unemployment has always in the past

43

ONE MAN'S WAGE INCREASE . . .

It is not simply the rise in the level of costs, such as wages, which determines how prices respond. Rather it is the increase in *unit* or average costs, i.e. costs per unit of output, which matters. The level and movement of output thus becomes a crucial additional consideration.

AN INTERNATIONAL COMPARISON

Compare the nature of the UK's inflation – and its causes – in the sixties with the performance of her major competitors. Would you put the blame for Britain's poor showing more on wage inflation or on lower efficiency?

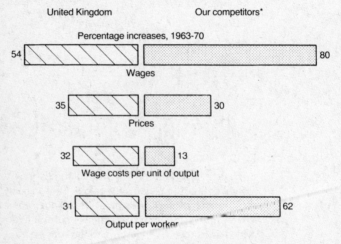

United Kingdom   Our competitors*

Percentage increases, 1963-70

54   80
Wages

35   30
Prices

32   13
Wage costs per unit of output

31   62
Output per worker

* Average of USA, Japan, France, West Germany and Italy

Wages rose considerably faster on average in the other countries, but wage costs in relation to output rose much more here than abroad. This is because output per worker only increased in the UK by half as much as in the other countries. The result is that prices rose rather faster here.

It can be argued that the most significant factor behind the UK's poor showing was the much slower rise in output per worker, rather than wages rising too fast.

So 'one man's wage increase' need not automatically become 'another man's price increase'!

'*Phillips curve*'

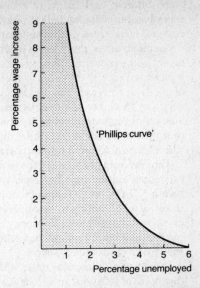

been associated with lower wage increases.) Rather higher unemployment might just prove to be electorally acceptable because everyone suffers from inflation whereas there would be only a few thrown out of work. And Chancellors are paid to take stern but necessary measures . . .

Ten years later

By 1975, the situation facing the Chancellor had become more complex and more serious. Unemployment *had* risen – to the 4 per cent which some had predicted would be sufficient to kill off inflation. But instead prices had risen faster and faster, and by 1975 were exploding at 25 per cent per annum. The Phillips relationship had broken down.

As usual there were different explanations for the rapid increase in inflation.

● *Demand*-pullers pointed to the tax cuts and public-spending increases of the 1971–2 'Barber boom' as the trigger.

● *Cost*-pushers saw the fourfold rise in the price of oil in 1973–4 as the obvious cause.

● Both agreed that *expectations* of worsening inflation by businesses and workers were self-fulfilling as they set their prices and wage claims accordingly.

But there now emerged, or re-emerged, upon the scene an elderly actor whose performances of half a century ago had been scathingly criticized. But with a change in name (he used to be called the Quantity Theorist) and much hard work, here he was again.

The Monetarist came armed with a mass of statistical data and a third

45

quite different explanation of inflation. He agreed that spending was excessive, but what made that possible? As to trade unions and other cost pressures, these were symptoms rather than the root of inflation.

Monetarism   For monetarists, the cause of inflation is simply that there is *too much money* in the economy. Money is like any other commodity. If its supply is increased excessively then its value falls and it buys a smaller quantity of goods and services than previously, i.e. their price rises.

Led by Professor Milton Friedman of Chicago University, a growing number of economists subscribed to this view. They produced volumes of statistical evidence suggesting that inflation has 'always and every-where' been associated with increases in the money supply.

Thus for example between the beginning of 1971 and the end of 1974, the money supply grew by 92 per cent. Between 1972 and 1975 prices rose by 77 per cent. There certainly seems strong circumstantial evidence of a link between the two. And according to monetarists, it is a *causal* link: it is an increased money supply that makes excess demand or exorbitant wage settlements possible. To control inflation you must curb the growth of the money supply.

What was a Chancellor to do when offered three radically different diagnoses of inflation? In 1975 it was Mr Healey who was faced with the choice and in effect he hedged his bets by a combination of policies:
- public-spending cuts, partly as a result of pressure from the International Monetary Fund;
- the 'Social Contract', a form of prices and incomes policy that lasted until the winter of 1978;
- the setting of targets for the growth of the money supply.

When inflation then fell from 25 per cent to less than 10 per cent it was therefore possible for each of the three protagonists to claim that their theory had been vindicated.

The Thatcher years   However, with the advent in 1979 of Mrs Thatcher's Conservative government the way seemed clear for an experimental test of the kind that economists dream of.
- *Politically*, 'squeezing inflation out of the system' was given paramount priority over all other economic objectives. It was argued that employment, growth and the balance of payments could safely be left to market forces once government got prices under control.
- *Technically*, reducing inflation was to be achieved by monetarist techniques. Demand management or prices and incomes policies were dismissed derisively as irrelevant or harmful tinkering.

With a single policy objective, reducing inflation, having been pursued through a single policy instrument, restraint of the money supply, we should now be able to judge quite unequivocally whether the monetarist explanation of inflation is right or wrong. Unfortunately it is not so straightforward. To see why this is so we need to look at the record of the Thatcher years with regard to prices, output and employment, and the behaviour of the money supply.

NO SUCH THING AS A FREE MONETARIST EXPERIMENT

The House of Commons Treasury and Civil Service Committee noted the cost of controlling inflation by monetarism:

The Treasury's evidence from its model of the economy suggests that the cost of reducing inflation by policies designed to reduce the growth of the money supply is high. After four years a lasting fall in the rate of inflation of about 1 per cent per annum can be achieved at a cumulative cost over four years equivalent to 4 per cent of a single year's gross domestic product and a year's additional unemployment for 2.5 per cent of the labour force (650,000 man-years).

Source: *Third Report from the Treasury and Civil Service Committee, Session 1980–81, Monetary Policy*, House of Commons, 163-1, HMSO.

Falling inflation

Prices are certainly rising far less rapidly. In 1979 inflation was running at the rate of 9 per cent per annum. Since then it rose to some 16 per cent in 1980, fell to 4 per cent in 1983 and has subsequently risen slightly again. Inflation has not been eliminated. But after an initial hiccup, the record on prices at first sight seems to justify the policies that have been followed.

Output and employment

Unfortunately, the attempted application of monetarist policies to begin with affected *output* and *employment* much more than prices, as producers were faced with falling demand and dearer finance. Only subsequently did price rises begin to moderate. However, monetarists would argue that rising unemployment was the result of the perversely 'irrational' behaviour of trade unions. If trade unions had accepted that government policy *would* reduce the rate of inflation and if they had modified their wage claims accordingly, then the impact of monetarist discipline would have fallen directly on prices rather than employment and output.

Controlling the money supply

So far we have been assuming that in these years the government *was* achieving successful *control over the money supply*. In fact, great difficulties were encountered in implementing the monetarist doctrine. To analyse these properly requires an understanding of how money is created (explained in the Appendix to this chapter) and of the detailed methods by which the government attempted control (spelled out in the following chapter).

For now we shall mention just one quite basic problem: what *is* this 'money supply' that is to be controlled? Money is anything that is generally acceptable as a means of payment or settlement of debt. But what should that include? Coins, banknotes, current and deposit accounts at banks, Post Office accounts, credit cards, building society

47

deposits – the distinguishing line between 'money' and 'non-money' is not easy to draw.

This might be regarded as an arid definitional matter of no great concern – but not for monetarists who believe that controlling the money supply is *the* key regulator on which governments should concentrate. For them, it is obviously vital to be clear about what it is that should be controlled.

The Bank of England in its financial statistics offers an embarrassment of choices, ranging from a very narrow definition M_0 (notes and coin) through to a much wider M_6 hold-all of most of the items listed above. In practice the authorities chose at the start to concentrate on something in between, sterling M_3 (£M_3) consisting mainly of notes, coin, and current and time bank deposits in this country. Subsequently, although £M_3 has continued to command considerable attention the government now takes into account the way in which the whole range of 'monetary aggregates' is behaving.

● In fact they have often moved not only in different proportions but even in different directions.

● The monetary targets set by the government were not to begin with met and *yet* inflation fell.

● It was only *after* the fall in inflation that the money supply seemed to be more under control.

Pure monetarists are therefore able to claim that their theory has not after all been tested. Critics, on the other hand, view the episode as a demonstration of the impracticability of regulating the money supply and also of the damage that can be inflicted in the attempt to do so.

Deflation

For them, there is an obvious alternative explanation of why inflation has fallen. Efforts to apply monetarism have engineered an old-fashioned *deflation*, Keynesianism in reverse, with public-spending cuts and high interest rates severely restricting the level of total demand in the economy. With rapidly rising unemployment and falling demand it is not surprising that wage pressures were moderated or that firms found it difficult to raise prices. But what must be doubted is whether this represents a permanent change in attitudes that will persist if and when output increases and the rise in unemployment slows down.

The cost of achieving lower inflation has been very high. In Chapter 6 we shall ask if it will prove a worthwhile sacrifice with a more competitive industry being capable of bringing back into employment those who have been thrown out of work. Or have we in the process of fighting inflation destroyed the industrial foundation on which such a recovery would have to be based?

But first we look at the mechanics of attempted 'monetarism' in the public sector of the economy. It is here that the root of inflation and past lack of competitiveness has been alleged to lie.

The Money Supply

There cannot be many people who believe that the 'I promise to pay the bearer on demand the sum of . . .' printed on a bank-note has any real meaning, although there may be some who think that bank-notes are still 'backed' by gold held in the banks' vaults.

But we all quite happily accept bank-notes as a means of payment, and it is just this general acceptability that makes them (and anything else which is similarly acceptable) be classed as *money*. In fact, bank-notes are only a small part of what economists call 'the money supply'. They have become the small change of the system.

How banks make money

Far more important are bank *deposits* which banks have created, greatly in excess of their holdings of bank-notes. In other words, if we all go along to the banks tomorrow and withdraw our deposits, the banks simply won't have enough cash to meet our demands. The whole business of banking depends on us *not* all asking for our money at the same time. It's a gigantic confidence trick. How have they got away with it? How have banks managed to create 'credit money' unbacked by bank-notes? The answer looks very different according to whether we approach the question from the viewpoint of an individual bank or that of the banking system as a whole.

One banker's story

An individual bank, say Barclays, will describe its business like this:

'What we do is to attract customers to deposit cash with us – for safekeeping, convenience and, if they have a deposit account, to earn interest. Every day, we have people coming into our branches and withdrawing cash. But every day, there are others who make fresh deposits of cash. Over a long period of time we have learned that the two by and large cancel each other out, and that we therefore have to keep only a small proportion of total deposits as bank-notes in our tills to meet any excess of withdrawals over new deposits. Rather than leave the rest idle, what we do is to re-lend it to other customers by, for example, granting them overdrafts. Admittedly, in the unlikely event of a mass demand for deposits to be exchanged for cash, we would be temporarily embarrassed. But rest assured. We lend very carefully, and in due course we would be able to call in our loans and meet our customers' requirements in full.'

In other words, the individual banker claims that it is only after *you* have deposited cash that he can lend to others. He's not creating new money – just making what there is work harder.

The whole banking story

But the picture of how the banks operate collectively is very different. Suppose that Barclays grants an overdraft to one of its customers, who uses it to buy a car. The car dealer takes his £1,000 and puts it into his own bank account – at National Westminster. To them, it looks like any other fresh deposit of cash. National Westminster have no way of knowing that it is the result of lending by Barclays.

But, like Barclays, they know from experience that any £1,000 of deposits requires only a small proportion of bank-notes to be held in their tills. So they, in turn, re-lend the rest. And the customer who consequently gets an overdraft from National Westminster may use it to make a payment to a client of Lloyds – which enables them, after making the appropriate deductions of cash to be kept in their tills, to make further loans . . .

So when banks lend, and those loans are then used to make payments, they enable fresh deposits to be created elsewhere in the banking system. Collectively, they create 'credit money' (which has no physical existence other than as entries in their ledgers) far in excess of their holdings of notes and coin. But of course there is a limit to the process. They must always be ready to meet any demands for cash which customers are ever likely to make. However, because today (and it wasn't the case in the nineteenth century) we are confident that the banks are not in a state of imminent collapse, we don't keep going to the banks to check that our money is still there. That means that the amount of ready cash that the banks have to hold is relatively tiny – in practice, only about 5 per cent of their total deposits. On top of that, they also have a second line of 'reserve assets' which could be quickly converted into cash if needs be.

Banks are therefore literally manufacturers of money – and that's a profitable business to be in. However much your bank manager may sometimes give an impression to the contrary, banks *want* to lend money. It's no sin in their eyes for you to borrow. They depend on the interest you pay for their living. Left to their own devices, they would be constantly searching for credit-worthy customers to whom they could lend.

Controlling the supply of money

Generally, they have not been left to their own devices. For most of the postwar period, governments have thought that they could *regulate* the extent to which banks could make loans since the pyramid of credit they create is based on their holdings of cash (notes and coin) or other 'liquid assets' (like Treasury bills), the amounts of which are determined by the Bank of England. By creating more or less of such assets, the authorities hoped to control the total of bank deposits.

Controlling the demand for money

Their attempts to do so have been largely unsuccessful, with the banks finding ways round the various technical measures aimed at limiting their lending. That is why recent governments, pursuing monetarist policies, have instead aimed at controlling the demand for money. Since the demand comes from two sources – government and the private sector – the policy has been to:
• hold back public spending, and thereby reduce the need for governments to borrow from the banks;
• restrain borrowing by individuals and companies, by influencing the rate of interest that they have to pay on their loans.

What is money?

Apart from how money is created and whether governments can control it, there are three other major sources of confusion with regard to the money supply.
• What *is* money? As we saw in Chapter 4, it can be argued that bank-notes and deposits are only part of the total money supply, and that various other assets, like building society deposits, should also be included. Instead of there being a clear dividing line between 'money' and 'non-money', there is really a range of assets with different degrees of 'moneyness'. For monetarists in particular, this creates the problem of just what it is that they should be trying to control.

Money and
wealth

● Money is not the same thing as wealth. It is just one way in which we can hold our income or wealth – rather than, for example, by owning a house or stocks and shares. To see that this is so, imagine that tomorrow morning we woke up to a world without money – because overnight a plague of money weevils had eaten up every bank-note, coin and bank ledger in existence. It would be a world in which we were no poorer. The factories, the farms, the transport system and the shops would still all be there and capable of producing goods and distributing them. It would be a world very much more cumbrous and inconvenient to run because money is an extremely useful invention. But the consequences of a freak hurricane that destroyed all the physical means of production but left paper unharmed would be very different. Then we really would be poorer.

Money and
spending

● Money is not the same thing as spending. Certainly, as individuals, families, or firms, it is money that we use when we do spend on goods and services. But for the community as a whole, the total *flow* of spending is made possible by a much smaller total *stock* of money. That is because the pound notes or bank deposits which one person uses to settle bills are then re-used by others to do the same thing. The number of times that a given stock of money turns over in this way during a period of time is known as the *velocity of circulation* of money.

Monetarism
and velocity

Monetarist theory that it is the money supply which determines the price level depends on many assumptions. One of these is that the velocity of circulation of money is in practice relatively stable. On this basis, monetarists can argue that an increase in the money supply generates a similar proportionate increase in spending, which is then reflected in higher prices. If this were not true, and the velocity of circulation varied from time to time, then a rise in the money supply might instead be offset by a fall in the rate at which it circulated; a constant money supply could, on the other hand, support a higher level of expenditure if the velocity increased; the vital link between money and spending would be broken.

What are the facts of the matter? There is considerable dispute.

Evidence and
doubts

The resurrection of monetarism has rested heavily on the massive collection of statistical evidence compiled by Professor Milton Friedman and his disciples, showing that changes in the price level *have* historically been associated with changes in the quantity of money.

But these foundations of monetarism were severely undermined at the end of 1983 in a paper by Professor David Hendry and Neil Ericsson of Oxford University.* Referring to Friedman's main work (with Anna Schwarz), they comment on the 'dubious evidence' offered in reaching 'conclusions devoid of empirical support' – and claim that 'almost every assertion in the book is false'.

In particular, they argue that:

● Even on Friedman's own figures, the velocity of circulation of money shows enough flexibility to make it possible for any given quantity of money to support a variety of different price levels.

● The actual figures for money supply and price changes are arbitrarily adjusted (to take account of special factors like war, depression, price control and rationing) in such a way as to suit the relationship between money and prices that Friedman wants to demonstrate.

* *Assertion without Empirical Evidence: An econometric appraisal of 'Monetary trends in the United States and the United Kingdom' by Milton Friedman and Anna Schwarz*, David F. Hendry and Neil R. Ericsson, Bank of England, 1983.

Their general conclusion is that they are unable to 'find any evidence that money supply creates either income growth or inflation'. On the publication of the Hendry/Ericsson paper, a Bank of England spokesman was reported as saying that the study 'blows Friedman out of the water'. A Treasury spokesman said that the government had 'no intention of changing its monetary policy'.

5

Is Government Borrowing Too Much?

Is government spending a burden or a benefit? Do you feel cheated out of your hard-earned income by taxation to finance it, or do you recognize the contribution which it makes to your living standards?

Isn't it deplorable that the British government borrows *large sums of money year after year?*

Which of the following statements worries you most, and why?

● *Total public expenditure has been over 40 per cent of gross domestic product for many years. It must be pruned, both to prevent the state from dominating the economy and to enable income tax to be reduced.*

● *The quantity and quality of public services are increasingly inadequate. To bring them up to the standards we expect, higher levels of government spending are inevitable.*

● *Public spending leads to a rise in money supply as a result of an excessive public sector borrowing requirement financed through the bank sector. It also leads to either resource or financial crowding-out of the private sector.*

Your worry about the last of these statements may mainly stem from the baffling jargon. Sorting out this, and the general economic and political implications of public spending – and government borrowing in particular – are the aims of this chapter.

We have now become accustomed to government warnings of the need to control, indeed cut, public spending. And a constant emphasis on keeping a tight rein on the use of taxpayers' money has considerable popular appeal. Very properly, too, if by this is meant that central and local authorities should be eternally vigilant in avoiding extravagance and waste and giving the best value that they can in providing goods and services. (Although we hear less of them, similar strictures should equally apply to *private* sector production – so that consumers do not find themselves paying unnecessarily over the odds.)

For monetarists, however, holding back public spending is a matter of much more basic concern. For them, it is the fact that governments spend too much – and the way in which they finance their expenditure – that lies at the heart of our economic problems. The monetarist view is that governments are to blame, through their excessive spending, for:

- *inflation* – as a result of allowing too much money to chase too few goods;
- *lack of competitiveness* – caused by the state pre-empting resources and thereby 'crowding-out' the private sector where they could be more efficiently used.

Too much money

As we have just explained in Chapter 4, monetarism is a reversion to the pre-Keynesian theory that rising prices are due, not to trade unions or other cost-inflationary pressures, but simply to there being too much money swilling around the economy. And a key reason for this, according to monetarists, lies in the ability of *governments* to 'print more money' when it suits them to do so.

This has frequently been the case, so it is said, because in the past political parties have courted voters with promises involving ever higher levels of public spending – for better defence, more on law and order, improved hospitals and education, higher pensions and benefits. But when elected and faced with redeeming such pledges, they have been reluctant to foot the bill by raising taxes to the necessary level. Fortunately there is another, easier way out. What governments can do instead is to pay for any shortfall of taxation below spending by creating new money. And this, according to monetarists, is the cause of inflation.

Public-spending cuts

Believing this to be so, recent governments have deliberately aimed at avoiding adding to the money supply by their own actions. On top of this, they have been politically committed to *reduce* taxes – in order to leave consumers freer to spend as they choose, to increase incentives, and improve efficiency (arguments that we shall be looking at in later chapters). That is why spending cuts have therefore become the order of the day:

- to *balance* governments' budgets so that public expenditure does not exceed revenue from taxation, thereby requiring the creation of new money;
- to do so at a *lower level* that makes room for cuts in taxation.

PSBR

As a gauge of their success, governments have increasingly concentrated their attention on one main indicator – referred to time after time in official publications, in the speeches of the Chancellor and other Ministers, and in policy discussions – the PSBR. Only a small proportion of the electorate will have heard of it, know that it stands for the Public Sector Borrowing Requirement, or have the vaguest idea of what it means. But for those whose consciousness it has permeated, the orthodox message must surely have hit home – that a high PSBR is a bad thing, and that its ultimate elimination would be a triumph of economic policy. Why this is thought to be so, and whether it should be, are matters to which we now turn.

First of all, what *is* the PSBR? As we have already seen, tax revenues may fall short of the desired level of public spending, and to fill this gap government has to borrow. The PSBR is the total sum that has to be raised in this way by central government, local government authorities and the nationalized industries.

There is nothing new about public borrowing. It has been part of the process of public finance for centuries – particularly during wartime, but also on a regular basis with the extension of state economic involvement since 1945. There are several ways in which government can raise the funds that it needs:

Sources of borrowing

● Through loans from members of the general public, by inducing them to hold investment accounts with the Post Office Savings Bank or National Savings Certificates, or to contribute to save-as-you-earn schemes.

● Through the issue of gilt-edged securities – government bonds sold on the Stock Exchange. These are IOUs issued in £100 units and carrying the promise by the government to pay the holder a fixed rate of interest annually. They are 'gilt-edged' in the sense that such payments are absolutely guaranteed – and that holders will receive back the full amount of the loan at the end of the period for which it was issued; in the meantime, there is regular trading in second-hand bonds on the stock market.

● Through the sale of Treasury Bills. These are short-term (generally ninety-one-day) assets which are offered for tender each week and sold to the highest bidders, who then make a profit from the difference in the price they paid for them and the full face value they receive when the bills mature. This 'floating debt' as it is called is generally held by the banks and other financial institutions.

Borrowing, money and prices

What has been said so far should clear up two misconceptions that may exist about PSBR. First, public expenditure does not necessarily lead to a public sector borrowing requirement. It is *only* that part of public spending over and above government revenue from taxation and other sources that gives rise to any need for borrowing. This is a very small proportion of total public spending (less than 7 per cent) and an even smaller proportion of national income (3 per cent). And these figures for the UK are low by international comparison.

Second, the PSBR does not automatically lead to an increase in the money supply of an equivalent amount. Its effect on the money supply depends on whether government borrowing is from the public or the banks. Borrowing from the public is simply a transfer of spending power from them to the government. The money supply need not change as a result. It is borrowing from the banks which increases the money supply – as they pay for government bonds or bills by, in effect, giving the government bank deposits in return. But in fact governments in recent years have been successful in largely financing their borrowing requirement from non-bank sources.

The Least of the Big Borrowers: General Government Financial Balances as a Percentage of National Output, 1983
(The general government financial balance is the basis for the public sector borrowing requirement)

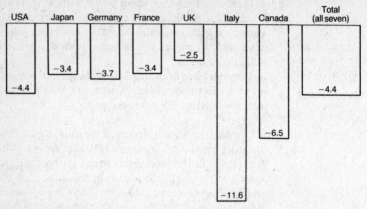

Source: OECD.

There are two further links to complete the complex monetarist chain of argument:

● That any increase in the money supply that *does* stem from the PSBR automatically leads to higher prices – a fundamental proposition which, as we saw in Chapter 4, is itself highly debatable.

● That it is government, through its PSBR, which is the main cause of an increase in the money supply. But the prime reason for the increase in recent years has been the massive rise in private borrowing – partly from companies, but more from individuals and families to finance the consumer 'boom' of 1983–4, caused chiefly by the relaxation of hire-purchase control. It is because of the demand for credit from these sources that bank lending has greatly expanded. So *if* too much money is the root of inflation, why has more attention not been paid to the *private* rather than the public sector borrowing requirement?

Crowding out?

If there are doubts, to say the least, about there being a close connection between the level of public borrowing and the rate of inflation, then what of the other main reason for official concern about the PSBR that was mentioned at the beginning of this chapter – that it leads to a 'crowding out' of resources from the private sector where they could be more efficiently deployed?

Certainly, in an economy running at full employment, greater use of any given quantity of resources in the public sector can only be at the expense of less being available for the private sector. But with 3–4 million unemployed and private companies working well below capacity the case for public spending cuts to 'release' resources is hard to understand – although it is sometimes expressed in such crude terms.

However, the crowding out argument becomes more plausible when the *rate of interest* is taken into account. Thus, it is claimed, governments can only borrow by paying competitive interest rates, and the greater the amount they need to borrow, the higher the rates they have to offer. But this then increases the cost of finance for private companies competing for funds in order to undertake investment. The private sector is thereby 'financially crowded out'.

But, for three main reasons, this argument is also highly questionable.

● It assumes that public and private sectors are fighting to get their hands on a *fixed* quantity of finance. But this would only be the case *if* governments had been successful in tightly restricting growth in the money supply (which, as we have seen, they have not been able to do because private sector demand for funds is capable of causing a corresponding rise in bank lending).

● It assumes that shortage of funds and consequently high interest rates have been a major factor inhibiting private sector investment. But there is no evidence of a shortage of funds (GEC, for example, has for several years been sitting on rising cash reserves, which now exceed £1 billion), and interest costs have been a far less important consideration than companies' low expectations about future profits on their investment in conditions where demand has been depressed as part of a general deflationary package.

● The interest rates that private producers have to pay are anyway only partly due to the level of public borrowing. There are many other pressures at work, at home and abroad. For example, the high rates offered in the US have attracted an outflow of funds in that direction; the upsurge in consumer spending in the UK has led to a rise in borrowing which banks have found more lucrative to finance than lending to industry. If crowding out *has* taken place, then why not blame the US government and British consumers rather than the relatively small proportion of UK public spending that is financed by borrowing?

Public versus private?

These technical discussions about the possibility of crowding out are a reflection of two more general views of the nature of public spending. First, there is the false notion that 'wealth creation' is located exclusively in the private sector on which the public sector is essentially parasitic. But the public sector includes major industries like steel, shipbuilding, aerospace, etc., as well as most energy and transport provision. Moreover, a large slice of public expenditure is devoted to assisting or improving the performance of private firms. Secondly, there is the

57

COMMON WEALTH

'Wealth creation' is often referred to as though it only takes place with the *manufacturing* of goods in the *private* sector. The rest of the economy is regarded as somehow 'parasitic' upon the efforts of the wealth creators.

It is a view similar to that of some eighteenth-century French economists who argued that only *agriculture* represented real wealth-creating economic activity. The 'physiocrats', as they were known, regarded the husbandry which created 'something out of nothing' – farm produce from a basic crop without any 'bought-in' materials – as the only real wealth creation.

Both viewpoints ignore the fact that wealth is created whenever 'value' is added to materials and other inputs by any economic activity. 'Value added' thus represents the increase in the original worth of such materials generated by the production or service process. Thus:

- services, ranging from hairdressing to education, as well as manufactured products, involve value being added to the input of materials, and therefore represent wealth creation; similarly, the car showroom salesman as well as the car factory assembly-line worker is part of the process of adding value and creating wealth;
- value is added by public sector economic activity, such as steel-making or electricity supply, just as it is in the private sector: both represent wealth creation;
- value is added in the provision of public services even if no market price is charged at the point of transaction, as with the National Health Service or public libraries.

The narrow view of wealth creation is thus founded more upon bias than economic analysis. There is a bias towards identifying the tangible output of manufactured goods as somehow 'superior' to services. And there is a bias against public-sector activity as somehow inferior or parasitic. This is compounded by our arbitrary way of accounting for public services in our national accounts. Changes in their outputs are measured by changes in the number employed by them. The implication of no change in productivity negates the principle of added value, and implies that no wealth is being created.

implication that social services make no contribution to efficiency. But how much less productive would the private sector be without, for example, a health service or an education system? It is perhaps more illuminating to stress the *interdependence* of the public and private sectors rather than the competition between them for scarce resources conjured up by the concept of crowding out.

Practical problems

In practice, attempts to reduce the PSBR – particularly in the years 1979–82 – met with remarkably little success. That was mainly because efforts to cut public spending simply reduced demand in the economy still further and added to the depth of the recession. The twofold result, as we have seen earlier, is:

- a loss of tax revenue with falling employment and profits;
- an increase in spending on benefits to finance higher unemployment.

RECESSION AND THE EXCHEQUER

A fall in economic activity reduces government receipts and increases expenditure, so tending to increase the PSBR for any given setting of expenditure plans and revenue policies. The following list, which is not exhaustive, sets out the main ways in which a lower level of economic activity increases expenditure and reduces revenues:

EXPENDITURE

(1) higher unemployment and supplementary benefit, because of higher unemployment;
(2) higher payments out of the Redundancy Fund, because of higher redundancies;
(3) a higher take-up of special employment measures, such as the short-time compensation scheme;
(4) larger loans to nationalized industries and to state-supported firms, because their internal finance – generated largely by sales revenue – is diminished by the fall in demand in the economy. If, however, these extra loans or grants are charged to the contingency reserve, then there need be no impact on the PSBR;
(5) earlier deliveries by private firms carrying out government contracts as a result of the fall in orders from the private sector.

RECEIPTS

(1) lower receipts of income tax and national insurance contributions because fewer people are employed and less overtime is worked;
(2) lower receipts from company taxes, because profits fall in a recession;
(3) lower receipts from expenditure taxes, because of a lower volume of sales;
(4) perhaps some delays in handing over tax due.

Source: *Treasury Economic Progress Report*, February 1981.

Together these tended to raise the PSBR which initial public spending cuts had aimed at reducing – and left the government chasing its own tail.

This is one of the reasons why public expenditure today represents a higher percentage of national income (43 per cent compared with 40.5 per cent) than it did in 1979 – and why the arch-proponent of monetarism, Professor Milton Friedman, is known to be disappointed with the performance of the British government.

Upward pressures on public spending

In addition, there are now long-term upward pressures on public expenditure that any government has to face:

● Britain has a rapidly aging population. The number of retired people has never been greater than it is today, and will continue to grow in the future. People live longer today, and there are more of them than ever for the active working population to support. As well as the extra pension payments which result, older people make disproportionate claims upon health and social services. In neither case is any conscious political decision to raise public spending involved; demographic change is the cause. Thus, for example, NHS expenditure needs to increase by 1 per cent per annum just to *maintain* standards in face of this structural change in our population.

● On top of this, sustained postwar affluence has led to a general expectation of *improved* quality of public service provision. To use the NHS once again as an example, the advances made in medical knowledge and techniques create an increasing demand for attention to cases which previously might have been regarded as untreatable.

The future

To make matters still worse, Britain has been suffering a period of low growth and there is no guarantee that traditional postwar growth rates will be regularly resumed, let alone increased. And tax revenues from North Sea oil are shortly due to begin to decline.

It is difficult to see how a government aiming at a balanced budget *and* reduced taxation can hope to achieve such objectives without the most radical dismantling of state provision of major services, so far discussed only in 'think tanks' and by groups of right-wing economists. Whether that is the direction in which we shall ultimately move, and whether that could be economically justifiable or socially acceptable, are matters we shall discuss in Chapters 11 to 14.

In Chapter 7 we shall consider the view that action so far to reduce the PSBR has been quite contrary to the recent needs of the economy and that governments should instead have aimed at spending more rather than less in the recessionary conditions we have been suffering. But first, the effects of recession, and of longer-term factors, on the state of British manufacturing industry.

6

Does the Decline in Manufacturing Matter?

Which of the following in your view best explains the decline of British manufacturing industries?
- *It is part of a long-term structural change which all other economies are also experiencing.*
- *It is due to the impact of the recent world recession.*
- *It is a consequence of the loss of competitiveness resulting from our poor industrial performance compared to other countries.*
- *It is the result of government economic policy, especially since monetarism became a central feature.*

If you find it difficult to single out just one of the above four explanations as the most accurate, this is hardly surprising as all four have contributed to the decline of British manufacturing. This chapter assesses the significance of these various influences, to see how much we should worry about the current manufacturing decline. It also asks whether the decline heralds future problems for a UK economy in which manufacturing can no longer be relied upon as a major provider of jobs and exports. Will other industries and services be able to take over these roles? Will manufacturing emerge 'leaner and fitter'? Is the manufacturing animal a duck-billed platypus or a phoenix?

British industry has taken a terrible battering. Of that there can be no dispute. It is not only the traditional manufacturing areas like the North, Clydeside or South Wales that have been laid waste. It is the more recently prosperous industrial heartland of the West Midlands that now presents the bleakest picture of industrial dereliction. The course of manufacturing decline is well charted.

Facts of manufacturing decline
- 2½ million jobs – almost one third of the total – have disappeared in manufacturing industries since 1970.
- Half of this loss has occurred since 1979.
- Net investment in manufacturing actually became negative in the

61

early eighties – less than sufficient even to maintain the existing stock of plant, machinery, etc.

● Output of manufacturing declined – by nearly 20 per cent – in the seventies and early eighties.

● By 1983, manufacturing output in real terms was running at a level below that achieved during the three-day-week period of the Heath government in the first half of the seventies.

● For the first time since the industrial revolution, in 1983 imports of manufactured goods into Britain actually exceeded exports of manufactures.

Some regard this dismantling of the 'workshop of the world' without anxiety, seeing it as a natural stage in the evolution to an economy better geared to a future of high technology and service production. Others are alarmed at the prospect of 'de-industrialization' leaving Britain hopelessly exposed to falling living standards when North Sea oil, masking the present seriousness of the situation, finally runs dry.

Causes of decline

But before looking at these quite different interpretations, some consideration should be given to the *causes* of British manufacturing decline. There is no shortage of explanations on offer – the difficulty lies in deciding which have been the most significant. Broadly they fall into three categories:

● long-term factors eroding the competitiveness of British manufacturing for decades, some indeed at work over the whole period since Britain's head start in the industrial revolution;

● the impact of the recent world recession;

● the effects of attempted monetarist economic policies.

Long-term factors

Commentators have been lamenting Britain's comparatively poor showing ever since the emergence, in the later part of the nineteenth century, of other industrial nations like Germany and the United States. The catalogue of alleged shortcomings, each attracting more or less attention according to the fashion of the day, makes long and dismal reading. Blame has been attached to all involved – management, workers and governments.

Management

Thus of *management*, it is said to have been amateurish, preferring the quiet life to risk-taking, lacking in vision and poor at communicating. Consequently, on the investment front, there has been a failure to use the profits of boom-times to re-equip for the future, poor selection of projects and an inability to foresee the changes required to stay competitive. It is not just that their prices have been too high; British manufacturers, it is claimed, have frequently neglected the importance of non-price factors – like quality control, design, delivery dates, promotion and after-sales service.

Workers

Workers, on the other hand, particularly through powerful trade unions, are held responsible for inflationary wage pressures, the frequency of disputes and strikes, the prevalence of overmanning and restrictive practices. They are accused of looking backwards to the past, being resistant rather than welcoming to change, applying outdated apprenticeship training and reluctant to accept the flexibility and mobility needed in modern circumstances.

Governments   And *governments*, too, have received their share of the criticism – in failing to provide a stable economic framework within which business can plan ahead with confidence, in mismanagement of the public sector itself, in interfering too much or intervening too little in the running of the economy.

The depressing fact is that most of these points have some substance. Some are narrowly economic and can be roughly quantified. But others, which may be as or even more significant – like the effects of our class-based educational system – are difficult to calculate. And it is also a problem to sort out what causes what. For example, British investment has been lower and industrial relations poorer than in West Germany, which has had a faster rate of economic growth. But was slower growth in the UK the cause or the result of these factors?

Whatever their relative significance, it seems clear that the British economy, and hence manufacturing industry, has suffered from these problems for a very long period – and to a greater extent than most of our major industrial rivals.

World recession   Starting from a position of relative weakness, it would not have been surprising for Britain to have been particularly badly hit by the oil shocks of the seventies and the subsequent world recession – apart, of course, from the fact that we were lucky enough to have our own North Sea resources ready to exploit at just the right time. But even so, the recession (which we shall look at in a little more detail in Chapter 8) has affected all industrial nations. The slow-down in the growth of world trade and competition for limited markets has certainly played its part in reinforcing the process of manufacturing decline.

Monetarist policies   And in addition to long-term factors and the general world recession, there are the effects of recent UK economic policy to take into account. As we have seen, the objective of recent governments has been to 'squeeze inflation out of the system at all costs'. How far their success in reducing inflation has been attributable to the *monetarist* principles that they espoused is debatable. But certainly their attempts to apply monetarist methods led, particularly during the years 1979–82, to a massive deflationary pressure on producers, with many manufacturers forced into difficulty as a result of three aspects of the policy that was being pursued:

● A fall in domestic *demand* caused by restrictions on public spending – with a consequent 'multiplier' effect on the rest of the economy. It has been estimated, for example, that every job loss in the public sector is accompanied by a similar fall in employment in the private sector.

● A rise in *interest rates* in an attempt to hold back the demand for

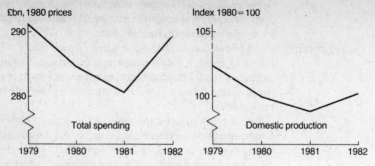

Source: *Financial Statement and Budget Report*, 1984–5.

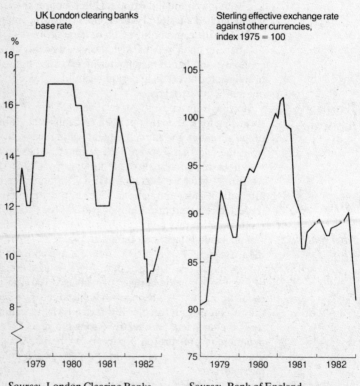

Source: London Clearing Banks.   Source: Bank of England.

money, which was a prime target of anti-inflationary policy. (In 1979–81, there seemed to be *some* recognition that private as well as public borrowing could push up the money supply.)

• A sharp increase in the *exchange rate* of the pound, making exports dearer and imports cheaper. This resulted partly from the way in which North Sea currency earnings were being managed and partly from an inflow of short-term funds from abroad to take advantage of Britain's attractiveness as a high-interest centre. It was argued at the time that this would force British manufacturers to increase their productiveness to counter the adverse effect in export and import prices. In fact, such was the immense loss of competitiveness involved that many of them were instead forced out of export markets altogether. And in the home market a great stimulus was given to imported manufactures.

Critics of this package of monetarist measures do not claim that it was this that caused the decline in British manufacturing, but suggest that it greatly accelerated that process and made the severity of the recession in the UK much greater than it need have been – or than was experienced elsewhere.

Against this, it is argued that longer-term competitiveness was restored by the fall in inflation, the weeding out of inefficient enterprises and the establishment of a platform for increased productivity in the

Where Did the Jobs Go?

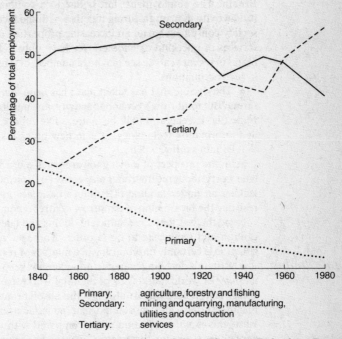

Primary:	agriculture, forestry and fishing
Secondary:	mining and quarrying, manufacturing, utilities and construction
Tertiary:	services

Source: *The Manpower Implications of Micro-Electronic Technology*, Department of Employment, 1979.

future. The jolt to the system was therefore beneficial and necessary. That view we shall discuss shortly.

For the moment we shall concentrate on the main issue of this chapter – does the decline in manufacturing *matter*? The optimistic view is that it doesn't, and that alarm and despondency are misplaced. There are a number of grounds on which such optimism may be based.

Grounds for optimism

● The decline in manufacturing industry's share of *employment* is nothing new. It has been taking place for several decades and should be regarded as a natural stage in the evolution of modern economies. After all, it was in farming that most people found work before agriculture gave way to manufacturing as the main source of employment. Today a similar shift is taking place away from manufacturing into the 'tertiary' or service sector of the economy. The agricultural worker of the early nineteenth century would have found it hard to believe that the UK would one day be able to provide for half its food needs using only 2 per cent of the working population. And yet it has happened. Tomorrow's manufacturing base will be similar, although equally difficult to envisage. Already no more than one in four workers is engaged in manufacturing, and this falling share of total employment is likely to continue.

● Similar trends exist in other economies – it is in no way peculiar to Britain. The employment shift is due to a combination of increased productivity in manufacturing together with the fact that in an affluent society consumers spend an increasing proportion of their incomes on services of one kind or another. We have only to look at the United States in recent years to see that huge numbers of jobs have been created in such occupations.

● The decline that has taken place has been in *traditional* manufacturing. But tomorrow's economic activity, and much of the international trade that it generates, will be in areas like robotics, microelectronics and information technology. It is in new processes and new products that Britain's future will lie.

With the prospect of moving towards such a brave new world, those who worry about recent trends may easily be depicted as the faint-hearts lacking an understanding of Britain's basic economic problems, and resisting the blossoming of tomorrow's entrepreneurs.

None the less they raise sufficient doubts and queries for a degree of caution and scepticism to be in order. To begin with, the *immediate* situation is certainly unpromising in a number of respects.

Some doubts

● Britain's declining manufacturing has not been a decline simply in its *share* of world markets or of the total workforce. Certainly both of these have fallen, but so also has the absolute number employed in manufacturing – and, most important, manufacturing *output*. So far, at least, this is *not* a situation to be compared with what took place in agriculture – or, for that matter, what is happening in other leading industrial nations.

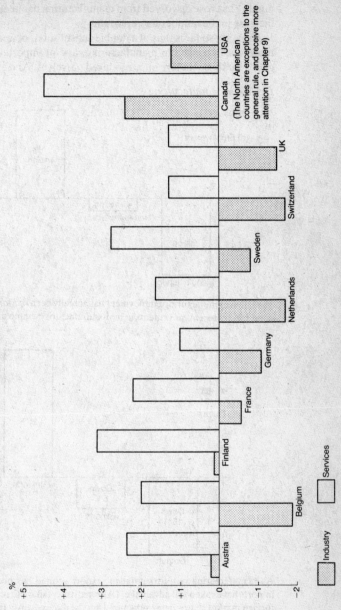

Average Annual Percentage Change in Employment, 1970–80

Austria Belgium Finland France Germany Netherlands Sweden Switzerland UK Canada USA

(The North American countries are exceptions to the general rule, and receive more attention in Chapter 9)

%
+5
+4
+3
+2
+1
0
−1
−2

Industry   Services

Source: OECD.

67

- Jobs have not been emerging in service occupations at anything like the rate of their disappearance from manufacturing. Virtually the same number as those disgorged from manufacturing has been matched by an increase in the number unemployed.

The story so far is thus of a double substitution: of unemployment for those once engaged in manufacturing, and of imported manufactured goods for those that we once produced ourselves. And even if this is just

Decline in Manufacturing

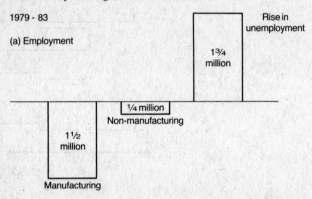

The fall in manufacturing employment has actually been *reinforced*, not compensated for, by recent movements in non-manufacturing employment.

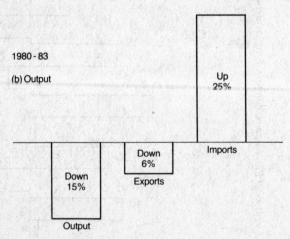

As manufacturing output has fallen, export volume has been reduced while imports have taken full advantage. (Alternatively, failure to retain domestic and foreign market shares in manufactured goods, reduced anyway by the recession, has been reflected in a sharp fall in manufacturing output.)

(c) Trade

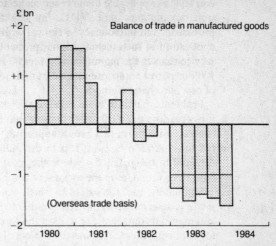

£ bn

Balance of trade in manufactured goods

(Overseas trade basis)

From its traditional enjoyment of a surplus in foreign trade in manufactures, the UK has slipped into the position of a net importer.

Sources: (a) Department of Employment; (b) Department of Employment; *British Business*; (c) *Financial Times*, based on *Overseas Trade Statistics*.

part of a painful transition towards the new pattern of employment and output that the optimists envisage, there are two key questions that require answering – more urgently than ever as the prop of North Sea oil is gradually removed:
- Will services provide the necessary number of jobs?
- Will we be able to earn sufficient foreign currency from exports to pay our way?

Employment   With regard to employment, the increasing application of new micro-electronic technology (still only just beginning) makes it unlikely that there will be a reversal in the trend towards fewer jobs in manufacturing. This is not certain, because tomorrow's technology may yet prove to create more jobs than it destroys. After all, that was the effect of technical change in the past, with reduced costs and prices and new products all stimulating demand and therefore the need to employ more labour. However, the arithmetic this time is not encouraging, with the potential labour-saving of new techniques being of a quite different order from what we have experienced before.

What must also be remembered is that the service sector will not remain immune from similar developments. Whereas previous technological change was focused mainly upon manufacturing production (mechanization, assembly-line methods and computerized control), today's microelectronic and information-oriented technological change is at least as applicable to many service sector and non-manual activities (micro-computers and VDUs in banking and insurance, word-processors and microfiches in clerical work, for example). Indeed the application of such techniques has probably been greater so far in the service than in the manufacturing sector. As a small illustration, some 100,000 petrol pump attendants lost their jobs through the introduction of new automatic methods.

Problems may also arise because the characteristics of new service jobs (predominantly female, non-manual and part-time) are in sharp contrast with those that are disappearing – mainly male, manual and full-time. And in the past it is in the public sector – now apparently destined to be curtailed – where the most 'labour-intensive' activities have been found, as in the social services, health and education.

Balance of payments

Ultimately, too, the extent to which work can expand in the service sector is determined by our ability either to produce manufactures, food and materials ourselves, or to earn the foreign currency needed to pay for importing them. This was the subject of Chapter 2, and it is *the* most important consideration in deciding whether or not the decline in manufacturing matters. It has already been suggested
- that services are less likely to be exportable than manufactures;
- that the scope for increased export of services – like finance, transport and tourism – even together with other 'invisible' returns on overseas investment, is simply not likely to fill the gap left by any continuing decline in the contribution from manufacturing;
- that anyway the UK surplus on invisible trade has in recent years not been improving at the rate in those other countries most actively competing in this area.

The production miracle?

The retort of the optimists to these doubts and suspicions is that they assume manufacturing output *will* continue to decline. On the contrary, they might argue, it is only *traditional* manufacture that is due for contraction. And in time it will be replaced by a variety of new, vigorous, high-technology industries that may not solve the unemployment problem but which will certainly provide the base for financing an extensive development of the service sector.

On this view, greater reliance on market forces has already begun to bear fruits. The weak have been weeded out, and more effective performance demanded from the survivors. British industry is 'leaner and fitter', capable of taking on foreign competitors in both domestic and export markets.

A rosy picture . . .

British Steel is a much cited example of what can be achieved. The Corporation is now breaking even rather than running up losses of £1 million a day. Closure of excess capacity, slimming down the labour force, resisting union pressure for increased pay, and cutting out loss-making parts of production: all have made their contribution, along with

ALL'S WELL THAT'S OIL WELLS

Again North Sea oil disguises the underlying problem. The surplus on oil in the UK's balance of payments of £7 billion (1983), together with a more modest surplus on invisibles, are currently capable of covering the deficit on manufacturing and other trade. But after the peak of North Sea oil production around 1990, can manufacturing ever again provide the kind of trade surplus capable of covering an oil deficit, as we used to have, of £4 billion? The decline in manufacturing industry experienced by the UK is hardly a springboard for achieving this total turnround on the oil account of £11 billion.

Francis Cripps and Wynne Godley of the Cambridge Department of Applied Economics, writing in the *Guardian* of 14 March 1983, highlighted the dangers:

> Everyone knows that North Sea oil will eventually run out but this fact plays little part in the current discussion of economic policy. Yet the onset of oil decline is quite close: North Sea oil production, already near its peak, is expected to fall quite rapidly in about three years' time – i.e. half-way through the term of the next Parliament. Oil decline will pose colossal strategic problems for the British economy. And it is these which should be dominating the discussion of economic policy – not the questions of whether the Budget should give away £2 billion or £3 billion, or whether GDP will rise by 1½ per cent or 2½ per cent between now and the first half of next year.
>
> Short-term forecasts are peculiarly and more than ever inappropriate, because by magnifying each quarterly movement up or down they completely remove any sense of perspective about the major structural changes in which our economy is caught up . . .
> . . . Unless the last three years of the oil peak are used to start an intensive reindustrialization, the North Sea episode will have left Britain with no benefits whatsoever, facing yet another severe intensification of the slump.

advanced technological developments and more flexible working practices, so that output of steel per worker sets new records and even outstrips the Germans.

And there is evidence that this epitomizes the process at work throughout British industry. Thus, during the sixties and seventies, there was an 'underlying growth of productivity' in UK industry of rather below 2 per cent per annum. That was the average percentage increase that took place in output per worker each year as a result of all kinds of improvement in efficiency. But the early eighties saw a dramatic

71

increase in productivity growth – to something like three times its previous level. Such a startling rise seemed a clear vindication of the rigour with which recent economic policies have been pursued and of the regenerating effects of releasing market forces.

Unfortunately, there are a number of reasons for doubting that this is the 'economic miracle' for which we have long hoped. There is for a start the likelihood that the jump in productivity has been a statistical freak, the result of a 'one-off' shake-out of labour and a rash of factory closures, mostly in 1980. Since these were mainly the less efficient, the average output per worker of those plants remaining automatically registers an increase. It has been compared with raising the batting average of a cricket team by excluding the five who have so far scored least well.

To change the analogy, it could be compared with injecting an army with a virus that carries off half its numbers. Most of those lost will have been the least healthy to begin with – but the casualties may well have included younger recruits or those particularly exposed to the virus; likewise the shake-out of the early eighties included in its victims not only the least efficient enterprises but also some which were rapidly growing and therefore more heavily dependent on expensive external finance, and some especially committed in export markets where the exchange rate turned so sharply against them.

Both the cricket team and the army are certainly leaner – but are they any longer sufficiently numerous and fitter to do the job for which they were intended? What about British industry?

Total capacity has been reduced – with the danger that the main beneficiaries of the shock therapy may be foreign competitors seizing their opportunity to penetrate the UK market further. Even back in earlier booms, like that of 1973, an early bottleneck to expansion was often the inadequate capacity of the home steel industry to meet the rising demand of its customers. The result each time was a surge in imports of steel, which subsequently held their UK market share as a 'ratchet' effect, with consequent damage to British Steel; the remarkable productivity improvement that has taken place in BSC since then has been accompanied by a virtual halving of its capacity.

Whether British manufacturing is 'fitter' as well as leaner depends on the extent to which the slimming process has led to increased investment and other improvements in remaining enterprises – and to the emergence of new, more efficient firms. So far there is little clear evidence that this is happening. Investment is still at very low levels compared with the seventies; and, as we shall see in Chapters 15 and 16, investment overseas continues to be regarded as a more attractive proposition by many.

Similarly, there is little hard support for the view that Britain is at long last producing the right products with up-to-date processes and marketing them appropriately. After all, it was not productivity limitations that lost North Sea oil steel orders to Japan, or yielded domestic colour television and video recorder markets to the same country. Quality, reliability, product development, marketing – and government support were also key factors.

The current orthodoxy is that the market will do the job – in 'picking the winners' and ensuring the establishment of a new industrial base yielding high output with relatively little labour, but enabling surplus workers to be engaged in a growing service sector.

Whether this represents a viable strategy for the UK's economic future depends on the ability of 'market forces' to perform two functions:

● to handle the economic and social consequences of the structural shift in employment and its distribution that would be entailed;

● to create and sustain high levels of output and productivity growth – without the support of government measures to stimulate overall demand.

7

Can We Spend Our Way Out of Trouble?

Tight control of money supply, and consequently of economic activity and spending power, has been the hallmark of the monetarist approach. In support of such policies it is claimed that:

● *Governments which have set out to reduce unemployment by reflating the economy have always finished up increasing it, as unemployment followed inflation upwards.*

● *'Pumping money into the economy' makes no contribution to improving our economic performance, and merely represents spending beyond our means.*

● *There is therefore, it is argued, no alternative to monetarist policies.*

Against this it is pointed out that the longest ever spell of prosperity, full employment, rising production and relatively low inflation was enjoyed between 1945 and the late sixties.

● *This was a period in which the economy was run according to Keynesian policies of demand management.*

● *Other countries such as Sweden, Norway and Austria have continued to apply such policies more recently with favourable results.*

● *Present levels of unemployment and unused capacity are indictments of monetarist policies, and endorsements of abandoned Keynesian principles.*

Which of these two viewpoints commands your sympathy? This chapter looks at the Keynesian record, and the case for a fresh attempt at applying such policies.

In 1984 it is estimated that in the UK there are 7½ million people living at or below the level of supplementary benefit; hundreds of thousands are technically homeless and many more live in substandard dwellings; wards in hospitals are being closed through lack of staff. At the same time industry is working below capacity and there are 3–4 million out of work, including large numbers of construction workers and even doctors and nurses.

Altogether, there is a vast number of unfulfilled needs and wants. And, as we saw in Chapter 1, unemployment on the present scale is enormously expensive. What prevents this crazy paradox from being resolved – by paying workers to produce rather than to do nothing?

The Keynesian heyday

We certainly used to believe it possible. Government after government during the postwar period up to the mid-seventies accepted that it was *their* responsibility to achieve the 'high and stable level of employment' laid down as a priority objective in the famous White Paper of 1944. They did so because they thought they now had the understanding and techniques to prevent the re-emergence of mass unemployment – on the principles of Keynesian demand management which we set out in Chapter 3. Were they wrong?

Well, for twenty-five years after the war Britain enjoyed quite unprecedently high employment. Unemployment never rose above 3 per cent and for most of the period was much lower still. When it is remembered that during this period the labour force grew by some 2½ million, the record is even more remarkable.

Admittedly there were a number of favourable factors at work:
● postwar reconstruction and pent-up consumer demand;
● government spending on the welfare state;
● the arms race;
● introduction of new technologies;
● rapid growth of world trade.

All of these meant buoyant demand that might have led to high employment had Keynes never written a word. Several of them had also existed in the years after the First World War, but the resulting boom at that time was only short-lived. The fact that full employment was *sustained* so successfully in the decades after 1945 must be at least partly due to the Keynesian techniques being practised, not only in the UK but in all of the major Western economies.

Demand management

Keynesianism consisted of trying to manipulate spending in the economy to a level just sufficient to buy all the output that could be produced with full employment. This was done in two main ways:
● *Monetary policy.* By altering the rate of interest or the availability of credit like overdrafts or hire-purchase facilities, it was hoped to influence the amount of consumption and investment that took place.
● *Fiscal policy.* This consisted of changes in government spending, taxation and borrowing. If the aim was to stimulate spending then it might be done through cutting income or business taxes, redistributing income to lower-paid groups most likely to spend more, investment grants and allowances – all within the framework of a balanced budget in which government spending was matched by its tax revenues. But it was also open to governments to spend *more* (or, in inflationary conditions, less) than they received from taxation and inject further purchasing

power into the economy by deliberately unbalancing the budget. Whether it is proper or prudent for them to do so is a matter we shall return to very shortly.

Limits of
Keynes

Just how effective were these techniques? What became obvious during the Keynesian years was the relative crudeness of monetary and fiscal measures. Reduced interest rates or increased investment grants, for example, might be expected to have *some* effect in stimulating businesses to install new plant and machinery. But just *how much* influence and precisely *when* investment would increase were altogether less certain.

Even worse, Chancellors of the Exchequer could never be quite sure what change in demand they should be aiming to achieve. The data on which they had to form their judgements was not very reliable. This was not due to the incompetence of government statisticians but simply because collecting information about huge totals like national income or consumption or investment is bound to be subject to time lags and a substantial margin of error.

Consequently, a Chancellor pondering over future policy could not be certain even where the economy was now let alone precisely how it would change in the future.

With mass unemployment as in the thirties the bluntness of Keynesian techniques would not have mattered. It was obvious then that not only was spending insufficient but that the deflationary gap was a huge one. The problem was simply how to persuade governments to inject the required amount of demand.

Fine tuning

But during the postwar period, with mass unemployment seemingly conquered, Keynesian techniques were being asked to do a much more delicate job – one of 'fine tuning' demand to *just* the right level. Too little, and the full employment target would be missed. Too much, and the result would be demand-pull inflation.

Stop-go

In practice, governments did very frequently get their sums wrong. Thus a Chancellor anticipating a shortfall in spending might boost demand and then find that private consumption and investment were greater than predicted. Realizing that this was so, he would apply the brakes and try to reduce demand – only to find that once again this was coinciding with an unforeseen cutback in private spending.

This is part of the explanation of the fluctuations in the economy that took place in the heyday of Keynesianism and came to be labelled 'stop-go'. And although they were relatively minor deviations around a high level of demand, the uncertainty that they created was at times undoubtedly detrimental to business confidence.

Conflict of
objectives

Postwar governments aimed at a complex of objectives:
- full employment
- economic growth

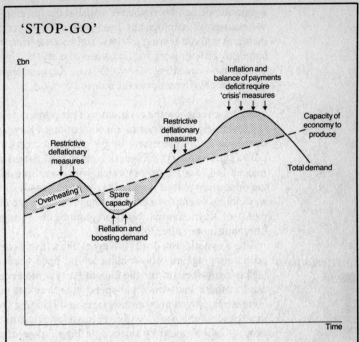

'STOP-GO'

£bn

Inflation and
balance of payments
deficit require
'crisis' measures

Capacity of
economy to
produce

Restrictive
deflationary
measures

Restrictive
deflationary
measures

Total demand

Restrictive
deflationary
measures

Overheating

Spare
capacity

Reflation and
boosting demand

Time

Government policies to deal with overheating or spare capacity in
the economy have to be well judged in timing, size and impact if
they are not to over-compensate. Failure to achieve this balance is
the root of the 'stop-go' rhythm.

- a sound balance of payments
- price stability.

Keynesian policies might be successful in achieving the first of these –
but could they enable the other objectives to be met simultaneously? Or
were they necessarily in conflict?

For example, raising demand to maintain full employment and stimulate growth might suck in more imports without a corresponding rise in
exports. The balance of payments would deteriorate and governments
be forced into cutting back on spending in order to restore balance.

But it was the compatability of full employment and price stability
that was most called into question. Inflation had occurred throughout
the postwar period, albeit at modest rates, and by the seventies was
rampant. As we saw in Chapter 4, there are different views about its
causes. But all of them to some extent or other associated inflation with
attempts at demand management:

77

- because demand periodically overshot the full employment mark;
- because full employment gave unions the power to push for wage increases without fearing job loss, and because firms could pass on cost increases without worrying about loss of markets;
- because – according to monetarists – Keynesianism was financed by unwarrantable increases in the money supply.

We have seen how the experience of the postwar years, particularly of the seventies, has led not to a modification of Keynesianism but to its overthrow and replacement by the old monetarist-cum-market orthodoxy. The centenary of Keynes's birth in 1983 passed largely unnoticed. Instead 1983 was the year in which, with over three million on the dole, the opposition parties singularly failed to persuade the electorate of the workability of employment-boosting programmes containing large elements of Keynesianism. Such programmes were regularly derided as 'throwing money after jobs'.

Is Keynesianism dead?

So is Keynesianism dead? Is Keynes himself now one of those 'defunct economists' against whose influence he once warned? Was Mr Callaghan right when he told the Labour Party conference in 1976 that 'We used to think that you could spend your way out of a recession and increase employment by cutting taxes and boosting spending. I tell you in all candour the option no longer exists, and that in so far as it did ever exist, it only worked by injecting a bigger dose of inflation into the system'?

Present-day advocates of spending our way out of trouble must convince disbelievers on two basic points:
- Where does the money come from?
- What are the effects of spending it?

Government borrowing

The money would come from government borrowing. That is the answer normally given. And it is the simple truth. But it is an unfortunate term that carries with it the connotation of getting into debt, failing to balance the books, imprudence, indeed even immorality on the part of government. It appears quite contrary to the canons of good housekeeping to which most people think they subscribe.

But although matching expenditure to income may be our puritan ideal of how a household or a nation should be run, it is certainly not the way that most of us actually behave. The majority of families borrow extensively. Some do so through hire purchase or other credit to finance the buying of cars, electrical gadgetry or even holidays. But the largest borrowing is generally for house purchase, which is generally regarded as virtuous thriftiness – even though it is the building society depositors who have done the saving in the first place. And it is also thought perfectly sensible for an individual or family to borrow for business purposes, expecting that the returns will be sufficient to service the loan as well as provide income.

Indeed businesses in general are very big borrowers to finance new plant and machinery, stocks of materials, even to pay wages. Why is that not frowned upon as bad housekeeping? Why is it only state borrowing that is seen as a vice and a sign of mismanagement?

Perhaps it is because people think that government borrowing must be from foreigners – going cap in hand to the International Monetary Fund or to other governments. But that is not what is generally meant at all. Government borrowing, as we saw in Chapter 5, usually takes the form of issuing various kinds of IOUs ranging from National Savings Certificates through to long-dated government bonds on the stock market.

Government borrowing is therefore within the family. It is *our* savings that we voluntarily lend to the government in response to the interest rates offered. Only to the extent that governments sell bonds to the banking system does the process even lead to an increase in the *money supply*. And that is only a problem anyway on the simplistic monetarist argument that more money automatically means higher prices (in which case more attention should be paid to holding back *private* borrowing which also adds to the money stock).

Effects of increased spending

Where the money comes from is not really the key issue in whether we can spend our way out of trouble. Much more important is the second question – about the effects of spending it. In a simple Keynesian model, a budget deficit creates incomes, part of which is subsequently re-spent to create further incomes. Total demand is raised through a multiplier process over and above the initial injection. The increase in demand will then lead to higher output to meet it, and a corresponding rise in employment. (The result may well be that the original borrowing becomes self-financing as social security payments are reduced and more people and businesses come back into the tax brackets.)

So what objections can there be to governments attempting to reduce unemployment and increase economic activity by deliberately raising demand? Critics argue that such a policy will not work for three main reasons:

● it would cause balance of payments problems;
● it would lead to inflation rather than new jobs;
● it ignores 'supply-side' considerations.

Balance of payments

In the first place, then, how seriously should we take the dire predictions that are made about the effects of a Keynesian reflation on the balance of payments? The answer must be – *very* seriously. Indeed it is accepted as a major problem by those advocating such a policy as well as by its critics.

The UK has a high propensity to import. That is, as demand rises, a large proportion of extra spending goes on imported goods and services rather than those produced at home. Partly this is a natural short-term result of British producers increasing their stocks of imported raw

PROPENSITY TO IMPORT

A country's *propensity to import* is the relationship between its income and its imports.

Its *average propensity to import* measures *overall* spending on imports as a proportion of total income. This tells us how much of total income is devoted to spending on imports.

Its *marginal propensity to import* measures how much of each *additional* slice of income is spent on imports. This tells us how much of each extra unit of income is devoted to spending on imports.

The 1984 Budget Financial Statement included the following figures:

	Total final expenditure	(£bn, 1980 prices) Imports of goods and services
1981	280.7	55.5
1982	287.9	57.6
1983	298.0	60.4

● The *average propensity to import* is given by expressing the import figure as a percentage of the total spending. This gives 20 per cent for each of the years shown, and indicates that 20p in every pound is devoted to imports.

● To identify the *marginal propensity to import*, we need to look at the changes from year to year.

	Increase in final expenditure	£bn, 1980 prices Increase in imports
1981–2	7.2	2.1
1982–3	10.1	2.8

Expressing the import increase as a percentage of the increase in total spending gives a figure of 29 per cent for each year's changes. This tells us that 29p of each additional pound of spending is devoted to imports.

● The marginal propensity to import is thus significantly higher than the average propensity. The higher our income, the more of each extra pound is devoted to spending on goods and services from abroad.

materials to meet higher demand for their goods. Partly, now, it would be a case of imported goods filling the gap in the market left by the recent decline in British manufacturing capacity. And partly it is simply a preference by British consumers for foreign goods on grounds of price or quality.

Those favouring spending our way out of trouble make three points in response:

● The balance of payments impact depends to some extent on the *type* of increased spending generated. Thus it is often proposed that the initial demand boost should be given through increased public investment in projects that essentially use home-produced rather than imported materials or which directly increase UK producers' capacity to meet higher demand and to export.

● The earnings from North Sea oil provide a surplus of foreign currency earnings that offer an immediate cushion while the economy is adjusting itself to higher demand. Unfortunately this was more the case than it is now and the best opportunity for a major reflationary approach to our problems has already been wasted.

● Buying British should be made more attractive by engineering a substantial fall in the rate at which sterling exchanges for other currencies. Such a devaluation would make imports dearer and exports cheaper. (An alternative or additional method of dealing with the balance of payments would be through the imposition of import controls along the lines considered in the next chapter.)

Inflation   The second major objection to stimulating demand through deficit financing is that it would be a recipe for faster inflation. For monetarists it would be an inevitable consequence. At least at the level of political debate, government borrowing is equated with increases in the money supply, which then feeds through into higher price rises. But as we have already explained, the money supply increases only to the extent that such borrowing is from the banks rather than the general public. And anyway the link between money and prices remains highly dubious.

But an alternative account of why prices rise also suggests that reflation might create inflationary pressures. Thus devaluation would lead to cost increases for producers, which they would then try to pass on, and to higher prices for consumers, who would then press for bigger income increases in compensation.

Against this there would be the beneficial effect of firms working again at full capacity and therefore able to spread costs over a larger volume of output. But reflationists generally accept that stimulating demand, while ultimately leading to higher real incomes and lower unemployment, would have to be accompanied by a prices and incomes policy to contain cost-inflationary pressures.

In the past such policies have failed. But those proposing a new attempt at prices and income regulation think that present conditions are more favourable.

● It would be offered as the *basis for expansion* rather than a response to an inflationary crisis.

● Workers would be more receptive to the idea, having now experienced the high unemployment entailed in the alternative strategy.

Producer response   The third big question-mark against pumping more spending into the economy concerns how British producers would *respond* to such a stimulus. Monetarists rightly emphasize the need for greater competitiveness and have tried to bring it about through letting market forces weed out inefficient enterprises. However, this sort of *supply-side* approach has done little to induce investment and increased productivity in remaining firms which have found themselves faced with stagnant or at times declining demand.

Naïve Keynesianism, on the other hand, relies equally heavily on a *demand-side* solution, banking on increased spending plus devaluation leading to an expansion of investment and productivity. But the past record of British industry suggests that to rely on such a dynamic response may be over-optimistic. Increasing demand may be a *necessary* condition for sustained recovery, but not in itself sufficient. Demand management may need supplementing by more specific intervention aimed at dealing with bottlenecks, improving efficiency and inducing high levels of productive investment.

But today higher investment does not automatically mean more jobs. The application of new technology may be highly labour-saving and there is no guarantee that those thrown out of work during the recession plus those who have subsequently entered the labour market will find jobs within the traditional pattern of employment. Whether we can ever return to full employment as conventionally defined is a question that we shall examine in Chapter 10.

PUSHING ON A PIECE OF STRING

Keynes recognized that some of the techniques of demand management operated much more effectively in one direction than another. For example, if a government wished to *bring down* the level of demand, particularly by reducing private investment, it had several possibilities:

- higher interest rates
- higher corporate taxes
- higher personal taxes
- higher indirect taxes
- tighter credit and HP controls, etc.

But if a government wished to *raise* the level of private investment, there was no guarantee that the reverse of the above list would have anything like their impact as 'carrots' than as 'sticks'. Keynes likened a Chancellor's attempts to raise private investment to 'pushing on a piece of string'.

Exchange Rates

'The pound had another poor day, falling two cents against the dollar, and also showing a decline in its trade-weighted index.' Every major news bulletin carries information like this. But what does it mean, and does it matter?

The rate at which the pound exchanges with other currencies, the amount of them that you can buy for a pound, is determined in the 'foreign exchange market'. This consists of the dealing rooms of the major banks where shirt-sleeved young men hold frenetic telephone conversations with their counterparts in other parts of the world, buying and selling huge quantities of currencies at prices that may fluctuate from minute to minute. But how do the orders to buy and sell arise in the first place?

Demand for pounds

The foreign exchange rate of a currency depends on the demand for it in relation to the supply of it coming on to the foreign exchange market at any one time. To begin with, we will concentrate on the value of the pound in terms of dollars.

In this case, the *demand* for pounds comes from those wanting to buy sterling and pay for it with dollars. The main sources of such demand will be:

● US importers of British goods and services who need pounds in order to settle their bills with those companies and individuals in this country from whom they have bought.

● Those at present holding dollars who wish to invest in British stocks or shares, or buy up British companies, or set up subsidiaries of their own companies in Britain.

● Those who have decided to increase the size of their British bank accounts and reduce their dollar holdings. They might do this because the interest rates payable in Britain are higher than elsewhere, simply because it is convenient for their trading purposes to do so, or in the hope of a speculative gain if the price of pounds subsequently rises.

All of these demands for pounds will exercise an upward pressure on the price of pounds, i.e. will increase the number of dollars that will have to be exchanged in order to obtain a given quantity of pounds.

Supply of pounds

On the other hand, there will be similar downward pressures on the value of the pound resulting from the *supply* of pounds coming on to the market from those wishing to purchase dollars – to pay for imports from the US, to invest in US stocks and shares or companies, or to increase their dollar holdings, possibly in the hope of a rise in the value of the dollar, or for fear of a fall in the value of the pound.

The actual exchange rate will therefore depend on the relative strengths of these upward and downward pressures. For example, a fall in the pound against the dollar could be due to a number of causes:

83

- weakness of the British balance of payments, with imports exceeding exports;
- an outflow of investment capital in excess of the inflow;
- the relative attractiveness of US interest rates;
- speculation in favour of the dollar and/or against the pound.

Dollar and trade-weighted rates

The rate at which the pound exchanges for the dollar receives particular attention, partly because of the amount of trade that we do with the United States, and partly because many other international transactions (e.g. the price of oil) are set in dollar terms. But it is quite possible for the pound to be falling in value against the dollar while it is rising against other currencies. The 'trade-weighted' index takes account of this, being an average of the movements of the pound against all the major currencies allowing for their different significance in terms of the amount of trade that we do with the various countries.

Import and export prices

A 'strong' or 'high' pound sounds like much better economic news than a 'weak' or 'falling' pound. But this is not necessarily so. There is generally a case that can be made for either a higher or a lower exchange rate. In understanding such arguments, it must be remembered that a higher exchange rate means higher export prices and lower import prices. For example, an American exporter wanting $1.50 for his product can sell it for £1 if the exchange rate is £1 : $1.50, but would have to charge £1.33 if it is £1 : $2. Similarly, a British exporter can sell a £1 product more cheaply in the US at the lower exchange rate than at the higher rate. (How *much* more or less will be sold depends on whether demand is sensitive to price – what economists call the 'elasticity of demand'.)

The case for a high pound

The case for a *high* exchange rate was outlined in Chapter 6:
- Low import prices help to keep down inflation. Consumers pay less, and cheap raw materials and components reduce manufacturing costs and pressures for wage increases.
- High prices for our exports give producers the incentive to maintain their competitiveness by increasing productivity and to resist excessive wage claims.
- British exporters may be pushed 'up-market' into high-technology, superior-quality products where price considerations are not so important.

Against this, critics argue that a high exchange rate weakens the balance of payments, forces some British producers out of export markets – or even out of business altogether – and creates unemployment.

The case for a lower pound

The case for a *lower* exchange rate, as advocated by the devaluationists, is that it would:
- strengthen the balance of payments and allow reflation of the economy to take place;
- by increased competitiveness, encourage greater investment by British producers;
- increase employment as consumers turn to home-produced goods and services rather than imports which the lower exchange rate makes more expensive.

The key question, discussed in Chapter 7, is whether the inflationary pressures that a lower exchange rate might cause could be contained, for example by a prices and incomes policy.

8

No Island is an Island?

- *Is the British economy, along with other countries, the innocent victim of world recession?*
- *Is world recession inevitable and irresistible?*
- *Is it equally inevitable that things will get better if we wait for them to?*
  OR
- *Have governments added to the adverse impact of recession through their own policies?*
- *Is world recession the actual consequence of such policies?*
- *Are governments compounding the scale and period of world recession by their negative responses and inactivity?*

Which of the above two perspectives offers the best account of what has been going wrong with the world economy and the best way of dealing with it? This chapter explains the nature of the problems involved and evaluates some of the options now open. How can we get the world working again?

Britain is deeply enmeshed in the world economy. There are a few very large countries like the USA or the USSR that are relatively immune from what goes on elsewhere. But for the rest, mostly heavily involved in international transactions of one kind or another, our economies are often profoundly influenced by events in other parts of the world, by the policies of other governments and international bodies, by the activities of giant firms bestraddling national frontiers.

One result of this interdependence is undoubtedly to limit the freedom of any one nation to pursue an individual style of economic policy – as we shall see in due course. But this is not to say that countries now have no choice in the way in which they react to global pressures, and that they have lost all control over their own economic destinies.

But this is more or less the way that an increasing number of people in Britain have come to view the economic situation. The optimism that economic matters are amenable to rational control, and that the economy can be deliberately manipulated in ways that make it behave as we want it to, has given way to a passive acceptance that we are in the grip of blind and unpredictable economic forces that we are unable to regulate.

World recession

Thus mass unemployment, stagnation and our other economic ills can all be put down to a 'world recession' inflicted like some biblical curse, about which there is nothing that we or others could do. There *is* no alternative to unshackling market forces from government interference and then waiting patiently for the economy to self-right itself and chug again along its own natural path.

This is dangerous fatalism, and the greater the general understanding – about the nature of world economic problems, their relative impact on Britain compared with others, and how others have and are trying to cope – the less likely we are to remain impotent pawns in the economic game.

Let us look to begin with at the 'world recession'. To attempt an adequate explanation would be a daunting task even for the world's leading economists who, as we know, have difficulty enough in agreeing about even relatively simple matters like what causes inflation. But it is worth just pointing to some broad factors that must have played a significant part – if only to show that it did not arise as a malignant bolt from the blue, but from a complex of human decisions and actions which *could* have been different and led to another outcome.

For nearly twenty-five years after the war, the world enjoyed a colossal boom. It was a period in which there were vast increases in production – of manufactured goods, foodstuffs and materials, energy supplies. In the industrial nations, employment reached new peaks, there was unprecedented economic growth, and standards of living doubled or more. There were occasional international payments crises but, in a relatively unrestricted framework, trade between nations flourished as never before.

Development gap

It could be claimed that even the less developed countries shared in this general leap forward – aided by investment and aid from the rich to a breakthrough into modern economic growth. But in fact the absolute gap between rich and poor countries continued to widen; much of their increased prosperity was confined to relatively small enclaves of modernization; the mass of people – their numbers greatly increased by reductions in the death rate – continued to live at near-subsistence levels and in many instances were becoming still worse off.

Inflation

Overall, much more concern was shown about a far less important blemish of the system, but one close to the hearts of those responsible for the financial operation of the world economy. The postwar boom showed a growing susceptibility to *inflation* – extreme in the case of many less developed nations, but creeping ever upwards even in the majority of the already industrialized countries.

Oil prices, 1973–4

It was against this background that the first wave of oil price increases hit the world in 1973–4. Partly as a result of a new degree of unity brought about by the Arab–Israeli conflict, the leading oil-producing countries, mostly of the Middle East, finally formed a common front, establishing OPEC (Organization of Petroleum Exporting Countries) and securing for themselves a much larger slice of the proceeds from the exploitation of their resources by limiting production and forcing a *fourfold* rise in the price of oil.

OIL AND THE BALANCE OF PAYMENTS

These problems were acknowledged in the UK Public Expenditure White Paper of January 1975:

. . . the balance of payments deficit has been greatly aggravated by the oil crisis. The increase in the price of oil since the autumn of 1973 now represents a claim on our resources equivalent to roughly 4 per cent of our national output. This, together with the previous deficit, has meant that our absorption of resources last year was around 6 per cent in excess of national output . . .

. . . Since 1973, the increase in oil prices has greatly increased the external deficit. This cannot be dealt with all at once. Until the oil-producing countries are able to absorb goods and services to match their new wealth, massive international borrowing is inevitable.

Source: *Public Expenditure to 1978–79*, Cmnd 5879.

This was a profound shock to the world economic system that had been booming on the basis of hitherto cheap and abundant energy. It had three main effects.

● It represented a shift in spending power from oil-consuming to oil-producing countries on a massive scale. But the enormous revenues created for the OPEC countries (giving them claims on the output of oil consumers) were too large for them to spend immediately. Strenuous attempts were made to 're-cycle' surpluses, i.e. for the OPEC countries to lend unspendable surpluses to those oil-consuming countries now facing balance of payments difficulties as a result of their higher oil import bills. But these were only partially successful, and the overall impact was therefore *deflationary*, with total world spending dampened down.

● The oil price rises meant a major increase in their cost of production for the industrial nations. This could have been accommodated by them accepting a once-and-for-all cut in their standards of living – but instead led to great cost-inflationary pressures as workers and firms sought compensatory income and price rises.

• Governments in oil-consuming countries, trying to control inflation and meet their rising import bill, frequently resorted to deflationary policies, holding back demand to achieve a new balance. In Britain, for example, where extra spending on oil at this time amounted to some 4 per cent of national income, increasing balance of payments difficulties and problems of growing international indebtedness led to the imposition by the International Monetary Fund of an agreed package of public expenditure cuts and control over the money supply in return for temporary bailing out.

DEAR IMF

Denis Healey as Chancellor of the Exchequer signed the 'letter of intent' of 15 December 1976 to the International Monetary Fund (IMF):

The Government of the United Kingdom hereby requests of the International Monetary Fund a stand-by arrangement under which for a period of two years the Government of the United Kingdom will have the right to purchase from the Fund currencies of other members in exchange for sterling up to an amount equivalent to SDR 3,360 million.

Translation: Can we borrow some money, please?

Since the summer of 1975, the Government, with the support of both sides of industry, has pursued a medium-term strategy whose objectives are to reduce the rate of inflation and to achieve a sustainable growth in output, employment and living standards based on a strong expansion in net exports and productive investment. In order to secure this strategy, the White Paper on public expenditure published in February 1976 (Cmnd 6393) indicated the Government's intention in the years ahead to reduce the share of resources taken by public expenditure. It is also part of this strategy to reduce the public sector borrowing requirement so as to establish monetary conditions which will help the growth of output and the control of inflation.

Translation: We promise not to spend it ourselves, but to use it to allow a breathing space to get the economy going again.

In carrying out the annual survey of public expenditure programmes in 1977 and in preparing my 1978 Budget, I shall continue to be guided by the need, which is an essential element in our strategy, to shift resources into the export and investment sectors and I shall, therefore, take full account of the prospective growth of output and ensure that nothing stands in the way of this shift of resources. In particular, if the forecast rate of growth from the beginning of 1978 to the end of 1979 is in excess of 3.5 per cent per annum, I shall – in order to allow for it – make an additional fiscal adjustment in 1978/79 of between £500 million and £1,000 million at 1976 prices. The exact figure would depend on the buoyancy of aggregate demand.

Translation: If and when the economy does get going again, I'll deflate it.

The Government believes that the policies set out in this letter are adequate to achieve the objectives of its programme, but will take any further measures that may become appropriate for this purpose. The United Kingdom Government will consult the Fund in accordance with the policies of the Fund on such consultation on the adopting of any measure that may be appropriate. In any case, the United Kingdom authorities will reach understanding with the Fund before 16 January 1978, on their policy intentions for the remaining period of the stand-by arrangement.

Translation: We'll do whatever you say.

POSTSCRIPT

In the event the government adopted a tighter control of money supply and public borrowing than the IMF were promised, and, as a result of the introduction of cash limits on public expenditure as well as actual reductions, cut public spending by twice the amount the IMF were promised.

The combined result was a vicious downward pressure on the level of world economic activity, a shattering experience then repeated in the second round of oil price rises in 1979 and 1980 which further doubled the cost of imported oil from its 1974 level.

NICs
To make matters worse, the seventies and eighties have seen the emergence on the scene of a new group of countries aggressively joining the competition to *supply* the now less rapidly growing world demand. These have become known as the newly industrialized countries (NICs) and include some of the fastest growing economies in the world, like Taiwan, South Korea and Brazil. These and other members of the group are countries into which vast amounts of capital have been poured by firms, governments and banks in the already industrialized world. They have not generally represented the reduction in international inequalities that those concerned with world development have sought, since the mass of people in most NICs have not been the beneficiaries of the concentration of new industries in relatively narrow modern urban sectors. But they have been highly attractive to foreign capital as a result of their political regimes, their docile labour forces and freedom from constraints on private enterprise activities. We shall have more to say about these attractions in Chapter 16.

Two factors contributing to the world recession have therefore been the rise in oil prices and the growth of competition from new low-cost producers. The third element is the change that has taken place in both the priorities and the techniques of governments in the course of reacting to the new situation.

World monetarism

That reaction has essentially consisted of a new emphasis on the need for financial discipline. The objectives have been first, to reverse and ultimately eliminate the inflationary process, and second, to maintain competitiveness and international balance by cutting real wages and other costs – or reducing the level of employment and activity. The methods we have already examined in the case of the UK – a reversion to monetarist beliefs in the effectiveness of restricting the growth of the money supply and reducing budget deficits.

But since more or less all the leading nations are simultaneously engaged in similar exercises the result is to *reinforce* the depressive effects that we have already seen to be at work. In other words, in an attempt to solve their problems, governments have in fact become involved in *competitive deflations* – adding to the collapse of demand for each other's output.

Controlling economic forces

These are highly complex matters which obviously require far more detailed consideration than we can give them here. But a key point is that the circumstances of world recession are the result of *human* decisions, activity or inactivity. They are not the result of mysterious natural forces – but the outcome of human behaviour over which potentially we can therefore exercise control. Whether or not we simply succumb to economic forces set in motion by our own decisions is perhaps the most important choice of all facing us. Of late we have come perilously close to opting for a self-inflicted serfdom.

There is a close analogy with the events of the nineteen-thirties. In fact, so far at least, the world recession has been nothing like as severe as it was then (although, extraordinarily, the UK has suffered worse in many respects despite having its own oil). And once again it was Keynes who demonstrated the first steps to bringing order to an international jungle, in the same way that he had encouraged the management of economic forces at work within economies. For it was he who, towards the end of the war, was putting forward proposals for international institutions to manage world trade and finance in ways that would obviate the need for the competitive deflations of the kind we are now experiencing. The passivity of governments today, their acceptance of recession and unemployment as 'outside our control' are as if Keynes had never written a word.

Going it alone

In such a situation, it is very difficult for any single country to try to break out of the impasse by 'going it alone'. The problems can be compared with those of an individual firm in a generally depressed economy. For any single firm to make wage cuts in such circumstances will be to its benefit, as it reduces costs and prices and sells more. But if all firms are pursuing the same policy simultaneously, then total spending is consequently reduced, and none of them gains. And similarly, if a single firm expands its investment and output, and others do not follow suit, then it will find that it is out on a limb, unable to sell its higher output.

The case of France

The recent French experience illustrates the problems vividly. The new government elected in May 1981 was committed to extensive Keynesian reflation of the economy, based on increased public expenditure and stimulation of consumption through increased welfare benefits and a national minimum wage, relaxation of monetary controls, work-sharing and incentives to create new jobs, and price controls. But within little over a year, these policies had been put in reverse. A temporary expansion and a slower rise in unemployment were accompanied by major balance of payments difficulties, forcing devaluation, increased taxation and a host of other deflationary measures.

Critics argue that the programme was basically ill-planned and ill-timed anyway, but certainly a vital element in its failure was its being out of tune with policies pursued elsewhere. But it remains open to advocates of similar policies in this country to argue that what was impossible in France might still have proved feasible for Britain with its enormous North Sea advantages.

Import controls

Other economists in this country draw a different conclusion. In particular, the Cambridge Economic Policy Group argued strongly in the late seventies and the early eighties that expansion could only take place behind a barrier of import controls. They claimed that the long-term weakness of the British economy, made worse rather than improved by recent policies, had led to a situation where the choice before us was really about what *sort* of import controls we should have.

Import Penetration

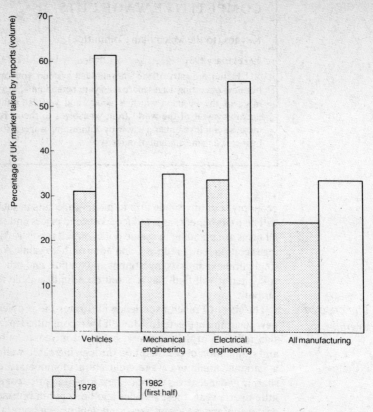

Percentage of UK market taken by imports (volume)

Vehicles — Mechanical engineering — Electrical engineering — All manufacturing

☐ 1978   ☐ 1982 (first half)

● Ever-increasing unemployment, reducing spending power, to keep imports in line with what we can afford, or
● formal limits placed on imports to restrict them to their present level, through the imposition of a general tariff.

On that basis, the Cambridge school argued that domestic expansion could then proceed along conventional Keynesian lines – and that such a reflationary approach would be far more likely to stimulate investment and productivity increases than the policies currently being pursued. In presenting their case fairly, it should be emphasized that the purpose is not to *cut* imports in order to make room for inefficient British producers and raise prices for home consumers. The object is to allow *future* growth of demand (which would not otherwise be possible) to be channelled into higher home production, rather than lead to a balance of payments crisis (as a result of higher imports) which would force such expansion to be nipped in the bud.

Dangers of protection

There are two main criticisms that can be made of such a policy.

● The emphasis is wholly on allowing *demand* to be increased in the hope that efficiency will also then rise in response. But in the absence of 'supply-side' measures to deal with Britain's underlying competitive weakness as outlined in Chapter 6, might the effect not be the very reverse of what was intended? Knowledge that they would be protected from further penetration of markets by foreign imports might make British producers still more sluggish and even less capable of competing in *export* markets.

● It is difficult to envisage agreement with our major trade partners that we should pursue such a policy, given membership of the EEC, the General Agreement on Tariffs and Trade and other international organizations committed to the freeing of trade between nations. And unilateral action along such lines would be bound to invite massive retaliatory measures.

The dangers of *protectionism* are very great, with the possibility of a massive shrinkage of world trade such as occurred in the thirties. And the argument that Britain should be the first to move in such a direction is surely a second-best solution, to be turned to only in the last resort. That may still be necessary if:

● The persistence in current rounds of competitive deflations by the major economic nations leads to equally or even more undesirable consequences.

● Britain's *relative* competitive position is not improved by present policies and its underlying weaknesses become fully exposed with the exhaustion of North Sea oil.

Alternatives

The rationally preferable alternative for the UK and for the world economy must surely be on the basis of simultaneous action towards a coordinated and controlled reflation. The European Economic Community is a natural starting-point. Concerted progress within such a large grouping towards a more expansionary outlook could offer considerable benefits both for member states and, through the lead it would set, for the rest of the world. What is distressing is the parochialism of the issues that are discussed at European economic summits in view of the pressing nature of these more fundamental problems. (See the graph on the next page.)

COORDINATED REFLATION

The advantages of coordinated expansion of the world economy
would reduce the problems and constraints facing any one country
'going it alone' for growth. Here is what would happen to output
as a result of a 1 per cent increase in public investment, coordinated throughout Western Europe:

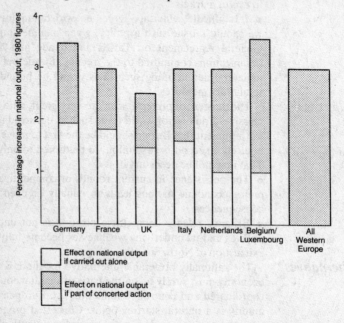

Effect on national output
if carried out alone

Effect on national output
if part of concerted action

Source: *TUC Economic Review*, 1983; calculations from OECD occasional study: *Fiscal Policy Simulations with the OECD International
Linkage Model*, July 1980.

9

How Have Others Coped?

Which of the following would the post-war UK economy have benefited from:
- *a stable and strong currency*
- *a high level of investment*
- *a high rate of output growth*
- *low unemployment*
- *stable prices and low inflation*
- *a high and rising level of productivity (output per worker)*
- *a strong increase in export volume of goods and services?*

None of them would have come amiss, of course! But other countries for example Austria, seem to have been much more successful in achieving them.

How can the Austrian success be explained?
- *Is it the consequence of cooperation between government, businessmen, banks and unions, and of the institutional promotion of consensus politics?*
- *Or are the chicken and the egg the other way round, with economic success and achievement promoting more cooperation between vested interests (which seem to have become even more polarized in Britain)?*

This chapter looks at the Austrian success story and also sets the UK's poor performance in the context of other countries who have survived the recession less painfully.

There is no doubt that during the past decade the British economy has been struggling. And as we have seen, it is common and all too easy to lay the blame for our difficulties over recent years at least on the impact of a world recession – as though that were the product of natural global forces over which we and other nations have had no control. That we have already disputed: much of the recession has been due to a collective failure of economic policy, and the best hope for recovery lies in a concerted reflationary approach that has not so far been attempted.

Who's fared worst?

Whatever its origins, the general effects of the recession have certainly been felt world-wide. However, the suffering has not been equally shared. Some countries have been relatively little affected. Britain, on the other hand, amongst the main industrial nations, has been one of the hardest hit. This is surprising, since one of the main causes of the recession was the shock of oil price increases. With its own new-found reserves of oil and gas, it might therefore have been expected that Britain would be relatively immune.

That is very far from having been the case, as we can see by comparing the chief aspects of British economic performance with what happened in other OECD countries. (It should be explained that the Organization for Economic Cooperation and Development is simply a loose grouping of the main industrial nations – West European, N. America and Japan. It serves as a forum for debating issues of common interest and produces a vast quantity of statistical data and official reports to which frequent reference is made in the media. The 'OECD major seven', used as the basis for our comparisons, consists of the US, Japan, Germany, France, UK, Italy and Canada.)

Percentage Unemployed

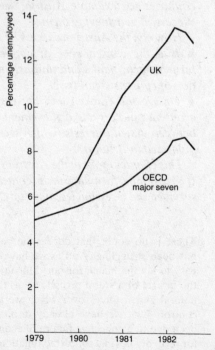

Source: OECD.

Unemployment

● *Unemployment*. The common view that unemployment has risen sharply throughout the industrial countries rather than just in the UK is certainly correct. But its extent in the UK has been far worse than generally experienced elsewhere. Thus, from being roughly in line with the OECD average in 1979, Britain has shot up this particularly unflattering league table to occupy an unenviable second place only to the Netherlands. The 14 per cent official recorded unemployment in the UK (which, as we have suggested, almost certainly underestimates the real total) is *not* the typical picture. In the worst of the recession years, 1979–82, the percentage rise in unemployment in the UK was from 5.7 to 12.4 – as compared with an increase from 5.0 to 7.4 in the OECD major seven. Moreover, whereas in most other OECD countries total *employment* rose during these years (i.e. the number of jobs increased but not by enough to absorb the growth of the workforce), the UK was again one of the few to record actual falls.

Output

● *Output*. As we have already seen in Chapter 6, the recessionary years greatly accelerated the decline in UK manufacturing industry. But what emerges from a comparison with the other major OECD countries is that for them, the recession was a hiccup in their previous expansion, a *slowing down* in their rate of economic growth. In the UK, on the other hand, there was an absolute decline. The fall in industrial output (which would have been still greater if North Sea oil production was excluded) was, in particular, much more severe than that experienced on average elsewhere.

Fall in Industrial Production, 1979–82 (first quarter)

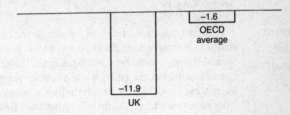

Source: OECD.

Inflation

● *Inflation*. It might be expected that considering the high priority given in the UK to a reduction in inflation and the particularly tight monetary policy that was attempted, prices would have been brought more effectively under control than elsewhere, to that extent accounting for the greater sacrifice of employment and output that had been made. But this was not the case. Starting from a rather high rate, inflation first increased very much more rapidly in the UK, in 1979–80, and has since fallen, but only to a level which is still in excess of that found on average in the other OECD major economies.

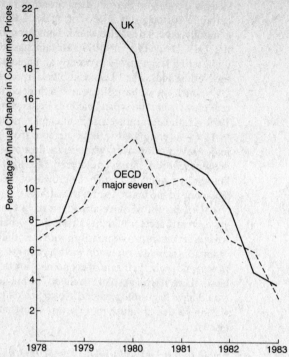

Percentage Annual Change in Consumer Prices

Source: OECD.

<table>
<tr><td>Weathering
the storm:
the case of
Austria</td><td>If Britain has fared relatively worse in the recession than most of its major industrial competitors, the contrast is even more marked if we look at the most successful, such as Japan. However, closer to home, the example of Austria provides a possibly more relevant case study, suggesting that there *is* an alternative to what we have undergone. A brief analysis of the Austrian record may help to give some further insight into the nature of our own economic problems and the appropriateness of the policies that have been pursued.</td></tr>
<tr><td></td><td>Austria is, of course, a much smaller country than the UK, with a population of some 7½ million. But it has a similar distribution of employment between primary, secondary and tertiary sectors. It lacks Britain's energy reserves but does, on the other hand, benefit from very high foreign currency earnings from tourism.</td></tr>
<tr><td>Postwar
record</td><td>Its general postwar economic performance has been far superior. For example, its growth in income and output has been consistently higher than that in most other western countries and over double that of the UK – 4.1 per cent per annum during the seventies as compared with 1.9</td></tr>
</table>

per cent in this country. The result of this faster growth rate can be seen in the fact that in 1970 the average Austrian earned 12 per cent less than the average Briton; by 1980 it was 12 per cent more. And during the worst years of the recession, the effect was to reduce the rate of Austrian growth rather than to cause an actual drop in output. (Nor does this much better growth record seem to have been achieved at a cost to the 'quality of life' in which Austria in 1982 was ranked third after Norway and Denmark in a survey of some 107 countries.)

At the same time, Austria has escaped the ravages of mass unemployment. In 1976, the percentage out of work was 2.0. Astonishingly, by 1980 it was slightly lower still – 1.9 per cent. Since then, it has certainly risen, to 3.7 per cent in 1982 and to over 5 per cent in 1983. But that is still a far cry from the thirties-type level experienced in the UK.

Percentage Unemployed

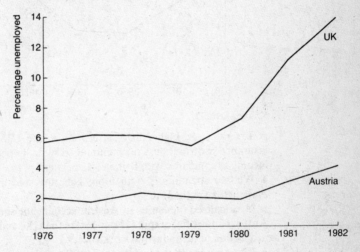

Source: OECD.

Current thinking might suggest that these much lower levels of unemployment in Austria would be at the expense of higher inflation. But that is not the case. Austria, too, suffered from the oil shocks of the seventies – and did not share Britain's good fortune in discovering it had reserves of its own. However, that has not prevented Austria from containing inflation altogether more successfully – with prices rising at 7.3 per cent in 1976, 3.7 per cent in 1979 and 5.4 per cent in 1982.

Why has Austria coped better? Substantially higher growth, lower unemployment, lower inflation. This is an impressive record which cannot be explained simply by the absence in Austria of one or more of those many bugbears that it is claimed have bedevilled the British economy. Thus, for example:

99

Percentage Annual Inflation Rates

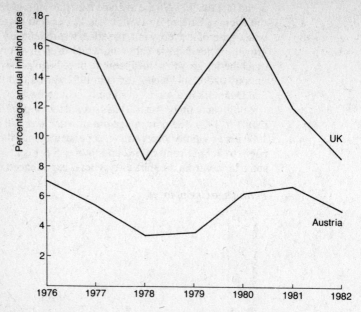

Source: OECD.

- Tax rates are higher in Austria than in the UK. Including social insurance contributions, they amount to some 49 per cent of national income as compared with Britain's 42 per cent.
- Welfare spending is both more generous and more extensive in Austria than in the UK.
- Nationalized industries in Austria account for some 20 per cent of Austrian industrial output (11 per cent in the UK) and employ a greater proportion of the industrial workforce.
- The Austrian economy is even more dependent on foreign trade than the UK: 40 per cent of national output is exported (34 per cent in the UK). And yet, despite having to import two thirds of its energy requirements and a policy of keeping the schilling in line with the DM, the Austrian balance of payments remains in surplus.
- Austria has a much higher proportion of the workforce in trade unions than the UK – some 60 per cent as against 45 per cent. However, there are only fifteen unions in Austria (over 400 in the UK); votes for union representatives show a high turn-out rate of up to 90 per cent; and the structure is centralized, with little shop-steward activity in opposition to the official representation.

Social partnership

So what *does* explain the Austrian success story? The starting-point must be to look at the distinctively Austrian notion of *social* or *economic partnership* which is so central to the way in which the economy is managed. What this represents is a cooperative approach to all aspects of economic policy between the various parties involved – government, industry and labour.

Since 1957, the social partnership has had its most concrete expression in the Joint Commission on Wages and Prices, or so-called Parity Commission. The Commission is made up of four members from the government and two members from the four bodies representing economic interests:
- farmers – represented by the Presidential Conference of Chambers of Agriculture;
- industrialists and employers – represented by the Federal Chamber of the Economy;
- workers – represented by the Council of Austrian Chambers of Labour.

(Membership of these 'Chambers' is compulsory, and the subscription that, for example, a worker pays to the Chamber of Labour, finances research and representation of worker interests over a wide area.)
- trade unions – separately represented in the Parity Commission, with the Austrian Trade Union Federation working closely with the Chambers of Labour but having exclusive responsibility for wage policy.

It is within the forum of the Parity Commission and its many subcommittees that *all* important matters of economic policy are discussed and agreed before implementation. These include, as well as wages and prices, changes in taxes, welfare benefits, exchange rates, etc. Decisions of the Commission must be unanimous, which encourages a spirit of compromise and consensus rather than confrontation.

There is an obvious similarity in the composition of the Commission to our own National Economic Development Council – but there the similarity ends. For although, extraordinarily, decisions of the Parity Commission have no legal status, government in practice refers to it all key questions of economic policy and then acts on the basis of its conclusions. Partly this power of the Commission derives from the interlinking of its membership with that of the major political parties involved in government. Essentially it stems from a determination to emphasize the extent to which all are concerned with common rather than competing interests. This is a matter we shall return to shortly, but for the moment what needs to be stressed is that the Commission is certainly not just a 'talking shop' or there simply to rubber-stamp decisions already determined in advance by government.

Investment
A further element in the postwar Austrian economic 'miracle' is the remarkably high rates of *investment* that have taken place. Investment, the process of adding to the capital stock in the economy rather than consuming output immediately, was running at an average of some 26.6 per cent of GDP throughout the sixties and seventies. This placed Austria in second place amongst the western industrialized countries,

behind only Japan – and it was a rate well in excess of the UK's 19 per cent.

Economists remain uncertain about the relationship between investment and economic growth. Some argue that it is high growth that stimulates high investment rather than the other way round. But clearly Austria has succeeded in achieving a virtuous circle of investment, productivity increase and fast economic growth that the UK has singularly failed to establish.

Finance

An important factor contributing to this may be the role of government and the banks in financing new investment projects. The banks in particular have been much more prepared than their British counterparts to involve themselves heavily in long-term industrial investment. The two largest banks are nationalized, and in effect own several industries themselves (not to be confused with the nationalized industries directly responsible to the government). And the biggest non-state-owned bank is owned by the trade unions.

Commitment to full employment

Finally, Austrian economic priorities have been both more consistent and generally agreed to than in the UK, and its style of economic management has been much less susceptible to wild swings in economic fashion. In particular, one of the main reasons why Austria has weathered the economic recession more successfully must be its *continued* adherence to the commitment to full employment. Increases in unemployment in Austria, far from being used as an instrument of policy, have been viewed with genuine alarm, with economic policies adjusted to minimize them. The approach has been pragmatic but basically reflects an 'Austro-Keynesian' approach rather than the wholesale conversion to monetarism that has characterized the economic policy of so many other leading industrial nations. In Austria there is little anxiety about growth of the money supply or the level of the PSBR – although ironically, the latter represents a smaller proportion of the GDP than in Britain, probably because of higher tax hauls and the need to spend less on unemployment and associated benefits.

Consensus policies

More generally the practical success of the social-partnership concept is based on a recognition by the partners of their *common* interest in matters like controlling inflation and achieving high economic growth. It seems to have involved a tacit agreement *not* to pursue vigorously aims that would inevitably lead to conflict and confrontation. Thus there is an implicit agreement that the present degree of 'mix' in the economy between public and private enterprise is an acceptable one. The political left and the political right do not actively push for radical changes through further nationalization or privatization; there is a similar truce about the broad pattern of income and wealth distribution. Such a consensus is in direct contrast to the polarization of political thinking in the UK – and, whatever its critics may say, it does provide a platform of stability and continuity in economic policy on which it is a great deal easier to build a successful and efficient economy.

*Why has
Britain fared
badly?*

Myths

*Swings in
policy*

None of this is to suggest that it would be possible or even desirable for Britain to emulate the Austrian model. All that this brief comparison can do is to offer some pointers to the reasons why Britain has fared relatively badly and others relatively well.

First, a wider survey would reinforce the conclusion that we came to earlier, that Britain's poor showing is *not* to be explained by simplistic reference to over-taxation, the debilitating effects of the welfare state, or too large a public sector. Contrary to popular myths, the level and extent of British taxation, public spending and government economic involvement are not peculiarly out of line with those found in most of the major industrial economies.

What does, on the other hand, seem to have been true is that by the onset of the world recession Britain was in a structurally weaker position than many of its competitors – that we had not enjoyed during the boom years the degree of success that others had managed to achieve. And the response in the late seventies to our relative economic decline was a switch in economic policy objectives and methods much more radical than that occurring elsewhere. Others, too, may have paid lip-service to the monetarist counter-revolution but it has been in Britain that the

---

WELFARE SUPPORT

Others have put this argument more strongly still:

The 'crisis of the welfare state' is essentially political in character, not economic . . . For the paradox is that the perception of crisis seems to be sharpest in the two countries – Britain and the United States – whose levels of public expenditure on welfare are amongst the lowest in the advanced industrialized nations of the West. In both these countries, total public welfare spending was less than 20 per cent of gross domestic product at the end of the seventies, compared with over 30 per cent in Sweden, the Netherlands and Denmark. Furthermore, there appears to be no evidence whatsoever of a systematic relationship between economic performance and the level of public expenditure on welfare. There is no correlation between expenditure and either growth or inflation rates. What really matters, it seems, is the ability of the political system to make given levels of expenditure – and the consequent tax rates – acceptable without provoking a backlash in terms of either votes or wage demands. Given strong labour movements effectively incorporated into the process of public decision-making, governments appear able to sustain much higher levels of spending than in Britain without either damaging economic performance or being voted out of office: the pattern in Sweden and Austria, for instance.

Professor Rudolph Klein, 'Privatisation and the Welfare State', *Lloyds Bank Review*, January 1984.

---

most dogmatic emphasis has been placed on its basic tenets. Nowhere else has quite such exclusive reliance been put on attempted monetary control and regulation of public borrowing. Nowhere else has the cost of mass unemployment been so accepted as the price to be paid for bringing down inflation. In this, North Sea oil has played an important role – not in providing a cushion against the impact of the world recession but in avoiding the costs of unemployment being clearly seen to fall on those remaining in employment. To this extent, it is possible to argue that the intensity of the recession suffered in Britain has been self-inflicted.

Institutions and attitudes

But perhaps what emerges most strongly from a comparison with an economy like that of Austria are the deep-rooted differences of British institutions and attitudes – the adversarial and sectional nature of our trade unions, our sometimes strident and short-sighted management, the arm's-length approach of financial institutions to industrial investment. These are matters we shall look at in more detail in later chapters. Above all, the failure to achieve any common sense of purpose has led in turn to swings in economic policy aimed at dealing with the problems of economic confrontation rather than creating the stable continuity which might create the basis for sustained economic success.

The general conclusion is that Britain has suffered particularly acutely from a recession that its oil advantage might have been expected to cushion – and yet has been relatively unsuccessful in achieving the policy objectives that its emphasis on tight monetary discipline was aimed at.

Moreover, to date, the British revival has proved to be weak and stuttering. This is true also of the other main West European economies which, although they may have weathered the recessionary storm better than the UK, have not so far engineered a strong recovery. As we saw in the last chapter, there has been little attempt at concerted action – and the French example illustrates the difficulties of any one country going it alone.

Getting out of trouble: the case of the US

All of this is in extraordinary contrast to what has been happening in recent years in the United States. There, 'Reagonomics' was initially seen as a monetarist strategy consisting of tax cuts, reduced public spending, balanced budgets and controlling inflation through regulation of the money supply. These were the aims. The practice has been very different.

Early on, the administration did make its promised cuts in personal and business taxes. But these were not then financed by corresponding reductions in public expenditure. On the contrary – partly because of the additional welfare payments made necessary by the effects of world recession, but principally because of a massive increase in defence spending, the Federal budget soon moved into enormous deficit, which has so far shown little sign of contracting.

Priming the Pump: USA General Government Balance

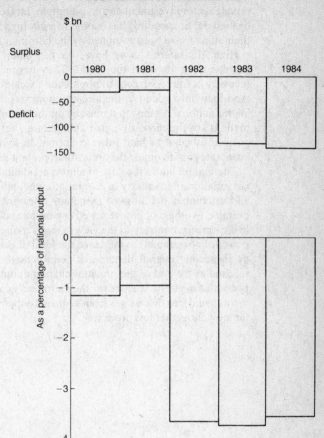

USA General Government Balance

Source: OECD.

Here, whether it was intended or not, were the main elements of a traditional *Keynesian* fiscal response to a recessionary condition – with the government increasing total demand by stimulating private spending through lower taxes, and itself helping to fill the deflationary gap by spending more than it received in taxation. And the results have been falling unemployment (despite a rapid increase in the size of the US workforce), a dramatic increase in industrial output and a rate of economic growth dwarfing that being achieved by European economies. Moreover, it has not so far been accompanied by any significant rise in the rate of inflation.

105

Interest rates, meanwhile, have remained at very high levels although whether this is due to the size of the deficit or to continued attempts at tight monetary policy is debatable. What is clear, however, is that private sector investment and consumption, far from being crowded out by high public spending, has boomed *despite* high interest rates because their effects have been swamped by the buoyancy of demand.

High US interest rates have, on the other hand, created great problems elsewhere in the world. They have served as a brake on recovery in European countries reluctant to adopt reflationary policies. And they have added to the already enormous debt burdens of Third World nations. Against that must be set the stimulus given to exporters to the US by the currently high exchange rate – but it is clear that this will not be sufficient to haul other countries on to a path of more rapid economic growth unless they relax their present deflationary policies.

The United States is a case of almost accidental, unplanned Keynesian reflation. Particularly in its strange combination of lax fiscal policy and attempted tightness of monetary discipline, it hardly offers an example to others of how renewed expansion should be organized. But in illustrating, contrary to the view of many monetarist economists, the power of government to influence the level of employment and output by increasing overall demand, it reinforces the conclusion that we reached at the end of the previous chapter about the favourable prospects that might be in store for the European economy if only governments could free themselves from dogmatic adherence to policies that so far look altogether less promising.

10

Can We Ever Get Back to Full Employment?

Which of the following explanations of unemployment appears most persuasive to you?

● *Unemployment is the result of workers pricing themselves out of jobs by pursuing high wages which employers cannot afford.*

● *Unemployment is due to inadequate demand in the economy, resulting from public expenditure restrictions, holding back consumer demand, and failing to promote investment.*

● *Unemployment reflects the 'structural' inability of the economy to offer jobs in sufficient numbers to an ever-increasing number of people seeking work.*

Which of the following policy responses is appropriate to each of the above explanations?

● *Reduce work time, share existing employment more equitably, and seek to develop more labour-intensive services.*

● *Encourage more spending by consumers and government, and more investment in both private and public sectors.*

● *Resist pay increases, cut wages, restrict trade union activity, and offer even higher unemployment as the only alternative.*

Is your first answer still the same? This chapter aims to clarify some of the issues involved and the future they point to.

For twenty-five years after the war, young people could confidently expect to find work by the end of the summer in which they left school or college. They could look forward to a secure working life, not necessarily in the same job or area but with ample alternative opportunities on offer. The parents of the present generation came to regard this as the normal state of affairs. The fear of a return to the bad old days of mass unemployment receded year by year.

But was it after all just a brief and exceptional phase? Are we now doomed to permanently higher unemployment? There is no certain answer but instead many views about whether or not the restoration of

Youth Unemployment

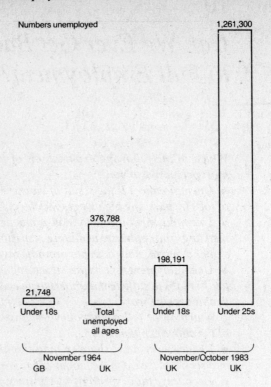

Numbers unemployed

1,261,300

376,788

198,191

21,748

Under 18s   Total unemployed all ages   Under 18s   Under 25s

November 1964
GB   UK

November/October 1983
UK   UK

Source: *Department of Employment Gazette.*

Percentage Unemployment Rates by Age, January 1984

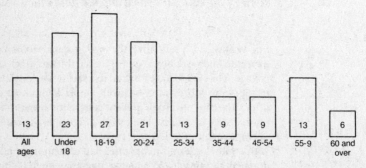

| 13 | 23 | 27 | 21 | 13 | 9 | 9 | 13 | 6 |
| All ages | Under 18 | 18-19 | 20-24 | 25-34 | 35-44 | 45-54 | 55-9 | 60 and over |

Source: *Department of Employment Gazette.*

full employment, as conventionally defined, is practicable, how this might be achieved, and what should be done if it is not.

All that we can do here is to speculate about the likely outcome of present policies and the main alternative proposals that are put forward. This will involve drawing together many of the threads of argument that have appeared in previous chapters.

Can the market do the job?

Full employment has not been part of the vocabulary of recent governments, which have been reluctant to predict even when unemployment might begin to stabilize, let alone whether it can ever be eliminated. That is because of a belief that governments are not themselves capable of employment creation. 'Real jobs', it is frequently asserted, can only arise from increased competitiveness as a result of three key conditions being achieved:
- reduced inflation
- increased efficiency
- lower real wages.

It is the first of these that is government's prime responsibility. Reduction of inflation is to be achieved through regulation of the money supply via tight control of the government's own borrowing and spending. In the course of such policy it contributes towards increased efficiency by releasing resources for use in the private sector and by transferring activities from the public sector through the process of privatization. With the addition of appropriate tax incentives market forces can then be relied upon to weed out weaker companies and encourage the remainder to become still more competitive through investment stimulated by higher profits.

As we have seen in earlier chapters, many of the links in this argument are, to say the least, debatable:
- There is considerable doubt about the causal relationship between the money supply and inflation.
- Government borrowing does not necessarily increase the money supply.
- Attempted public spending cuts tend to be offset by higher social security outlay as a result of the consequent increase in unemployment.
- Releasing resources from the public sector does not automatically ensure that they are re-absorbed by the private sector, which faces declining demand as a result of cuts.
- Investment has not so far responded to market signals.

However, even if government is successful in controlling inflation and industry responds by becoming more efficient, the effect on employment depends according to current orthodoxy on what is happening to real wages.

Wages and jobs

It will be recalled from Chapter 3 that the theory is that the labour market is the same as any other and will 'clear' itself only if the wage rate

109

is sufficiently low to match the demand with the supply being offered. In other words, unemployment can only be eliminated by a fall in real wages to the level at which businesses find it profitable to employ those at present out of work.

Governments can assist in this process, but only to a limited extent:
- by holding back the wage increases of their own employees below the current rate of inflation;
- by weakening union power through legislative restrictions and creating an economic climate in which expectations of income increases are dampened;
- by removing artificial constraints on wage levels like minimum wage restrictions or wage councils.

WHY PAY MORE?

Recent examples include:
- A zero pay offer to the lowest clerical grades in the civil service by the government in the 1983 pay negotiations, on the grounds that unemployment amongst young workers was so high.
- The introduction of Employment Acts in 1980 and 1982 restricting union rights on closed shops, industrial action and picketing.
- The critical review of wages councils, the abolition of the Fair Wages Resolution of 1981 and Schedule 11 of the Employment Protection Act of 1975, all of which underpinned by comparative reference the limits below which wages were deemed to be unfair.

Can wages be cut?

So far attempts by government to work along these lines seem to have been remarkably unsuccessful in restraining wage increase in the private sector. There, by 1983–4, earnings were rising by well in excess of inflation. As Keynes recognized in the thirties, the *practicability* of reducing real wages is a problem in itself – quite apart from whether it would create jobs if it were achieved. Even in times of high unemployment, those who remain in work may still secure real wage increases – from firms able and willing to pay them.

The fact of the matter therefore seems to be that wages are 'rigid' or 'sticky' despite weakened union bargaining power. They lack that 'downward flexibility' that tends to be built into economic models and enables predictions to be made that, for example, a 10 per cent cut in real wages would lead to the creation of 2¼–2½ million new jobs.

Would wage cuts work?

Whether wage cuts, if they could be achieved, *would* increase employment is anyway highly dubious.

110

• If it is to work by making British industry more competitive *vis-à-vis* its foreign rivals, then it depends on what is happening to real wages in other countries. If they too are pursuing a similar policy it is only the winners in the competition to reduce the wages of their workers who will be successful.

• For an individual firm, wage cuts might well induce it to increase employment. But if wage cuts are general then the immediate effect is to reduce spending in the economy. Firms will be faced with lower labour costs but at the same time less demand for their products.

• Similarly, government attempts to lower wages by deflationary policies also depress demand and add to the tax burden of financing the increased unemployment which is the initial result.

The argument of previous chapters and what has in fact happened so far do not support much hope of a spontaneous economic recovery based on a lowering of real wages. The more probable outcome seems to be that the government persistently chases its own tail – public spending cuts holding back demand and leading to higher spending on social security benefits and therefore indicating the need for yet another round of public spending cuts. What is more, such cuts tend to be concentrated in sections of the economy that are 'labour-intensive' and release resources for a manufacturing sector which is less and less in need of them.

In any case, those advocating such a market strategy for clearing the labour market do not claim for it that it would restore *full* employment but only bring a reduction of the number jobless to a 'natural rate of unemployment' compatible with preventing prices rising faster. This natural rate is currently suggested to be some 8 per cent.

Back to Keynes?

We have already looked at the broad alternative approach to the problem of reducing unemployment. It derives from the Keynesian premise that governments should increase the level of spending in the economy by sufficient to buy full employment output. Reflation rather than deflation should be the order of the day – with additional demand being injected through lower taxes and interest rates, general public investment and benefits, more grants and allowances to encourage private investment. This would aim at creating new jobs directly in the public sector, and indirectly in the private sector as businesses found their order books swelling. Productivity and efficiency improvements would come from the higher investment undertaken as the 'animal spirits' of entrepreneurs were roused by rising demand for their products.

Problems of Keynesianism

We have also examined some of the difficulties that might arise with the application of this currently unfashionable approach. Higher demand may be a necessary condition for reducing unemployment but is it sufficient? 'Naïve Keynesianism', *simply* boosting the level of spending in the economy, might quickly lead to balance of payments problems and to renewed cost-inflation.

111

WHAT MORE DO YOU WANT?

In 1973, the Prime Minister, Edward Heath, addressed the Institute of Directors on the many incentives his government had offered to increase investment in industry.

> When we came in, we were told there weren't sufficient inducements to invest. So we provided the inducements.
> Then we were told people were scared of balance of payments difficulties leading to 'stop-go'. So we floated the pound.
> Then we were told of fears in inflation. And now we're dealing with that. And still you aren't investing enough.

These problems are fully recognized by advocates of a return to demand management policies who accordingly propose supplementary measures to deal with them:
• a large devaluation of sterling to restore our international competitiveness, coupled with the introduction of a prices and incomes policy to contain inflationary pressures; and/or
• the imposition of explicit import controls in place of the mounting unemployment which, it is claimed, is the alternative means of keeping the balance of payments sound.

But those favouring reflation do not suggest that it would lead to a quick and easy return to full employment. All that they claim for their policies is that there would be a marked reduction in unemployment compared with the deterioration that they predict will be the outcome of a continuation of the current strategy.

The underlying problem

The question must be faced: are *both* the 'monetarist' and the 'Keynesian' approaches inadequate or irrelevant in view of the nature and gravity of Britain's present economic problem? There are three underlying features of this problem to which we must give attention – the growth of the labour supply, the impact of technological change and the structural weakness of British manufacturing industry.

The labour supply

Getting back to full employment is not just a matter of finding work for those who are at present unemployed. It also means making work available for the sharply increasing number of people who will be seeking jobs during the coming years. There are two sources of this increased supply of labour:
• Female labour has greatly increased throughout the postwar period and the rate of growth in the number of women wishing to obtain paid work shows no sign of abating.
• Since the late seventies, there has been a massive increase in the number of young people coming on to the labour market, even allowing

for an increase in the number staying on in full-time education. This is a population trend, reflecting the second generation of the postwar bulge in births.

When added to those already unemployed, it means that no less than 700,000 jobs a year would need to be created over each of the next five years if unemployment were to be reduced to one million.

Investment and technology

This growth in the labour supply is taking place at a time when manufacturing processes are using more capital and less labour than ever before. This trend was apparent before the advent of so-called 'new technology'. For example, in the decade 1965–75, there was an increase

---

THE 'JOBS GAP'

The 'jobs gap' is greater than the number of registered unemployed workers for several reasons:
● employment has fallen more than registered unemployment has risen;
● this can be explained by unregistered unemployment and special employment schemes;
● labour supply will continue to increase as more young people leave school, even after allowing for greater numbers staying on in higher and further education;
● more women are seeking jobs or, in the quaint wording of the Manpower Services Commission, 'offering themselves to the labour market';
● productivity, or output-per-worker, can be expected to continue to grow, so that less existing employment will be offered in the absence of output growth.

Taking all these factors into account, 700,000 more jobs per year would need to be created to bring UK unemployment down from its 1983 level of 3.3 million to a 1988 level of 1 million.

Similar calculations have been done for Europe and the OECD countries:
● the EEC 'jobs gap' to bring unemployment down to 2 per cent by 1985 from its 1980 level of 6.4 per cent was estimated at 10.8 million;
● for Western Europe as a whole the corresponding figure was 14.9 million jobs;
● increased labour supply in OECD countries between 1984 and 1989 has been estimated at 18–20 million. To bring unemployment down to its 1979 level another 15 million jobs would be required. This gives a 'jobs gap' of 35 million, or '20,000 extra jobs, every day'.

of nearly 50 per cent in 'capital stock per operative' (i.e. the cost of investment backing each worker) while over the same period there was a decline in the number of workers and the hours they worked of 25 per cent. And this was despite the relatively *low* level of investment that characterized British industry.

The trend is bound to be reinforced with the application of robotics and micro-chip control systems. Moreover, this new technology with its ability to store and act on information is ideally suited to hitherto more labour-intensive service activities. Banking and insurance, retail distribution, public administration and lower management all lend themselves to microelectronic applications.

This means that much investment in the future will not be associated with increases in employment as it has in the past. Much of it will be job-destroying and how far this will be offset by job-creation as a result of new products and different servicing requirements remains to be seen.

Structural weakness

The third underlying feature of our present economic problem is the extent to which the decline that has taken place in manufacturing has been due to the structural weaknesses mentioned in Chapter 6. There is abundant evidence of the failure of British manufacturers to adapt to the requirements of a changing world. We have therefore been in the position of too often producing the wrong products in the wrong markets, with inadequate investment, inappropriate design and poor promotion.

Supply or demand?

All of these are essentially 'supply-side' problems. The merit of recent policies is that this point is fully recognized. What is altogether more debatable is whether they have provided the solution. A stiff dose of deflation has been effective in weeding out many inefficient producers. But the low demand that has been associated with the strategy has been unfavourable to that rebuilding of the industrial base on which expanded service employment can be generated.

Keynesianism, on the other hand, essentially relies on increased demand stimulating the structural changes that are called for. But why should such an approach succeed now when it has failed in the past?

We are therefore caught between two schools of thinking about what should be done:

● one emphasizes the supply side and suggests that demand will look after itself;
● the other stresses the importance of high demand in the hope that the supply side will adjust appropriately.

What they have in common is a belief that there will be a favourable response as a result of the operation of market forces. But in later chapters we shall argue that an economy dominated by powerful sectional interests, like big business, the trade unions and the City, is far removed from the textbook model of the market on which such a belief is based.

Radical
alternative

If that is so, it can be argued that a more radical alternative is called for. This would combine a Keynesian stimulus to demand with a range of interventionist measures – greater control over the capital market, planning agreements with major enterprises to ensure that they locate and invest according to the national interest, public enterprise and investment where the private sector fails to respond.

Such a radical approach has never been tried and in the present political climate would be unlikely to find electoral favour. Its advocates, however, argue that it offers the only possibility of a return to full employment as we once knew it.

Future
prospects

If they are right, or if the doubts about the effectiveness of the monetarist and basic Keynesian options prove well-founded, then what are the prospects for employment in the future? If there is insufficient demand for labour to provide full-time jobs for all who seek them, then how might the volume of available work be distributed? There would seem to be three broad possibilities.

Income and
work

● One extreme solution might be to sever the link between income and paid employment. A substantial number of people may want 'jobs' as traditionally understood *solely* in order to secure a required living standard. The state could therefore offer a guaranteed minimum income regardless of employment pitched at a level high enough for those without paid work to be in that position *voluntarily*. Many of these would not be 'unemployed' but engage in a variety of unpaid activities in preference to paid employment. Their incomes would be financed by taxation of those who chose to remain in paid work.

Work-sharing

● A second possibility is to revise our traditional notion of what is meant by full employment – that there should be jobs for all who want them occupying some forty hours a week, forty-eight weeks a year, for about fifty working years. Why not instead share out the amount of available work – through a shorter working week, longer leave, earlier retirement and similar means?

A divided
society

● Thirdly we can learn to accept a division of society into those in whole-time employment and with relatively high earnings and those unlucky in the job lottery and therefore living on minimal state unemployment benefits.

The first of these options is the most ambitious, and would require an imaginative and constructive governmental initiative to change traditional social attitudes towards work, activity and leisure. It is therefore the most unlikely. However, we shall look at it in more detail in Chapter 18.

The second option is more practicable in the short run but is unlikely to be achieved through the normal market process of free collective bargaining since work-sharing necessarily involves income-sharing as well. This is a matter that we shall touch upon again in Chapter 17.

The third option is the easiest since it requires no action or intervention from government. It is painfully inequitable and carries high political risk, concentrating unemployment as it does on the younger generation. More than five million unemployed under-twenty-five-year-olds across Europe is as appalling in its political and social implications as in its human and economic waste. Yet this is the option we have so far chosen.

The consequences may be profound. Fifty years ago, Keynes wrote: 'It is certain that the world will not much longer tolerate the unemploy-

EUROPEAN UNEMPLOYMENT

LONG-TERM UNEMPLOYMENT IN SELECTED OECD COUNTRIES AS A PERCENTAGE OF TOTAL UNEMPLOYMENT

	1979		1982	
	6 months and over	12 months and over	6 months and over	12 months and over
Austria	19.4	8.6	19.8	5.7
Belgium	74.9	58.0	75.3	59.5
Finland	41.5	19.3	33.9	11.4
France	55.1	30.3	66.5	39.8
Germany	39.9	19.9	46.4	21.2
Netherlands	49.3	27.1	59.4	31.6
Norway	8.4	–	11.2	–
Sweden	19.6	6.8	22.1	8.4
Great Britain	39.7	24.5	54.5	33.3

Source: OECD Employment Outlook, 1983.

UNEMPLOYED AGED UNDER 25 AS A PERCENTAGE OF TOTAL UNEMPLOYMENT, OCTOBER 1983

Country	
Belgium	39.0
Denmark	29.3
France	45.2
Ireland	30.7
Italy	49.9
Luxemburg	53.9
Netherlands	41.0
United Kingdom	40.7

Source: Eurostat.

ment which, apart from brief intervals of excitement, is associated – and, in my opinion, inevitably associated – with present-day capitalistic individualism.'* The warning is as relevant for the eighties as it was for the thirties.

* J. M. Keynes, *General Theory of Employment, Interest and Money*, Macmillan, 1936, p. 381.

11

Which Way for the Market?

What do you understand by the phrase 'market forces'?
● *Does it conjure up a picture of harsh, ruthless, cut-throat competition under which dog eats dog, the winner takes all and the weakest go to the wall? Is it synonymous with bankruptcies, closures, redundancies and unemployment?*
● *Or does it suggest a fair and efficient way of organizing the maximum freedom of choice for consumers, of obtaining the most efficient allocation of economic resources and of obliging producers to respond to consumer preferences? Is it a formula for consumer sovereignty?*

Is your answer influenced by your experiences in recent years, your behaviour as a consumer or your level of income? These are some of the considerations which will affect the role and appropriateness of market forces as an engine of economics, and which form the subject of this chapter.

The language of the market, like that of Eliza Doolittle, is strong and colourful. And when we move from the bustling vitality of the stall-holders in a market square to the more abstract notion of 'the market' in economics, we find that the terms used there are similarly robust and persuasive. Thus its advocates often refer to a 'free' market economy, the necessary 'discipline of the market' or the wisdom of 'leaving the market to get on with the job'. Above all, there is the suggestion of impersonal and powerful 'market forces' at work with which we interfere only at our peril.

The market has already been mentioned on numerous occasions in earlier chapters, and it is high time that some explanation was given of just what is meant by market forces and how they operate in practice. These are matters which, after all, economists over the centuries have spent a huge amount of their time studying in the minutest detail; scratch most economists and market analysis will soon gush out. Then again, a very large proportion of output in western economies is actually produced and sold in market conditions of one kind or another. And finally, it is important to understand its strengths and weaknesses because recent governments have been placing increasing reliance on the market's ability to bring the best out of people, companies and the economy.

The price mechanism

To begin at the beginning, just what is a market? It is simply the bringing together of buyers and sellers – physically, by telephone or by some other form of contact. But whatever the circumstances, a key role is then played by the so-called *price mechanism*. In a market system, prices are a gauge of how much consumers are prepared to buy and how much producers are willing to sell of various goods and services.

● Consumers in effect 'elect' a certain pattern of output by the way in which they 'cast their votes' (distribute their spending) amongst the alternatives on offer. How much they are prepared to pay is therefore a reflection of the strength of consumer preferences.

● The amount that producers offer for sale will depend on their costs of production. The prices they charge will therefore reflect the relative scarcity or abundance of the land, labour and capital that they need in order to produce for the market.

The interests of consumers and producers are directly in conflict. Consumers want low prices whereas for producers the higher the better. The market serves to strike a balance, with prices settling at levels that just match the strength of consumer preferences with the scarcity of resources. Moreover, changes in the relative prices of products signal the need for a different pattern of output. For example, increased popularity of a certain style of jeans may mean that market traders can charge a bit more; increased revenue for the producers means they can buy more materials and hire more workers so that output rises in response. A producer of an unpopular line, on the other hand, may be forced out of business by lack of demand.

Efficiency of production and consumer satisfaction are thus harmonized through the working of the market. Competition will keep prices down and prevent excess profits; it will weed out the inefficient or force them to improve; the successful go-getters will be rewarded and thrive. In this way, the economy's land, labour and capital are put to the best possible uses (what economists call an 'optimum allocation of resources') which maximize the benefits enjoyed by consumers.

And, almost magically, this is achieved without government intervention – through the natural operation of demand and supply. 'As if by an unseen hand', Adam Smith put it, the actions of millions of individuals each pursuing their own self-interest lead to the common good. No wonder the nineteenth-century economist, J. B. Say, concluded, 'That government is best which governs least.'

Command economy

The virtues of the market are commonly highlighted still further by comparison with the alternative basic system for deciding what should be produced and in what quantities. This is bleakly labelled a 'command economy' in which such matters are settled through administrative decisions taken by governments or planning authorities – according to what *they* think consumers want or need or ought to have. The picture that this conjures up – of red tape, coercion and muddle – is highly unattractive compared with the 'free' workings of a 'self-regulating' market mechanism.

DEMAND OR COMMAND?

What are the advantages of a market economy as compared to a command economy? The points below set out some of the disadvantages of each:

MARKET ECONOMY

● Production may be distorted so that the rich get what they want and the poor are left out (e.g. luxury office blocks rather than old people's homes).

● The market may operate to reinforce and widen these inequalities (e.g. concentration of personal ownership of shares into few hands).

● Market forces may be restricted by monopoly elements with undue power over prices and production levels (such as dominant producers of building materials or closed-shop industrial trade unions).

● Resources may not be sufficiently mobile to allow market forces to operate (this can apply to land, labour and capital).

● Consumers may have insufficient or incorrect information about goods and services (irresponsible advertising and artificial product differentiation are examples here).

● At the international level, market forces can leave great power in the hands of the 'multinational' companies (e.g. they can choose which country to take their main profit in as a result of their internal pricing policies).

COMMAND ECONOMY

● Resources may be wasted by not being used where their efficiency is highest (e.g. the deliberate encouragement of 'prestige' industries, such as aerospace, which have very high opportunity costs).

● Neither prices nor production levels may be responsive to changes in consumer demand (shortages and long waiting lists are symptoms of this).

● The planners' decisions may not closely reflect people's genuine preferences or their social priorities (e.g. improvements in public transport may be held back in favour of subsidies to agriculture).

● Production can become geared to *quantity*, with insufficient attention to quality or suitability (when Yugoslavia was a centrally planned economy after the war, the adoption of production targets for glasses led to over-production of glasses which were too small to contain a bottle of beer).

● Problems arising from the lack of incentives can emerge, as producers decide it is not worth making extra effort in the absence of extra profits (again quality can suffer and wastages occur).

● The power of the planners and of the key industries can lead to bureaucracy, privilege and corruption.

● The overriding of market forces in favour of certain kinds of production can lead to imbalance and unfairness in the context of international trade.

Mixed economies

And yet the fact is that no economy in the world relies exclusively on the market. Nor is there any example to be found of a pure command economy. Instead, everywhere we find *mixed* economies combining elements of both. Certainly, in the United States it is the market that largely prevails. But huge quantities of resources are directed into the output of, for example, armaments or the space programme – by governments rather than market forces. And similarly in the Soviet Union or China, where many more decisions are taken by planning bodies, there remain large areas, mostly in the production of consumer goods, where market considerations are dominant. The political argument, both globally and in the UK itself, is about what *degree* of the mix is the proper one.

LEAVE IT TO THE MARKET

A major aim of the government since coming into office in May 1979 has been the restoration of market forces throughout the economy.

Treasury Economic Progress Report, May 1982.

In Britain, recent governments have strongly argued the case for a wider application of market criteria. They have aimed at extending that part of the economy subject to market forces rather than decisions by the state. And on the basis of the picture of the market at work that we have presented so far, it is easy to understand its popular appeal.

121

Limits of the market

But there is another side to the story which casts serious doubt on the idea that everyone's interests are best served by the market mechanism and its forces of competition. There are two main grounds on which the efficiency claimed for market forces may be challenged:

● Do they work in practice – or have we been setting up an ideal, utopian model unlikely to be found in the real world?

● Even if they did work in practice, would the outcome be obviously acceptable or 'optimal' as the theory suggests?

Theory and practice

First, then, the question of how closely the market in practice resembles that of the economists' textbook model. In that model, there are a large number of conditions that must be satisfied if the market is to work as it should. Of these, three are particularly important:

● Consumers must be perfectly knowledgeable and aware of all the alternatives on offer, and choose between them in a rational way.

● Producers must be sufficiently numerous for none of them to be large enough to dominate any market, or be capable of influencing or collaborating with other producers.

● Resources, like labour and capital, must be perfectly mobile – able and willing to switch freely from one type of production to another.

Why must these conditions hold good if market forces are to be effective? Because if consumers are not rational and fully informed, then the way in which they spend their incomes will not clearly indicate how *they* want resources used. If producers are not in genuine competition, then it is open to them to pocket some of the consumer 'votes' for themselves (in the form of excess profits) and to rig prices for their own benefit rather than as clear signals to consumers about relative costs of production. And if resources are not perfectly mobile, then capital and workers will not respond to changes in tastes and other conditions by moving from declining to expanding areas and occupations. Instead they may simply become unemployed.

Unfortunately, it is all too likely that the real world *will* differ from the ideal market model in these key respects. In practice, it is very difficult for consumers to be as informed as they might wish; the goods they buy are often technically sophisticated, many important purchases like cars or houses are made irregularly so that it is hard to learn from past experience, and advertising may lead them into irrational or impulse buying. In practice, most industries are dominated by just a handful of firms, sometimes large enough to ignore market signals and able to avoid open competition. In practice, resources are frequently 'sticky' rather than mobile and cannot easily be switched from one application to another in the short run.

In later chapters we shall be looking in more detail at some of these many reasons why the unfettered competition and free working of market forces of the ideal model may not apply in practice. The existence of such blemishes and obstacles to it working as it should are plain to see. And yet those who advocate greater reliance on the market as the cure for our economic ills all too often argue as though they did not exist.

The market outcome

If the gap between market theory and reality is worrying, even more serious qualms arise when we consider the second major ground for doubting the wisdom of over-reliance on market forces. Three main points can be made which suggest that even if the market did behave in textbook fashion, the outcome might not be as economically efficient or politically acceptable as its proponents would have us believe.

Private v. external

● The only costs and revenues that are relevant in a market economy are *private* ones, i.e. those that appear in the balance sheets and the profit and loss accounts of firms. It is these that provide the sole criterion of success or failure, indicating whether a firm should expand or leave the industry. But contrary to simple market theory, what is good for ICI or the NCB is *not* necessarily therefore good for the economy as a whole. That is because the operations of one enterprise may impose

COMMERCIAL AND ECONOMIC

A striking example of the discrepancy between private commercial costs and wider social economic considerations is provided by British Rail. Increasingly claiming to be a 'business-led' corporation, British Rail announced its five-year plan in August 1983. It aimed at reducing its need for public subsidy by lowering costs through staff cuts and line closures.

Within the terms of reference of the British Rail accountant this is eminently rational, and represents sound commercial logic. But:

● at least one third of the reduction in public subsidy would be transferred to other headings of public expenditure, especially unemployment and supplementary benefits to railwaymen made redundant;

● loss of income tax and social security contributions to public revenue is not included in commercial accounting;

● no figures are placed by commercial criteria on the economic and social dislocation which might result from line closures;

● no account is taken of the economic and social costs of any additional demands, including congestion, placed upon alternative road facilities.

The overall economic appraisal of costs and benefits thus reaches far wider than the private profit-and-loss account of a commercial concern.

123

costs on *other* companies and individuals (e.g. pollution, unemployment benefits arising from redundancies, traffic congestion). Similarly, others may find themselves enjoying benefits such as the increased business done by local traders because of higher employment by a major firm in the area, or through sharing the power or transport facilities installed for it. These costs and benefits are *external*, not picked up at all in the accountancy of *commercial* profit maximization but equally *economic* in their significance. We shall have more to say about the divergence of private and external or 'social' costs and benefits in coming chapters.

Wants and needs

● The unregulated market is inevitably geared to satisfying wants rather than meeting needs. The price mechanism only recognizes effective demand, i.e. willingness to buy backed by spending power. Those who can pay can therefore influence the responses of producers, while the needs of those who can't will be discounted. Thus, for example, it could be said the housing market, by setting appropriate prices, ensures that the supply of dwellings is sufficient to meet the demand for them. But all that means is that the houses available match the number required by those who can afford to buy them. It tells us nothing about the extent of homelessness amongst low-income groups who do not form part of the housing market.

UNCOMMON MARKET

The European Community (Common Market) provides an interesting example of how the market cannot be relied upon or trusted to be the sole determinant of relating supply to demand.

● The Treaty of Rome (1957), which founded the European Economic Community, held as its aim the creation of a free, unfettered European market. No kinds of restrictions, such as tariffs, would be permitted to encroach upon the free operation of market forces.

● In practice, the Community has recognized the imbalances within its territories as justifying its intervention in the free play of market forces in several ways, including:

a social fund and social policy concerned with disadvantaged groups such as the unemployed, and with workers' rights;

a regional fund and policy concerned with disadvantaged territories such as southern Italy or Northern Ireland;

a range of community aid and assistance to particular sectors (such as textiles) and specific firms which qualify (such as research and development);

plans for the restructuring or capacity reduction of sectors such as shipbuilding, steel and coal.

Income
distribution

Moreover, it is not legitimate to argue, as some economists have tried to do, that the market leads to the most *efficient* use of resources – and that matters of *income distribution* are a separate 'political' question outside the economist's scope. That is because the market definition of the 'most efficient' use of resources is the pattern of output which is signalled by prices that themselves reflect the existing income distribution. Think what would happen if incomes were distributed much more equally. Then the demand for luxury goods would diminish and that for basic necessities increase. Relative prices would change accordingly and the 'most efficient' use of resources would be quite different.

Policy
objectives

● The market does not in itself guarantee that there will be full employment or price stability in the economy, or that it will be geared to economic growth. It is a useful way of deciding whether rather more of this or rather less of that should be produced – but the collective outcome of innumerable individual decisions may not be what we want from the economy. For Keynesian economists, certainly, it is extremely unlikely that an unregulated market economy will lead to full employment. And with regard to economic growth, the emphasis of the market may be on maximizing the short-term rate of return on investors' capital

COMMON AGRICULTURAL POLICY

The European Community provides an example of supply and demand overriding administrative intervention. Its Common Agricultural Policy (CAP) is a major target of criticism. It is claimed that it dominates the budget (CAP represents over two thirds of all Community spending); featherbeds farmers; and creates mountains of butter and lakes of wine.

The point to note, however, is that the social and political motivations underlying the CAP have served their purpose in maintaining farm support prices. These provide guaranteed incomes for farmers who might otherwise leave the land. But they also provide excesses of agricultural produce. Intervention in the form of price support may well enhance production levels by making farming a relatively more attractive proposition for suppliers. But it does nothing to create or even sustain demand for such produce inside the Community. Indeed, if anything, the higher prices *deter* consumers and divert them towards alternatives wherever available.

The moral is that intervention – as with planning – cannot *remove* or *override* supply and demand considerations. These remain in force, and can only be planned *through*, by manipulation.

through, for example, property speculation rather than the systematic development of the economy's productive base.

Assessing the market

These are all serious criticisms of the market. But to list them is in no way to suggest that we abandon the market as a method for allocating resources or even greatly reduce its present scope.

That would be stupid. For, like money, the market is a brilliant accidental invention of economic society – a mechanism better capable of deciding the pattern of production for a large proportion of our output than any other method that has so far been devised.

There are many areas where its application is inappropriate – as we shall argue in Chapters 13 and 14. And it must always be made to serve rather than rule our economic lives. There are three broad conditions needed to ensure that this is so:

● Governments can encourage the creation of conditions in which the market is likely to work better – for example, by stimulating genuine competition, helping to increase mobility of resources and by establishing what is generally regarded as a 'fair' distribution of income and wealth.

● The market does not consist of natural forces beyond human control. There is considerable scope for achieving objectives of economic and social policy through *manipulation* of market forces. To take housing as an example once again, a government decree setting a lower ceiling on house prices would not in itself solve the problem of homelessness. At the lower price, fewer houses would be offered for sale and more would be demanded. Market forces would simply expose the extent of a 'housing shortage'. To eliminate it, those forces themselves would have to be altered. Subsidies to housebuilders would increase the supply to meet that higher demand. Policy will have worked *through* the market rather than despite it.

● Governments must continue to assume responsibility for creating the broad framework of high employment, price and balance of payments stability and economic growth wherever the market can be seen to be working too slowly, unfairly or not at all.

The real question is not whether one is for or against the market but rather what role is assigned to it. Politicians who sloganize about the virtues of the market or who can only see it as an expression of ruthless greed must be viewed with equal suspicion. At a more thoughtful level, it is clear that many Eastern European economies suffer from a lack of the market's role in their workings, while it is equally clear from the experience of western economies that there is a considerable price to pay for the unbridled activities of market forces.

In recent years, governments in the UK have aimed at bringing about a radically new 'mix' in the economy, placing much greater reliance on market forces. It is important that the debate about this important switch should be as informed as possible. That is why, in subsequent chapters, we shall examine some of the economic and social implications of the new direction in policy and try to get behind the political rhetoric and dogmas that so often shroud the real issues at stake.

Demand, Supply and Price

Demand

The principle which governs the 'law of demand' in economics is that *the higher the price of a good, the less will be the demand for it*. This is because a higher price requires a greater sacrifice of other spending on the part of the consumer. Demand could refer to an individual, a retail outlet, a particular product, or total demand in an economy. To be meaningful, demand should always refer to a specified period (hour, day, week, month or year).

Consider a shop selling video tape recorders. If priced at £500, the shop might be doing well to sell just one per month. At £400, demand rises to two; at £300 four per month are demanded; and so on. Demand per month would be ten if price came down to £100. The lower the price, the higher the demand.

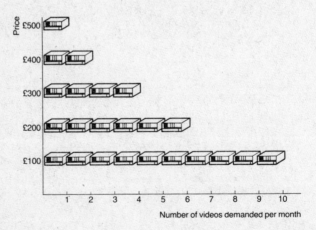

This kind of picture, or demand schedule, can be drawn more simply as a demand curve:

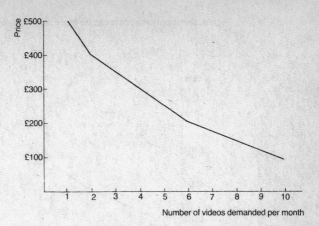

Number of videos demanded per month

Supply

The principle which governs the 'law of supply' in economics is that *the higher the price of a good, the more of it will be produced*. This is because resources are most profitably put to use where rewards are greatest. 'Supply' in economics could refer to a single producer, or to a particular product, or to total production throughout the economy.

Consider a firm producing video tape recorders and supplying the shop described above. At a price of £100, there is little incentive to produce and only one is supplied. At £200 it is worth the while of the producer to supply four, and so on. At £500 ten are forthcoming.

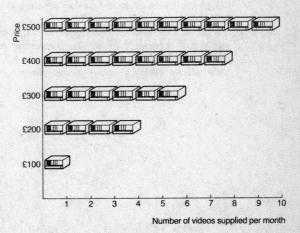

Number of videos supplied per month

Again, the supply schedule can be more simply drawn as a supply curve:

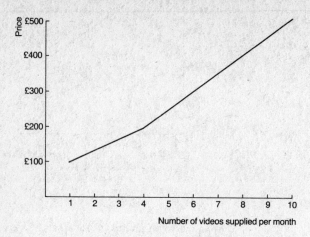

Number of videos supplied per month

Price

Price in economics is determined by the *interaction* of supply and demand: the market mechanism equates supply and demand through market price.

Diagrammatically again, this will be where the supply and demand curves cross each other: in our example the market price for video tape recorders will be £250, at which price five will be both demanded and supplied.

● *Above this price*, supply will exceed demand and there will be a surplus. Competition between producers must then be relied upon to bring the price down.

● *Below this price*, demand will exceed supply and there will be a shortage. Consumers in such circumstances may be willing to pay more, and the price can be pushed up.

It can thus be seen that at any price other than market price, which equates supply and demand, there will be competitive pressures at work amongst producers and consumers. These will have the effect of forcing the price back towards its market level – known in economics as 'equilibrium'.

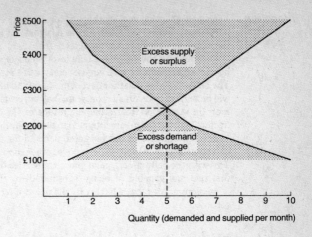

The power of supply and demand on market forces can be illustrated with reference to the point earlier in this chapter about the European Community's Common Agricultural Policy.

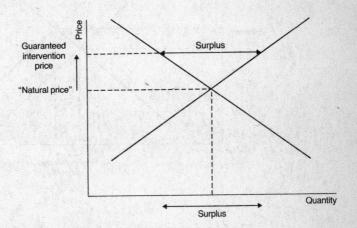

The diagram shows the effect of intervention in the market mechanism to provide guaranteed price levels for various agricultural products. A higher price is achieved by administrative mechanisms. These do not affect the position of the supply and demand curves, but merely encourage supply to exceed demand and thereby create surpluses in the form of butter mountains, wine lakes, etc.

As well as acting as a mechanism for equating supply of and demand for a particular product, price also acts as a 'signal' for influencing the allocation of resources between different products.

Returning to the original example of video tape recorders, consider what happens if demand for such goods increases as a result of consumer preference. The diagram shows that the effect of this (a shift to the right of the demand curve) will be to raise price. In due course this will attract more production and possibly more producers, so that economic resources (land, labour and capital – the 'factors of production') are attracted to this application.

The consequence of this increased demand for video tape recorders will be corresponding reductions in demand for other goods and services by consumers. This will especially affect similar goods and services in close competition with the first one and capable of being 'substituted' by it. In our example, cinema admissions may well be a likely casualty of any increased demand for video tape recorders.

Video Tape Recorders

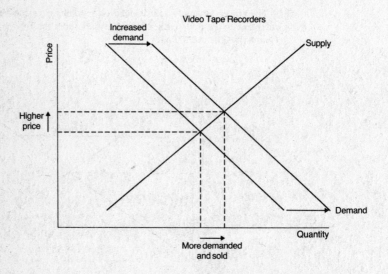

The diagram opposite shows the effect of this. This time a *reduction* in demand (represented by a shift to the left of the demand curve) will have the effect of lowering price. In due course, this will lead to a reduction in supply, i.e. the number of cinemas. Economic resources will thus be diverted away from this application.

In this way the price mechanism acts as a 'signal' for transmitting resources towards and away from different products in response to consumer demand.

Cinema Admissions

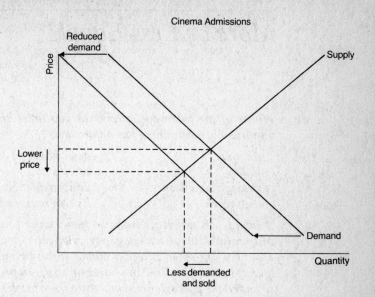

12

More or Less Equal?

Which of the following criteria do you think should be most important in determining pay differentials?

training	*dedication and commitment*
skill	*social status*
strategic significance	*difficulty/danger of work*
of work	*level of responsibility*

In practice, which of the above criteria are in your opinion most instrumental in determining pay relativities and differentials? Does this appear to reflect economic forces or more the kind of society in which we live? In what sense do they represent incentives to undertake particular jobs and to do them better?

In your view, are the differences in pay which attach to different occupations about right? Is there a case for widening them further? Or should it be the function of governments and the tax system to equalize rather than widen such differences?

This chapter looks at the influences upon relative pay levels in our economy, and at the cases for widening and narrowing them, with special attention to questions of incentives.

'A £240-a-week car salesman, Jack Jones, 35, was today charged with murdering his wife . . .' What on earth has his income to do with it? Nothing at all, but the tabloid press recognizes that most people are intensely curious about how much others earn compared with themselves. It reflects a concern about whether incomes are distributed *fairly* – whether it is right that a managing director of a firm may earn ten times more than someone on the shop floor, or that nurses are paid less than footballers.

Pay and the market

So what determines the way in which incomes from work are distributed? (We shall leave questions of inequalities in wealth to later chapters.) The economist's answer is that differences in pay are basically the result of market forces – the demand and supply conditions for the various types of labour on offer.

Demand for labour

In theory, the *demand* for labour, the number of workers of a certain kind that an enterprise is prepared to take on to its payroll, is determined by two broad considerations:

● The strength of demand for the product or service that the workers will be engaged in producing. In this sense, the demand for labour is said to be a derived demand.

● The contribution that workers make towards increasing output, i.e. the productivity of labour.

In practice there may be difficulties in putting exact money values on each of these. In the first place, the final output may not actually be sold. For example, in the NHS or state education, 'demand' is not decided by how many people are prepared to buy but by administrative decisions about the scale of service to be provided. Secondly, particularly in service occupations, it is often impossible to measure precisely what additional 'output' results from the employment of extra labour.

But in very general terms, the market mechanism will mean that enterprises usually employ more workers at a lower wage rate than at a higher wage rate.

Supply of labour

The *supply* of labour to an individual enterprise or industry will, on the other hand, tend to be greater the higher the wage rate offered. The actual numbers involved will depend on a variety of factors. One of the most important is the relative abundance or scarcity of the ability, skills and experience that are being called for. Another may be the non-pecuniary advantages or disadvantages attached to various jobs – whether working conditions are pleasant or unpleasant, the scope for job satisfaction, the existence of fringe benefits of one kind or another.

Pay as signals

The pattern of *differentials* within occupational groups and *relativities* between occupational groups can be seen as broadly reflecting these demand and supply conditions. For example:

● The financial controller of a large firm earns more than the shop-floor worker because the job requires specialist skills in short supply relative to demand (an equally 'skilled' specialist in medieval history cannot command the same premium because of lack of demand).

● Nurses remain relatively low paid because the numbers offering themselves for training in this demanding profession are considerable in relation to the jobs available in the national and private health services.

● University teachers have slipped down the pay league over the years because although the demand for their services greatly increased, the supply of fresh graduates capable of doing the job rose even more sharply.

● Car workers have also suffered a relative decline. But in their case it has been due to a falling demand for their services as a result of a sometimes uncompetitive domestic car industry and the application of capital-intensive methods of working.

In this picture of pay being determined by the market forces of demand and supply, the economic role of differentials and relativities is to act as signals, inducing labour to move from one type of employment to another. Thus a firm whose products are selling well may find itself short of labour and offer higher wages to bid workers away from other less successful enterprises in its area. Or a shortage of computer programmers may lead to high earnings which results in greater numbers undertaking training enabling them to enter this now more attractive occupation.

But what ought to happen in these circumstances is that, having played their part in bringing about the changes in employment dictated by demand, pay differences should then disappear as supply is adjusted. Movements of labour should be *equalizing* in their effect.

Persistent inequalities

Why then in the real world do wide inequalities in income from work persist over long periods of time? Are they really doing their economic job of signposting desirable shifts in labour use? Doubts that this is always or even generally the case are confirmed when we look at what lies behind the 'free market forces' that we have taken at face value so far. There are *human* and *institutional* factors to take into account that profoundly affect the pattern of income distribution and limit the effectiveness of pay differences as economic signals.

A FAIR DAY'S WORK . . . ?

A highly respected labour economist has tried to place the limitations of economics in explaining how pay is determined:

It is apposite to reflect how little support can be found in economic considerations for the more conspicuous inequalities of our wage and salary system.

Orthodox economic theory has not, at least in the present century, generally found itself on the side of drastic social change. The main effect of classical wage theories has been to justify an existing situation by explaining an imaginary one.

Lady Barbara Wootton, *The Social Foundations of Wage Policy*, Allen & Unwin, 1955.

Human factors

One obvious reason for the relative abundance or scarcity of various types of labour is that labour is not homogeneous. That is, we are not all equally endowed with the same strength, intelligence, dexterity, beauty, sensitivity or bossiness. This makes the world a more interesting place in which to live but also offers part of the explanation for persistent income inequalities.

Thus a large proportion of the labour force has the strength and other abilities needed for assembly line or other manual work. But few possess the talents to play a piano concerto or to reach a Wimbledon final or to paint a masterpiece.

But having the natural ability to play football like Pelé or George Best guarantees an earning capacity vastly greater than the average. It is a payment to labour in very scarce supply and also high demand. And it is a payment that includes a large element of so-called *economic rent*.

Economic rent

Economic rent is a concept first elaborated by the nineteenth-century economist David Ricardo. He originally used it to explain differing payments for the use of land but it can equally be applied to capital or labour. It denotes a payment to any of these 'factors of production' in *excess* of what is needed to keep them in their present use.

Suppose, for example, we ask of a pop star what he or she might earn in their next best occupation, i.e. if they were not in show business. The answer might be £120 a week as a bus conductor. If instead the pop star is earning some £2,000 a week delighting the fans, then £1,880 of that can be regarded as a 'rent of ability'.

The level of rent earnings depends on demand. But the really key point about an economic rent element in earnings is that it does not automatically cause an increase in the supply of the factor concerned – because in this and similar cases the supply is limited by natural factors that do not respond to price signals.

Human capital

At a more mundane level pay differences can be explained in terms of education and training – making the best of whatever talents we happen to possess. The supply of skilled machinists is more limited than that of general labourers because they have had to undergo periods of learning their skills. The number of graduates coming on to the labour market is far fewer than the number of non-graduates. Brain surgeons take even longer to train than general practitioners.

Economists sometimes analyse the resulting differences in skill as being due to 'investment in human capital' – the combined cost of the training involved and the loss of income that the trainee would otherwise have been earning. On this argument, many or most differentials can be accounted for as 'compensatory' payments, a reward for undertaking education or training that makes certain types of labour therefore relatively scarce.

However, the opportunity to make the 'sacrifice' which earns such rewards may be limited by institutional factors operating in the labour market to which we now turn.

Institutional factors

Trade unions or professional associations can try to limit the supply of labour in various occupations by imposition of stringent skill, experience or financial entry qualifications. More generally, differentials can be created and maintained by sheer industrial muscle-power, with workers in strategically key areas of the economy sometimes able to extract substantially higher incomes than those less strongly organized. Not dissimilar is the ability of top managers more or less to set their own level of pay with only occasional murmurs of dissent from shareholders.

But even more basic is the effect of *social* immobility that continues to exist in this country – the difficulty of moving from one class of occupation to another. It might be argued that the higher earnings of doctors may not lead to dockers taking up medicine but that it does provide an inducement for their children to do so. However, studies show that the prospect for a manual worker's children entering a professional or managerial occupation is still comparatively poor. The Nuffield Social Mobility Group researches, for example, suggest that eighteen out of every hundred boys from a manual worker's home will become a professional or managerial worker. On the other hand, sixty-two out of every hundred from a professional or managerial home will themselves find similar work.

BARGAINING POWER

● Perhaps the most commonly referred-to group of 'strategically' placed workers are Fleet Street printers. The key to the power they hold – and consequent pay levels which they command – lies more in the perishability of their product than in their printing skills. A newspaper not produced to its deadline is by definition out of date and out of demand.
● Similarly, the wage rate at the top of the league table in recent years has been that of exhibition stand contractors. Again the perishability of the product is the key. It is the day before the Motor Show or Ideal Home Exhibition opens . . . !
● By contrast there are other categories of worker who would possibly bring public relief rather than exasperation or hurt if they went on strike. Inland Revenue staff and traffic wardens might be good examples here. But they are nevertheless 'key' workers from their employer's point of view as, without them, governments and local authorities would face loss of revenue and mounting chaos.

Many markets

Instead of a single labour market, there are therefore a great number of fragmented labour markets. Within each of them there is a degree of mobility of labour which ensures a tendency for some equalization of earnings to be brought about. For example, in Oxford the wages paid by BL at Cowley will be broadly related to those earned by electricians, plumbers, transport workers and general labourers in the area. Marked disparities that might emerge would soon be ironed out by the movement of workers from one to another. Similarly, there might be a link between the salaries of lecturers in the University of Oxford and those received by higher civil servants (after allowing for the non-pecuniary advantages enjoyed by the former).

But between the various labour markets there is little scope for mobility. Therefore differentials often simply indicate the imperfections of the market and the extent of economic rent elements rather than act in their theoretical role of re-allocating labour more efficiently.

Taxation of incomes

It is recognition that the degree of inequality in income from work which results from the imperfect working of market forces has only limited economic justification which is the basis for the policy in this country and elsewhere of levying personal income tax at a *progressive* rate. That is, higher income groups pay not only larger absolute amounts of tax but a higher proportion of their incomes. Post-tax inequalities are consequently substantially narrower than pre-tax.

Moreover, for the greater part of the postwar period there has been a broad political consensus that inequalities should at least not be allowed to widen.

Incentives

However, 1979 marked a break from this consensus with the Budget announcement by the Chancellor of the first of the major principles on which future economic strategy was to be based: the 'need to strengthen incentives, by allowing people to keep more of what they earn, so that

---

TO HIM THAT HATH . . .

Between 1978 and 1984:
- Personal taxation rose by £9.1 billion in real terms.
- Only those with incomes above £21,503 saw their tax burden fall.
- The increase in the tax burden has fallen most heavily on the low paid. A family on half average earnings saw their tax burden more than double compared to a 6 per cent increase for those on average earnings.
- While the tax burden on the low paid rose, taxes on the wealthy declined – their contribution to total receipts declined by 25 per cent.
- These developments were accompanied by a growth in tax concessions to the better-off which stem from the array of reliefs which can be claimed against taxation.

Source: 'Setting Record Taxes Straight', *Low Pay Review*, No. 17, February 1984.

hard work, talent and ability are properly rewarded'. The tax changes then introduced to implement this principle increased inequality in three ways:

● by widening the tax bands at which higher rates of income tax became payable;

● by concentrating major cuts at the top of the tax scale;

● by a shift from taxation on income to indirect taxation like VAT – a proportional rather than a progressive type of tax.

The effect was that by 1982 a married man with two children on two thirds of average earnings was less than 5 per cent better off; on average earnings, rather more than 5 per cent better off; on five times average earnings, 22 per cent better off; and on ten times average earnings, 54 per cent better off.

Here, we are mainly concerned with the economics of the incentive

Shifting Burdens: The Incidence of Direct and Indirect Taxation, 1982

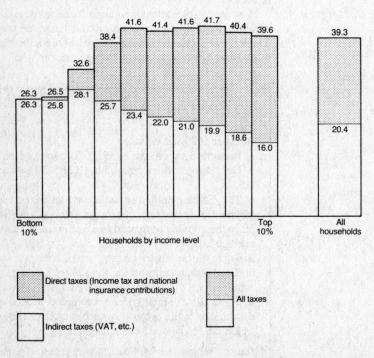

Percentage of income taken in taxes

Households by income level

Direct taxes (Income tax and national insurance contributions)

Indirect taxes (VAT, etc.)

All taxes

Source: 'The Effects of Taxes and Benefits on Household Income, 1982', *Economic Trends*, November 1983, CSO.

argument for greater inequality which aimed at meeting 'complaints about erosion of differentials, and the sapping of initiative and effort. In the government's view, it bears a considerable responsibility for industry's lack of competitiveness.'

Arguments against 'incentives'

From what has been said earlier it would seem that the argument is a dubious one.

● To the extent that differentials consist of economic rent elements, to widen such differentials simply increases the payment to recipients still further above that needed to keep them in their present occupation, while doing nothing to increase the supply of labour entering that field.

● It is doubtful whether higher income incentives are necessary to stimulate more effort in obtaining training and education. That is because most of the burden is generally borne by parents or taxpayers rather than by those who subsequently earn higher incomes as a result of their qualifications. For most people, their years spent in higher education are positively pleasurable and there has been no reduction in the supply of undergraduates even in recent circumstances of uncertain *employment* prospects (though unemployment may well have had mixed effects on those thinking about studying for lower level qualifications).

● There is no evidence that wider differentials have incentive effects in inducing upward movement *within* occupational groups; for example, that promotion up the managerial scale tends to be rejected because it would involve a shift into higher tax brackets.

● So is the case for lower taxation simply that it will give people the incentive to work harder or longer hours? There may well be circumstances where workers are deterred from overtime by the amount they know they will lose in tax, but in times of mass unemployment this can hardly be regarded as a pressing issue. And for those on a basic day rate or a salaried base it is far from obvious that greater effort would result from higher post-tax incomes. (Would our captains of industry, for example, *really* improve their performance with lower marginal rates of tax?)

We all like cuts in income tax – at least unless we recognize that they are being offset by increases in other types of taxation or by cuts in the volume or quality of valued public services. And indeed Keynesian economists would strongly recommend reductions in taxation in the present situation of mass unemployment and industrial recession. But they would do so on the grounds that they would be an important element in a package of measures to *raise demand* in the economy and thereby to stimulate recovery.

That is quite different from the incentives argument. We suggested earlier in this chapter that pay differences do play a role in allocating labour in the most efficient way, but only to a very limited extent. Many differentials and relativities have little economic justification – and even less in terms of what people may think of as 'fair'. If this is true about the *pre*-tax distribution of incomes that results from the operation of market forces, it is difficult to accept that there is a serious case for widening *post*-tax inequalities still further.

13

Welfare State or Going Private?

Are there limits to the application of the market forces, or are consumers' interests always best served by competition and the price mechanism? Health care is a good, if somewhat controversial, case for illustrating opposing viewpoints.

'. . . the best health services should be available to all . . . money should no longer be the passport to the best treatment.'

Labour Party Manifesto, 1945

'The NHS must fail to supply the British people with the best medical care they want because it prevents them as individual consumers from paying for the services that suit their personal family requirements, circumstances and preferences.'

Arthur Seldon, ed.,
The Litmus Papers:
A National Health Disservice,
Institute of Economic Affairs, 1980

Which of these two opposing standpoints do you sympathize with? If you tend towards the first, is it because you feel consumer interests are better provided for collectively through a National Health Service? Or because there are considerations involved other than – and more important than – consumer sovereignty?

If you sympathize towards the second, is it because you see a National Health Service as incapable, by its very nature, of being sensitive to consumer preference? Or because its current standards and attitudes fall short of what you would expect?

In an ideally working market system, it is consumers who rule the roost, and we do so by voting with our pockets. It is *we* who signal instructions to firms about which goods they should produce and in what quantities – and firms then pass on that message by getting hold of the amount of resources that *our* expenditure enables them to buy. In this way, resources are channelled into just those lines of production that *we* have dictated. It is consumers who are the kings and queens of a pure market economy.

This is the ultimate justification of the market and it is not therefore surprising that a key argument that is put forward in support of recent policies is that 'We need to enlarge freedom of choice for the individual by reducing the role of the state.'

It is an argument of simple intuitive appeal. In our present mixed economy, it is possible for Milton Friedman vividly (if misleadingly) to imply that people spend half their time working for the government – and to contrast that with the much more attractive prospect of being left 'free to choose' by having money in their pockets rather than the coffers of the state.

'Privatization' is a rather ugly addition to the English vocabulary that has emerged over the past few years to denote the mechanism through which the scope of the market is being extended – by the transfer of the production of goods and services from the public sector into private ownership or operation. In Chapter 14, we shall examine the other main claim that is made for it – increased *efficiency*. But for now we look at whether privatization does automatically enhance consumer sovereignty in the way that its advocates suggest.

A preliminary question is how far even in the present market sector consumer sovereignty is a reality or myth? This is a matter that we have already touched upon in Chapter 11 but it is worth restating some of the ways in which the ideal market mechanism is distorted in practice – because the vital conditions on which it depends are so often neglected in simple advocacy of its virtues.

There are four important limitations on consumer sovereignty in practice:

How real is consumer sovereignty?

● Consumers are often too ignorant to make rational choices between competing products. How many of us are able to judge the real differences between soap powders, cars or video recorders? And the continual introduction of new products and new models makes it difficult for us even to learn from past experience.

● Advertising can help to increase consumer knowledge of the alternatives on offer. But more commonly, it seeks to persuade us to buy without providing any hard information about the product itself. In these circumstances, it is all too easy for the tail to begin to wag the dog. Big business, instead of responding to our demands, can itself create new wants which we would never have dreamed up for ourselves. It can manipulate rather than simply respond to consumer preferences. The result may be that instead of consumers calling the tune, we have what the American economist J. K. Galbraith has called a 'revised sequence' – with supply determining demand rather than vice versa.

• The reshuffling of resources according to changes in consumer tastes that ought to take place according to ideal market theory will only do so if all those other conditions that we mentioned in Chapter 11 – like genuine competition and a high degree of mobility – hold good. In practice this is often not so.

• Inequality of incomes and wealth mean that some consumers have far more 'votes' than others to cast in the economic ballot of the market place. 'Freedom to choose' is a good deal more meaningful for the well-to-do than for those on low incomes.

So what is left of consumer sovereignty in practice? Undoubtedly there has been a shift in recent decades in the balance of consumer and producer power, but consumers do still retain the ultimate sanction of saying 'no' – by not buying the goods producers try to foist upon them. And with the help of consumer organizations and protection from the government, we can become better informed, less easy prey to the blandishments of the advertisers and more capable of judging products by their real quality and usefulness.

Despite the extent to which their freedom may be illusory, there is no doubt, too, that the great majority of people want to be left to spend their own incomes as individual consumers according to their own whims and wishes – making their own selection from the supermarket shelves, the car and electrical showrooms, the clothing stores and the travel agents.

Widening the market

In areas of consumption like these there would seem to be a clear case for 'leaving it to the market' – while at the same time introducing measures designed to make the market work more effectively and fairly. But the current thrust towards privatization raises much more fundamental issues. Increasingly, economists and politicians imbued with enthusiasm for the market mechanism, are suggesting that it could be appropriately applied to a whole range of what have for long been regarded as 'public services' – some of which, like health and education, form the basis of the Welfare State.

There is a new questioning about the need for so extensive a 'command' sector in the economy – that in which production and consumption decisions are made by government authorities rather than individuals and families. It certainly sounds the exact opposite of the consumer sovereignty which reigns in an ideal market system. But that is not strictly true.

• At least in a democratic society voters are able to express their broad preferences for more or less public or private provision of goods and services.

• Within the bodies administering the various public services, there is scope for representation of consumer interests. Whether the voices of users have in fact been sufficiently heard is a matter we shall return to.

The case for public services

But why, particularly in the postwar period, have we in this country (and the same has happened in many others) deliberately opted for greater 'collective consumption' – apparently limiting our individual consumer choice? What have been the main arguments for state rather than private provision?

● Certain services, like defence or the maintenance of law and order, have to be provided on an all-or-nothing basis. It is simply not practicable to allow individuals to decide just how much each of them should spend on weaponry or policing or the judicial system.
● The consumption of many goods and services has a social as well as a private dimension. This means that the free exercise of individual choice might be detrimental to others. For example, would we be happy to allow parents to spend as much or as little on education as they chose? In doing so, they would be asserting their own consumer sovereignty but possibly at the expense of their children. Similarly with health care, the

THE SOCIAL WAGE

The 'social wage' is the estimated value of benefits enjoyed per head of the working population and provided through public expenditure. The official definition in the late 1970s included housing, education, health and other categories, but excluded defence, foreign aid and other items. Its value was estimated at around £1,800 per year, or £35 a week, which represented about one third of average earnings then.

benefits of medical treatment are not limited to the individual recipient: his or her family, friends, employers or employees, indeed the whole national economy all stand to gain, too. The same is of course true in the other direction: failure to take advantage of educational opportunities or health provision (far more days are lost through illness than through strikes) can adversely affect society and the economy generally, and inflict penalties on others as well as the individuals concerned.

ROLLING BACK THE STATE

There are some economists who would deny that health and education are necessarily 'public goods'. Professor Patrick Minford of Liverpool University is one such:

The main services bought by the state for the people and passed on at free or subsidized prices but still not public goods are health and education services.

The statement that these are not public goods requires some qualification. There are elements of 'public good' in both: if your neighbour catches bubonic plague, you and many others suffer. If someone is unable to read or understand the spoken language, he may cause others a nuisance (e.g., by disregarding public safety orders). A lack of general education impoverishes society and not only the individuals involved. But these aspects are easily handled *without* public purchase of health and education services for all; minimum standards of hygiene and preventive medicine (such as inoculation), and of education can be set and subsidized directly. Inoculations for bubonic plague would naturally be 100 per cent subsidized; and education vouchers subsidize education directly. Thus the specific 'public good' elements are best handled by specific measures and subsidies . . .

Patrick Minford, 'State Expenditure: A Study in Waste', supplement to *Economic Affairs*, April–June 1984.

Minford's overall approach is summarized as follows:

1. There is inefficiency and waste in state *production*, mainly because monopoly inflates costs and prices, of from 3 to 10 per cent of the national product, or £6–18 billion.

2. There is inefficiency and waste in state *consumption* because there is over-provision or under-provision of goods and services, except in 'public goods'.

3. There is waste in state *taxation* – up to 60 per cent of the yield of additional taxes.

4. The cure in principle for waste in state *production* is ultimately complete privatization.

5. The cure in principle for waste in state *consumption* is to transfer consumption to the citizen, except for public goods.

6. To help the poor a negative income tax for those in work should replace the current family income supplement, etc.; for those out of work there should be a limit on unemployment benefits relative to income in work.

7. Taxation can be brought down by savings to the Exchequer from these reforms. Tax thresholds can be more than doubled, child benefits more than trebled, national insurance contributions abolished and VAT cut by 4 per cent.

8. The shift, in the ownership of nationalized assets and in the financing of state services, from the state to the citizen should be phased over five years to 1990.

9. The NHS, except for its element of public goods, should be replaced by competitive health insurance.

10. State education should be replaced by competitive private education.

11. Other central and local government services should be privatized.

12. Because of improved incentives output should rise by 10 per cent and employment by 2½ million.

13. These reforms should benefit rich, poor and middling because of the massive reductions in economic waste. Only pressure groups will lose.

14. They are essential if the British economy is to regain its dynamism.

Patrick Minford, 'State Expenditure: A Study in Waste', supplement to *Economic Affairs*, April–June 1984.

• The demand for some goods and services is created by the very extent of private consumption. Thus, most obviously, market choices lead to an ever-growing number of cars – but the costs of roads and traffic lights are difficult to recoup through market pricing and therefore are generally provided by the state instead.

• Above all, we have hitherto accepted that certain areas, once again health and education in particular, are too important in human terms to be left to individual choice. This is clearly a matter of values rather than purely technical economics – a belief that all should have a right of access to such amenities regardless of ability to pay.

More scope for the market?

Some economists claim that these arguments for the public provision of goods and services have been grossly overplayed. It has led to government spending on a wastefully extensive scale – and to a quite unnecessary restriction of individual free choice. Under our present system, state benefits like secondary education or health care are handed out on a universal basis regardless of individual circumstances. Wouldn't it be more sensible to concentrate help on those who need it and to leave the better-off to fend for themselves out of their own incomes? Benefits granted on a selective basis to only those consumers below stipulated income levels could massively reduce the present level of state spending.

The recent ideological climate has fostered a wide variety of suggestions for replacing state provision in areas like refuse collection, sewage disposal, road use, etc. All of these aim at reintroducing prices as the test of how strongly people *want* various services, and shifting the burden of providing them from taxpayers to the consumers who actually benefit.

Inevitably they have been of interest to recent governments pledged to cut personal and business taxes (at a time when North Sea revenues are due to begin their decline), and to reduce public spending just when the age distribution of the population and rising expectations about the quality of services are pointing in the direction of still greater public provision.

However, so far a radical dismantling of the Welfare State is no more than a gleam in the eyes of market-oriented economists. Official policy has up to now been confined to restricting the *growth* of public services through cash limits and the encouragement of:

• privatization of local government services like refuse disposal and of ancillary services (cleaning, laundering, catering) in the NHS and other major public providers;

• the development of parallel private provision of health care and education.

How do these developments, which may well be due for more radical extension in the future, affect the issue of consumer choice, which is our

present concern? There are two broad aspects to consider. First, we
must ask how far choice is increased for users of present private schemes
and what would be the implication of their further extension. And
second, are there ways in which private provision affects consumers
remaining within the public sector?

Sovereignty of private users

Even for private users, sovereignty is limited because of the type of
problems that we outlined earlier – which assume considerably more
significance when purchasing health care rather than a new car.
● Consumers may not be fully aware of what they are buying under
private schemes. They may be ignorant of the full range of what is on
offer and be misled by advertising and presentation. They may not be
able to anticipate their needs in advance, particularly with respect to

health care. They may therefore choose in a way they later come to regret. Both the quantity that they are buying (the scope of coverage and exemptions under a health-insurance plan, for example) and the quality (the adequacy and suitability of services offered) are difficult to define and compare. Value for money is not so easily evaluated with health care or education as it is for a tin of baked beans or a washing machine.

• If in some cases the standard of private education or health care may be lower than consumers believe they are buying (many private hospitals, for example, do not even have resident doctors), there is also the danger that provision will be more extravagant (over-luxurious accommodation, expensive drugs, consultants' fees) than patients would themselves choose. The possibility that provision is not finely tuned to consumer demands becomes greater because consumers often deal with producers at a double remove: increasingly, private education and health provision are offered on a group basis to employees (in some cases to trade union members) as a fringe benefit, with the company then contributing to an insurance scheme such as BUPA.

• Above all, the market only recognizes *ability to pay* as the criterion for the provision of services; its terms of reference do not include need. Lower-income levels are likely in practice to be associated with greater educational and health needs. But producers for the market will naturally concentrate upon the more lucrative targets amongst consumers. This will favour those with the greatest ability to pay but probably the least need, as against those who are more 'at risk' but with less means to pay. It is interesting to note that health insurance schemes are finding their prospects less profitable as they extend their clientele further down the social scale, and are having to increase their subscriptions accordingly.

But despite these limitations, there is no doubt that the extent of consumer choice and sovereignty of private users is enhanced by their membership of private schemes – by retaining access to state services while enjoying supplementary or alternative private provision. The question that we turn to next is whether these benefits are at all at the expense of those remaining wholly within the public sector. There are a number of ways in which this might be so.

Sovereignty of public users

• There is considerable financial assistance from the state to private health and education producers in the form of subsidies (e.g. for hospital building) and tax relief (e.g. for schemes to meet the cost of school fees). Taxpayers outside the private sector find *their* choice as consumers correspondingly limited by the reduction in their post-tax incomes.

• The private sector may drain resources from the public sector – in particular through the use of NHS trained doctors and nurses and subsidized pay-beds. It also provides additional resources of its own – but these may tend to be in the narrowly profitable areas and may distort

151

THE HEALTH LEAGUE

The following diagram gives the rank order of health quality in ten major countries in 1975. Health quality is measured by an index of health indicators including infant mortality, perinatal mortality and premature death.

The diagram also shows each country's total spending on health, and its health finance from the public sector, as a percentage of its national output (GDP).

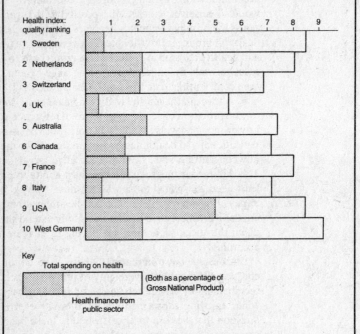

Key

Total spending on health

(Both as a percentage of Gross National Product)

Health finance from public sector

Source: Robert Maxwell, *Health and Wealth*, Lexington Books.

● The UK has the lowest proportion of national spending devoted to health care of all the countries covered.
● The proportion of health care financed by the public sector is higher in the UK than in the other countries.
● The UK does slightly better than average in terms of the nation's health.

public provision by encouraging specialization by NHS staff in those fields that offer the best prospect for private practice.

● Those opting for private education or health provision are likely to come from upper- and middle-income groups most aware of the deficiencies of state provision and vocal in articulating them. Their withdrawal into private schemes removes a major source of pressure for increased funding and improved standards in state services.

Thus even the coexistence of private health and education provision alongside state services may be detrimental to the majority of consumers while increasing the choice available to relatively few. We are all in favour of freedom of consumer choice, but can this greater freedom for the better-off amongst us be justified if it creates different levels of quality and standards in such vital areas of need and opportunity? In education in particular, private schooling represents the purchase of privileged access to a variety of occupations and therefore helps to perpetuate those very inequalities on which it is itself based.

Greater choice for all

Whether governments should provide more public services or less is a question that cannot be answered by economics alone. It is also a matter of political ideology. It involves a value judgement about the nature of the society in which we want to live. Is an individual's 'right to choose' sacrosanct even though it involves the absolute or relative restriction of choice by others? Do we really want to defend private health and education provision as an extension of a freedom of choice to which the great majority can have no conceivable access?

An alternative is to explore the extent to which more equitable freedom of choice might be achieved *within* state provision. There are many ways in which public services, and indeed government departments and nationalized industries, could be made more responsive to consumer preference, and to provide for more options and alternatives in the levels and forms of service provided. The management of these institutions does not have to be highly centralized and bureaucratic. Nor need provision of services be highly standardized and uniform. But little attention has been paid to such possibilities, and their neglect increases the danger of an extension of market forces to areas where their outcome would be inequitable and unacceptable.

14

Public or Private Enterprise?

Someone once said that nationalizing a privately owned industry was like setting out to make Marks and Spencer as attractive and efficient as the Co-op.

● *Is 'nationalized industry' a term which evokes a large, bureaucratic, lumbering inefficient concern in your book? Featherbedded by state finance and taxpayers' money and lacking competition and incentive?*

● *Is 'private enterprise', by contrast, a term which suggests the enterprising go-getter spurred on by the competition to provide better quality and service to the consumer at lower prices?*

These connotations are reinforced by media reports and increasingly by recent governments. But is the difference so wide and so sharp? And are we really comparing like with like?

This chapter looks at the aims and achievements of public ownership along with the case for and against privatization, with an emphasis upon economic *considerations and arguments. What should we expect and what do we get?*

Whether you would be happier if the next telephone bill to arrive through your letter-box were from a privately owned British Telecom rather than a nationalized British Telecom would mainly depend on whether it were for a smaller amount or whether you felt that the service had been of significantly higher quality or more suited to your needs. In other words, your principal interest would be in value for money – whether you were being served more or less efficiently.

Greater efficiency is the second major claim made by advocates of privatization. In Chapter 13 we looked at the argument that it would lead to wider consumer choice, and focused largely on the provision of welfare services. Here, we shall be mainly concerned with whether a transfer from public to private ownership *is* likely to lead to reduced costs and prices or improved quality of output in the case of the many major industries now scheduled or discussed as candidates for a return to the private sector.

Public enterprises prior to the present spate of privatization accounted for some 11 per cent of national output; for 14 per cent of all capital employed; and for 8 per cent of total employment. With the exception of steel and, more recently, shipbuilding, aerospace and specific companies such as BL or Rolls-Royce, nationalized industries have been engaged less in manufacturing than in the areas of energy, transport and communications.

The Nationalized Sector, 1981/2, £m Turnover

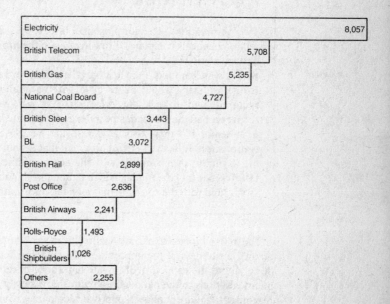

Electricity	8,057
British Telecom	5,708
British Gas	5,235
National Coal Board	4,727
British Steel	3,443
BL	3,072
British Rail	2,899
Post Office	2,636
British Airways	2,241
Rolls-Royce	1,493
British Shipbuilders	1,026
Others	2,255

Source: *Public Expenditure White Paper* (Cmnd 8789), HMSO, February 1983, and various annual reports and accounts, 1981–2.

Why nationalize?

The main thrust of nationalization took place in the 1945–50 Labour government's bid to capture 'the commanding heights of the economy'.
● Some industries were regarded as so crucial to Britain's postwar economic recovery that only public ownership, it was thought, could guarantee the necessary degree of control, coordination and planning.
 ● Several of these industries were badly run down and needed huge amounts of finance for investment in reconstruction and development. Neither the banking system, nor the stock market nor the profits of the industries themselves would be likely to raise the necessary funds, so the Treasury would have to take on this financing function.
 ● The economic scale of production needed implied monopoly status

155

in many cases, and the degree of state control required was most easily achieved through nationalization.

● Accountability and control were organized on an 'arm's-length' basis, with a nationalized industry chairman and his board intended to be responsible for day-to-day management, but broadly accountable to a Minister and his 'sponsoring department', who were to lay down general guidelines for the industry's operation.

A PRIVATE VIEW

Two observations of senior personnel of ICI, the leading private sector chemicals company, throw light upon the pros and cons of nationalization:
● Sir Paul Chambers, then head of ICI, is on record as saying that British industry would never have got the amount of coal it required, and at such low prices, for the post-war economic recovery, had the coal industry remained in private hands.
● A senior ICI man associated with the NEDO Study of UK Nationalized Industries (1976) observed that it would be impossible to run his own company with the degree of intervention and interference by government which nationalized industries had to suffer, and with the consequent doubt and uncertainty.

The initial impetus to nationalization lay in a combination of political dogma, awareness of the importance of rebuilding key industries and doubt about the capability of private enterprise to do the job. Subsequent additions to the nationalized sector have mostly been piecemeal responses to failure of important private companies. But as we shall see, what has been lacking throughout has been any systematic conception of how nationalized industries should behave – which has led to difficulties and unresolved problems for those industries and their relationships with governments, and have become part of the current case for privatization.

General case for privatization

That case can be advanced in three stages:
● that nationalization has been a failure;
● that private industry could do the job better;
● that privatizing offers a better option than seeking to improve the performance of public enterprise.

The failure of nationalization?

We shall look at each stage of the argument in turn. To begin with, the postwar experience of nationalization has certainly led to public enterprises being the butt for a wide variety of criticisms:
● they make losses and have to be bailed out by government with taxpayers' money;

- they are monopolies which can continue to run inefficiently, over-charge and otherwise exploit the consumer;
- they are huge, bureaucratic and unresponsive to consumer requirements;
- they employ more workers and pay them higher wages than necessary at the expense of the consumer or the taxpayer;
- industrial relations have been poor, with trade unions able to take advantage of the strategic importance of public enterprises in the economy.

How valid are these criticisms?

Feather-bedded?

While it is true that some nationalized industries have made losses, others have been commercially much more successful – and have then been attacked for profiteering! But what has never been conveyed to the general public is that a simple comparison of the results of a nationalized industry with those of a private company is generally unfair and misleading. That is because public enterprises have traditionally been obliged to borrow any investment funds they require at fixed rates of interest from the Treasury. Private companies, on the other hand, can raise part of

---

GAS TAX?

As well as charges of profiteering, it has been argued that govern-ments succumb to the temptation of using the pricing policies of monopoly nationalized industries as a way of boosting govern-ment revenue without increasing taxes.

Despite a further decline in industrial gas sales attributable to the recession, the Corporation remained highly profitable, financed all new investment from its own resources, and achieved the financial target set for it by the government. Far from being a burden on public funds, the Corporation made payments to the Exchequer during the year totalling £666.6 million for gas levy and taxation.

Foreword by the Chairman, *British Gas Corporation Annual Report and Accounts, 1982–83*.

This strategy was evident in the government's April 1980 *Public Expenditure White Paper, 1980/81 to 1983/84* (Cmnd 7841), which proposed:

By the end of the period the projection is that the nationalized indus-tries in aggregate will be making net repayments of borrowing, as current losses are reduced and underpricing of electricity and gas is eliminated.

The White Paper aimed at converting a nationalized industry borrowing figure of nearly £2 billion to a net repayment of over £½ billion over the period.

---

their capital through the issue of ordinary shares on which dividends are payable according to profitability. Therefore a public enterprise earning a surplus of revenue on its trading over and above its costs might none the less be declared 'loss-making' because the surplus was insufficient to meet its interest charges. A private company in an identical trading position would, on the other hand, simply declare only a low dividend. Similarly, a public enterprise just breaking even after meeting its interest charges would, as a private company, be able to announce a dividend of an equivalent amount.

PRIVATE AND PUBLIC ACCOUNTING

A private company and a nationalized industry may report exactly the same level of operating performance in their accounts:

Turnover	£100 million
Operating costs	£ 90 million
Operating profit	£ 10 million

• In the case of the private company, if financed entirely by share capital, the whole of the £10 million (after tax) will be available for new and replacement investment or for distribution as dividends to shareholders. Either way 'good news' can be reported.

• The nationalized industry by contrast is obliged to borrow long-term at fixed rates of interest from the Treasury. It may therefore find that much of – and sometimes all or even more than – its operating profit is taken up in interest payments to the Exchequer. This can lead to an overall accounting loss and yet another 'bad news' story.

• The difference between the two is thus not one of *performance*, but rather of the method of financing and its accounting treatment. Yet this is seldom taken into account when such comparisons are made.

Further considerations militate against the commonly held view that nationalized industries are 'featherbedded' by government support. First, nationalization often excluded the more potentially profitable related activities of an industry which were left in private hands, such as coal distribution, steel stockholding and parts of road haulage. Second, unlike a private company, a nationalized industry is not free to diversify into new ranges of products or other activities without special ministerial permission and statutory provision. Although, therefore, a private firm might be more likely to go bankrupt than might a public enterprise, it is arguably less likely to be trapped into a continuing loss-making situation in the first place.

Monopolies?   Some public concerns, like British Telecom, are undoubtedly monopolies. But most of the rest are quite wrongly labelled as such. British Rail, for example, is in intense competition with road transport; coal, oil, gas and electricity fight for their shares of the domestic market; others, like steel or shipbuilding, face fierce competition from foreign producers.

Bureaucratic?   The charge that nationalized industries tend to be unwieldy, bureaucratic and unresponsive to consumer needs is more difficult to rebut. We have all at times suffered from petty officialdom and been frustrated at being unable to communicate our wishes or complaints. But similar problems also arise with many large private companies, and high priority should be given in applying in the public sector any lessons that those more successful private firms have learned in overcoming such difficulties.

Overmanned?   Although the charge might have had some substance in the past, it is hardly the recent experience of employees in nationalized industries that they have 'soft' employers! Many of them have been in traditional sectors needing major structural change; productivity has shown great advances, mainly due to staff reductions, and now compares well not only with the domestic private sector but also with equivalent undertakings abroad.

Bad industrial relations?   Nor has pay in the nationalized industries moved markedly out of line with settlements in the private sector. But the picture on the industrial relations front has certainly been of a disappointing failure to break with the traditional 'them' and 'us' barriers that characterized the industries prior to nationalization. Management has not initiated and workers have not demanded that degree of participation in decision-making that would have instilled a genuine sense of involvement in the enterprise for which they work. Indeed, division and hostility have often been sharpened by the identification of management with the government of the day – with a consequent blurring of industrial issues with disagreements on general economic policy.

Objectives of nationalization   In part, such difficulties are the symptom of a more basic problem of identity. What are nationalized industries for? How are they different from private companies? It is the fact that there are no clear answers to these questions that is surely the greatest failing of postwar nationalization – with government after government, of both parties, fudging the issue time after time.

● The statutes of the nationalized industries have generally laid down *both* that they should pursue conventional commercial objectives *and* that they should aim 'to further the public interest in all respects'. But the potential inconsistency between the two is very considerable.

● At the beginning, it was the general intention that Ministers should

STEEL OBJECTIVES

A remarkable, though not untypical, example of the 'fudging' of commercial objectives and national interest can be found in the Statutes setting up the British Steel Corporation in 1967:

3. (1) It shall be incumbent on the Corporation –

    (*a*) to promote the efficient and economical supply by the Corporation and the publicly owned companies of iron and steel products, and to secure that such products produced by the Corporation and the publicly owned companies are available in such quantities, and are of such types, qualities and sizes, and are available at such prices, as may seem to the Corporation best calculated to satisfy the reasonable demands of the persons (including those in Northern Ireland) who use such products for manufacturing purposes *and to further the public interest in all respects*.

Iron and Steel Act 1967, Chapter 17, HMSO (our italics).

lay down broad policies to guide the nationalized industries, but not intervene in their implementation, with management being left responsible for the day-to-day running of the industries. But the practice

COSTLY INTERFERENCE

The House of Commons Select Committee on Nationalized Industries reported on the British Steel Corporation in 1973. It found:

● The Corporation's Chairman had had to deal with a succession of no less than five ministers in his first six years of office.

● In the fixing of its prices the Corporation had had to submit to direction from outside on five occasions in less than six years.

● Enforced delays and reductions of price increases which the Corporation had considered proper will have cost it between £150 and £200 million.

● The benefits to the economy of keeping down steel prices have not been conclusively demonstrated. The savings to industrial consumers may have been used less to hold down prices than to accede to inflationary increases in wages. On the other hand the harm done to the commercial well-being of the Corporation and the morale of its workers is well demonstrated.

House of Commons Paper 141, 13 February 1973.

has often been almost precisely the opposite of this. Governments have been reluctant to offer clear policy guidelines about how public enterprises should in general behave, but Ministers have exercised close involvement and intervention in the management process, especially on matters of pricing and investment.

The upshot has been a changing emphasis from time to time on the industries' commercial and public obligations, the setting and continual readjustment of a variety of financial targets, manipulation of long-term investment programmes to help achieve short-term objectives, the use of public enterprises as an element in prices and incomes policies. Those responsible for managing nationalized industries have been tasked to the limit by changes in policy not only between different governments but even within the lifespan of the same administration.

The case for privatization

The various shortcomings of the nationalized industries, many of them not of their own making, have created a highly unfavourable public image. It is therefore easy for politicians to present privatization as almost synonymous with improved efficiency. But is this true? What in fact is the substantive case for asserting that a transfer back into private ownership will lead to better run industries? There are two main arguments put forward:

● greater *competition* will act as the spur to increased efficiency as private firms unable to reduce costs and prices to the extent of their rivals will find themselves forced out of business;

● the *profit motive* of private enterprises provides an unambiguous incentive to the managers of companies and a clear yardstick of their success or failure.

'THE PUBLIC SECTOR FOR THE PUBLIC'

Under the above, perhaps provocative, headline, the Treasury Economic Progress Report of May 1982 offered the following official general arguments for privatization:

'It remains our purpose, wherever possible, to transfer to the private sector assets which can be better managed there.'

Sir Geoffrey Howe, Chancellor of the Exchequer, Budget Speech, 9 March 1982

'Privatization represents by far the most effective means of extending market forces, and in turn of improving efficiency and the allocation of resources.'

Lord Cockfield, then Minister of State, Treasury, 19 November 1981

'It must be right to press ahead with the transfer of ownership from the state to private enterprise of as many public sector businesses as possible . . . The introduction of competition must whenever possible be linked to a transfer of ownership to private citizens and away from the state. Real public ownership – that is ownership by people – must be and is our ultimate goal.'

Mr Nicholas Ridley, Financial Secretary to the Treasury, 12 February 1982

The article went on to elaborate on ways in which the policy was being pursued:

A major aim of the Government since coming into office in May 1979 has been the restoration of market forces throughout the economy. In this, the return of industries, assets and activities to the private sector has played – and continues to play – a crucially important part. This policy of 'privatization' has taken a number of forms, including the sale to private individuals of shareholdings in former nationalized industries, the disposal of public-sector shareholdings in companies and the contracting out of services previously administered by government departments and local authorities. In addition, the Government are taking a number of steps to open up areas remaining in the public sector, by abolishing statutory monopolies and allowing private enterprise to compete.

METHODS OF OPENING UP THE PUBLIC SECTOR
TO MARKET FORCES

Public sector activities and assets can be *returned to the private sector* by a number of means including:
- public issue of shares on the Stock Exchange (e.g. British Aerospace, Cable and Wireless);
- sale to employees/management consortium (e.g. National Freight Company);
- placement with institutional investors (e.g. government's minority shareholding in British Sugar Corporation);
- sales of physical assets (e.g. British Rail's hotel properties, New Town industrial and commercial properties);
- joint ventures (e.g. Allied Steel and Wire Ltd, an independent company in the private sector set up by the British Steel Corporation and GKN; merger of British Rail's hovercraft service with Hoverlloyd);
- contracting out of public services by central government and local authorities.

Where shares in companies are being sold, the government may retain a holding, but make it abundantly clear that they eschew control.

Competition   However, the simple equation of privatization with greater competition is misleading. First, as we have noted, several public enterprises already operate in highly competitive circumstances which privatization would do little to enhance. Second, where monopoly conditions do prevail, transfer of ownership may simply result in a substitution of private for public monopoly power; this would be a poor swap and immediately create the need for public regulation to avoid abuse of the privilege – as indeed has already been recognized in the case of British Telecom where privatization is to be accompanied by a new overseeing Office of Telecommunications. Third, there are dangers in creating more competitive conditions of wasteful duplication of services (which it was sometimes the original intention of nationalization to eliminate). And finally, the greater the competition to which a privatized concern is likely to be exposed, the less attractive the sale of a public enterprise will be to potential private buyers!

Profit and   efficiency   As to profitability, at least in competitive conditions, it provides a straightforward test by which the performance of an enterprise can be assessed. But the criterion is narrowly commercial, with 'efficiency' in the private sector being based only on the costs and revenues that appear in the company's own accounts. And yet, as we argued in Chapter 11, there may be a wide divergence between private and *social* costs and benefits which should be taken into consideration in drawing up a broader economic as opposed to commercial balance sheet. For, although it is not always easy to put precise figures on them, these wider costs and benefits *are* economic, in the sense that they represent real

---

FARES FAIR

A striking example of the different terms of reference of private and social costs and benefits was the decision of the Law Lords not to permit the GLC to reduce its London Transport fares structure. Both the narrowness and the legal priority of commercial costing were evident from the decision in favour of Bromley's and other ratepayers and against the lower fares. For only those costs and benefits arising directly for the commercial organization were considered relevant to the decision. Wider economic questions of the overall efficiency of transport systems, investment strategies and transport policies, congestion, pollution, delays and road wear-and-tear were inadmissible in deciding the legality of the GLC's 'fares fair' initiative. And yet these wider social, as opposed to private, considerations are crucial to an overall economic balance sheet and general economic rationality.

163

gains and losses to other parties affected by an enterprise's activities and decisions. Indeed in principle (although the practice has often proved very different) it might be thought that it was its obligation and ability to operate within this wider definition of efficiency that should distinguish public from private enterprise.

It should not be expected of those running private enterprises that they should consider the repercussions of their decisions on the nation's employment level or its regional distribution; on its balance of trade between imports and exports; on the fortunes and welfare of its workers or suppliers. What they are legally appointed to do is to maximize the return to their shareholders. But unless those narrow legal responsibilities are modified by government intervention, social costs and benefits will be neglected.

Sometimes commercial and economic criteria coincide – but not always. And it was when, in the past, private enterprises failing to meet the test of commercial profitability were judged as worth saving on broader economic criteria, that many of them were taken into public ownership.

To sum up, it is as dogmatic to assert that privatization guarantees greater efficiency (without reference to the degree of competition or nature of efficiency) as it is to claim that it automatically increases consumer choice.

Other arguments for privatization

There are two further strands in the official case for privatization which need not receive much attention here:

● Privatization will lead to wider share ownership. Thus, for example, employees are to be given preferential arrangements for the purchase of former public assets, providing a 'major boost to wider share ownership'. However, the evidence to date offers little evidence of any significant impact in this respect – and certainly does not support the view of privatization as 'the public sector for the public' which is the Treasury's disingenuous description of the process.

Reducing the PSBR

● It is also argued that privatization 'can help to reduce the burden on the Exchequer' – both through the receipts from the initial sales of public enterprises, and by 'the removal from the Public Sector Borrowing Requirement (PSBR) of any future borrowing by the bodies concerned'. This is questionable on several grounds. First, any immediate relief is a once-and-for-all benefit to revenue out of capital – akin, as some have put it, to 'selling off the family silver to pay the rent' – or to a farmer selling seed corn. Second, since newly privatized enterprises will still be raising capital from the same markets and the same institutions, it is difficult to see what real economic significance the change in status of the borrowers will make. Third, although by these means it will be possible to achieve a lower level of PSBR, it was shown in earlier chapters that many economists regard the British government's obsessive concern with this total as arbitrary or misguided.

SELLING OFF THE SEED CORN?

The meagre extent to which privatization provides funds – albeit on a once-and-for-all basis – which can be offset against public expenditure is evident from the February 1984 *Public Expenditure White Paper* (Cmnd 9143).

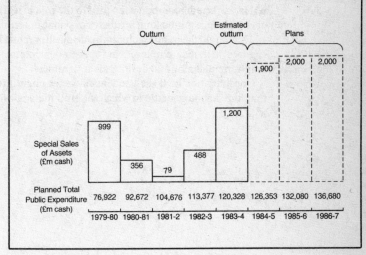

	Outturn			Estimated outturn	Plans		
Special Sales of Assets (£m cash)	999	356	79	488	1,200	1,900	2,000	2,000
Planned Total Public Expenditure (£m cash)	76,922	92,672	104,676	113,377	120,328	126,353	132,080	136,680
	1979-80	1980-81	1981-2	1982-3	1983-4	1984-5	1985-6	1986-7

For the political right, nationalization is an obvious evil and privatization is therefore often presented as self-evidently preferable. The political left hold the opposite view with a similar degree of ideological fervour.

But as we have seen, the economic record of nationalized industries has left much to be desired. And the economic arguments for privatization are not compelling. Economically, it would seem that the *conditions* under which enterprises operate are of far more significance for their performance than who owns them. It is therefore disappointing that in the current debate there is little reference to any but the extreme alternatives.

Alternative questions

● Is there scope for decentralization and competition *within* public enterprises?

● How can the distinction between 'commercial' and 'public interest' obligations of nationalized industries be clarified and separated to avoid the morale-damaging consequence of 'losses' which stem from their wider obligations?

● Should parallel social cost and benefit considerations be required in the accounting of private enterprises?

● Could public control be combined with private operation (with or without transfer of ownership) by parts of industries or services being auctioned off for limited periods of franchise? This could in principle be applied even to the loss-making 'public service' elements, with operators receiving the appropriate subsidy from public funds (although, as the experience of privatizing local cleaning and refuse disposal has shown, it would be important to exercise tight control over quality standards and the protection of employee rights and conditions).

● Has sufficient attention been paid to the role of workers and consumers in the decision-making processes of public enterprises?

● How could the public sector be made more immune from the frequent changes in policy emphasis and day-to-day interventions that make long-term planning and development so difficult?

Consideration of these and similar issues might prove more fruitful than the dogmatic battle in which the rival ideological factions are now locked.

15

Is the City Doing a Proper Job?

The City of London has always had a high profile – in more ways than one. Historically it has been the earliest, leading and most sophisticated capital market, serving a wide range of savers and borrowers. Its activities have always made a major contribution to the 'invisibles' surplus of the UK's balance of payments, and it was one sector unreservedly expected to benefit from UK membership of the European Community.

● Does this correspond with your image of the City? Does it serve the needs of the British economy as well as it could? Does it act in the best interests of domestic firms, your pension and your children's jobs?

● Or are you sceptical about its priorities? Does it tend to put financial and short-term rates of return at a higher priority than the longer-term development of our own productive capability? Is it indifferent between domestic industry's needs and the more opportunistic applications of funds in property and overseas investment? Is it selling Britain short?

This chapter looks at the role and function of City institutions and their terms of reference and priorities, and matches these against the needs of the domestic economy. Do we want the City, or is the City wanting?

What does somebody who is 'something in the City' actually *do*? Narrowly speaking, it means that he (for the chances are that it is not a she) works within the famous Square Mile itself – which is still the main London address of nearly all our major financial institutions. Bustling during the week but deserted on Sunday because nobody lives there, this tiny area is the hub of all the financial wheeling and dealing that goes on in the UK and much that goes on outside it too.

The importance of the City

The very substantial earnings of the City of London come from a wide variety of activities. For it is a place where you can charter shipping, insure it at Lloyds and use it for shifting quantities of commodities produced abroad for sale on the great markets of London like the Baltic

167

Exchange. It is where huge amounts of money can be lent or borrowed for periods ranging from hours to years, where dealings take place in all the major currencies of the world, the meeting place for buyers and sellers of stocks and shares of governments and companies.

But what has all this to do with 'ordinary people' who seldom even meet their own bank manager (if they have one) and certainly make no direct call on most of the esoteric services provided by the City? Only 1 per cent of the population own stocks or shares – and yet the news bulletins throughout the day regularly inform us of the latest movements in the 'FT Index'. At one level this is ridiculous since the great majority of those listening have no conception of what it is, let alone what it implies. But it is a somewhat bizarre reminder that in fact the City does play a vital part in our everyday lives. City opinion is a key element in financial decisions which in the end determine, for example, the availability and price of the funds with which we buy houses, cars and other consumer durables, and whether Spain or Yugoslavia will be cheaper for this year's summer holiday.

FINDING IT IN THE INDEX

The most heavily and regularly reported barometer of stock market prices is the *Financial Times* Industrial Ordinary Share Price Index. It is reported every evening on TV and radio (often coupled with its US counterpart, the Dow Jones Index) and in the following morning's press: it is graphed on an hourly basis by the *Financial Times*; and its current value is available to subscribers by telephone.

It is an average measure of the price movements of thirty key leading industrial ordinary shares, including such companies as ICI, Shell and Unilever, taking their 1935 values as 100. The Index can thus be regarded as measuring the average percentage rise in share prices since 1935.

- On 26 June 1940 it struck an all-time low of 49.4.
- On 23 August 1968, it passed 500 for the first time.
- On 3 May 1984 it reached a new record high of 922.8.
- In the week closing 25 May 1984 it recorded its biggest ever loss with a fall of 46.5.

But what do these movements in the Index really tell us?

- To the shareholder, the Index may or may not be representative of his or her own holdings, as it is based upon a very narrow sample.
- To the rest of us, the Index merely tells us how the City feels that particular day, which in turn is based upon its opinion about the future.

And what do they *not* tell us?

● Although stock market opinion is certainly very powerful and influential, it may be right or it may be wrong; it does not actually create events.

● The Index does not, as so often alleged by news reports, tell us how many millions of pounds have been wiped off or added to the value of British Industry in a day's share trading. Share prices are a reflection of mood and opinion rather than measures of the worth of companies.

Other indices published by the *Financial Times* include government securities, fixed-interest securities and gold-mine shares. Along with the London and Edinburgh Institutes, the *Financial Times* also calculates and publishes other detailed series of price indices, earnings and dividend yields for a variety of stocks, shares and commodities.

These indices are widely used by pension-fund managers and others who wish to follow movements in the values of share portfolios.

More profoundly, the views and actions of the City are a powerful influence on general economic policy, affecting the number of jobs, the amounts of investment in new factories, our basic standard of living.

Above all, it must be remembered that the huge sums that the City handles are mostly made up of *our* money, what *we* have deposited with the banks or building societies, *our* premiums to insurance companies or contributions to pension funds.

It is therefore a matter of general concern to know just what the City does with our money. Does it use it to *our* best advantage? If not, what can be done about it? In what sense, if at all, is the City publicly accountable for its activities?

Home and foreign investment

These are very large questions and in this chapter we shall focus on one major issue. How can the following facts be explained:

● in 1980, total investment in the UK stood at just over £11½ billion, of which only a tiny proportion was in manufacturing industry;

● in 1980, British investment overseas amounted to no less than £10½ billion.

How was it that at a time of severe recession, with massive and mounting unemployment and a rapidly shrinking home industrial base, British funds were flowing abroad in such vast quantities – creating jobs and economic activity there rather than here? The question involves looking at how effective the City is in one of its prime roles, as a *capital market*, bringing together savings from a variety of sources and channelling them into productive investment uses. It might be expected that this activity would be concentrated in the London Stock Exchange, the

The capital market

CAPITAL CITY

The capital market of the City of London is a market for long-term lending and borrowing. It is neither a single institution nor a single location. Rather it represents the relationship between long-term savers and long-term borrowers. These are depicted in the diagram below (which is not intended to be comprehensive and is somewhat simplified):

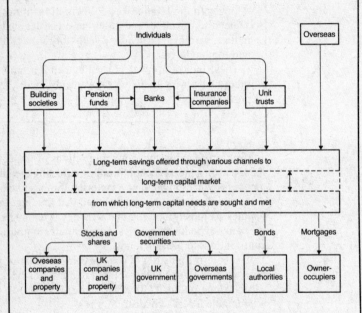

Points worth noting are:
- The market is that for *long-term* capital; short-term lending and borrowing takes place through other channels (referred to in Chapter 5).
- The market is not concerned simply with *new* claims on capital; the majority of its transactions represent dealings in *existing* claims, especially stocks and shares.
- The international dimension of much capital market activity is increasingly significant, involving both overseas investment opportunities and foreign funds for investment.

second largest in the world, serving as a reservoir into which new savings flow to match a corresponding outflow into new investment.

To some extent this is what happens, but the reality is infinitely complicated by the range of other financial institutions involved, by the variety of forms that 'savings' and 'investment' can take, and by the mixed functions of the Stock Exchange itself. For example:

● *Personal* savings are frequently placed with banks and building societies which only to a small extent then pass them through the stock market. More usually they bypass it and undertake lending operations themselves.

● A substantial element of personal saving is that done through life insurance and contributions to pension funds. The volume of funds handled by these *institutional investors* is very large indeed and a considerable proportion of them is channelled through the stock market.

● *Corporate* savings are those undertaken by companies. Their 'undistributed' profits may be subsequently invested by themselves in their own businesses (either here or abroad) *or* through the stock market.

● *Government* may also be an important agency in creating savings through taxation, or drawing on savings through the issue of bonds – in either case to finance public-investment projects or for current spending.

● On the stock market, a large proportion of sales and purchases are of second-hand securities rather than the injection of funds into *new* investment.

WHERE DOES ALL THE MONEY GO?

Increased savings opportunities, especially the development of pension funds, have not represented an *increase* in finance available to firms. New shares account for only 5 per cent of new company capital each year. Moreover,

● total company issues for 1979–80 were equivalent to only 7–8 per cent of insurance companies' and pension funds' net investment in those years.

● For 1980, three quarters of new share issues were for international trading and property companies, with very little being raised for new industrial capital expenditure.

Basically, the institutional shareholders and the stock exchange have not been the leading source of new capital for industrial investment in the UK. British firms tend to rely much more on their own retained earnings and, increasingly, on bank loans.

Based on Richard Minns, *Take over the City*, Pluto Press, 1982.

Instead of pursuing these institutional complexities still further, we shall return to the main question that we set out to answer – whether the fact that in recent years British investment overseas has greatly exceeded that taking place within the domestic economy is evidence that the system is badly malfunctioning and failing to serve the national interest.

Exchange controls

Until 1979 the outflow of British capital was regulated by *exchange controls* which laid down criteria which had to be met before official permission was forthcoming for the purchase of foreign currency which would be needed for buying foreign stocks and shares (portfolio investment) or for 'direct' investment in land, plant, machinery etc., in other countries.

Pounds Across the Sea

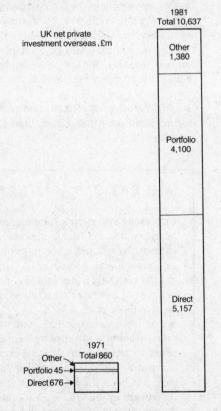

UK net private
investment overseas , £m

1981
Total 10,637

Other
1,380

Portfolio
4,100

Direct
5,157

1971
Total 860

Other
Portfolio 45
Direct 676

(Other = oil companies and miscellaneous)

Source: *UK Balance of Payments* ('Pink Book'), 1982.

The abolition of such controls in that year led to a remarkable upsurge in both types of overseas investment. This can be seen by looking at both the total figures and the uses that some of the major financial institutions made of their available funds.

Case for foreign investment

Although at first sight it might seem unarguably obvious that these massive outflows damage the British economy, in fact a strong case can be put forward for such foreign investment on two grounds:

- that real benefits to the UK economy result from it;
- that if it did not take place, there would be no guarantee of a corresponding increase in home investment.

During the late seventies and early eighties, Britain earned large surpluses on the balance of payments as a result of North Sea oil. This meant that the amount of foreign currencies being exchanged by British exporters for pounds on the foreign exchange market tended to exceed the demand for foreign currencies from buyers who needed them to pay for imports. As we saw in the appendix to Chapter 7, a situation like this leads to a rise in the exchange rate, and this is just what occurred, with British industry suffering a consequent loss of competitiveness as export prices were forced up and imports became relatively cheaper.

Exchange rates

The first benefit that can be claimed for high foreign investment is therefore that it helped to stem the rise in the exchange rate. The abolition of exchange controls encouraged an outward flow of capital which involved an additional *demand* for foreign securities – and from firms undertaking direct investment overseas. To that extent it staunched the deterioration in competitiveness that had previously been taking place.

Moreover, since the balance of payments gains from the North Sea will decline over the years as the oil reserves become depleted, it is clearly prudent to provide for the future. Overseas investment is one way in which this can be achieved.

Invisible earnings

Investment abroad, as we saw in Chapter 2, is the basis for a reverse flow in the future of a stream of 'profits, interest and dividends'. These are payments *by* foreigners, a return on British capital, which comprise 'invisible exports'. The effect on the balance of payments is the same as if we had instead exported goods to them. Thus the argument for foreign investment is that the rundown in foreign currency earnings as North Sea oil dries up will to this extent be offset by higher invisible earnings helping to maintain our capacity to import.

But would it not be better still if instead of investing overseas, British capital was channelled into home industry, re-equipping it to compete more effectively in foreign markets and preparing for the post-oil era in a more positive fashion? This seems more attractive in creating employment and activity at home rather than strengthening our foreign competitors.

THE BENEFITS OF DOMESTIC INVESTMENT

The Benefits of Domestic Investment

Rate of return	Value added is the value added to raw materials and bought-in supplies by the production process. It is measured by SALES minus BOUGHT-IN MATERIALS and COMPONENTS, and is broadly equivalent to WAGES AND SALARIES plus PROFITS.		Value added
Multiplier effect			Multiplier effect
Value added	The multiplier effect was explained in Chapter 3.	Rate of return	
UK investment		Overseas investment	

- The financial rate of return (profit, interest and/or dividend) on an investment overseas may be greater than that arising from home investment.
- But the value added from the undertaking of the process domestically is lost to the UK and goes to the overseas economy.
- So too do the multiplier effects of the original investment and the spending from pay of jobs created or maintained.
- The result is that the *economic* advantage of domestic investment, as opposed to the mere financial rate of return, is sacrificed by overseas investment.

Why not home investment?

However, the choice is not quite so simple. Supposing that a total ban were to be imposed on the transfer of capital overseas, then financial institutions with funds available would no longer be able to purchase the foreign currencies needed to undertake portfolio investment (although, as we shall see in the next chapter, multinational companies might find a way around the ban and continue direct investment abroad). In that case, there would be three options open to, for example, the manager of a pension fund seeking a profitable outlet:
- to buy non-financial assets like land, property or objets d'arts (in the hope they would appreciate in value);
- to buy 'second-hand' stocks and shares on the Stock Exchange;

• to buy newly issued shares in British companies which would then finance real investment in re-equipment of industry.

There is no guarantee that they would exercise the third of these options. Partly this may be due to a judgement that it was more profitable for them not to do so. But the opportunity would anyway be limited by the extent to which British firms were *demanding* additional finance and coming to the capital market for it.

Here we come close to the nub of the matter. British investment has been low in comparison with that of our major competitors for most of the postwar period, and in recent years there has actually been disinvestment in manufacturing industry (a rundown in the stock of capital used). But there is no evidence that this has been due to a shortage of finance.

Traditionally, British firms have financed their investment out of profits to a higher degree than elsewhere. But in the years when profitability was high, investment did not take place in industrial restructuring to the extent that subsequent events have proved necessary. It is not only those on the left who would indict British management for failing to use periods of prosperity to build for the future, to recognize the need for continuous modernization and change, and to invest accordingly.

More recently, it is even easier to understand a reluctance to invest. The application of monetarist policies since the later seventies has faced British industry with a combination at times of severely deflated demand, an uncompetitively high exchange rate and high interest rates.

On this argument it is therefore industry and governments which should bear the blame for Britain's economic plight rather than the City. It is not the City which has 'starved' industry of investment finance but industry itself, operating in an adverse climate partly created by governments, which has shown a marked lack of appetite for investing in the future.

Criticisms of the City

However, critics of the City have more to say, even if the simplistic view that foreign investment is automatically at the expense of home investment does not bear careful scrutiny. The City, it is claimed, *is* responsible for industrial failure in two respects:

• It is a powerful interest which frequently influences general economy policy in ways which are detrimental to the industrial health of the economy;

• its institutions and attitudes are based on narrowly short-term considerations which do not assist in the long-run restructuring of the economy that is called for.

Thus it is argued that the City, with its international orientation and traditional concern with financial 'soundness', may promote objectives which conflict with the healthy growth of the home economy. For example, governments of both parties throughout the sixties 'defended the pound' at its existing exchange rate, encouraged by a City view that a

RULED OUT OF COURT

An example of the limitations placed upon the influence of members of a pension fund to control its application arose in 1984. The President of the NUM, Arthur Scargill, in his capacity as a union trustee on the management board of the NCB mineworkers pension fund, had sought to prevent funds being invested in competing energy sources and in overseas locations. The High Court ruled against him, holding that a pension fund's responsibility was to maximize the financial rate of return on members' funds.

Thus, although the pension funds had grown from 3 per cent of company shareholdings in 1957 to 20 per cent in 1978, there is real doubt over the members' ability to control the investment of their funds through token representatives. The orthodox financial measure of a rate of return is the commercial criterion to be upheld, and the wider economic and social costs and benefits are again 'ruled out of court'.

devaluation would injure its standing and business as an international financial centre. This often meant cutting back on home demand to curb imports. But such 'stop-go' policies were highly unfavourable to industry – which most economists at the time thought would benefit from a substantial devaluation. This in fact is what happened, when the pound *was* devalued in 1967. Furthermore, the City's judgement of the effect of devaluation on its own position proved, in any case, to be wrongly pessimistic.

More recently, the City has been vocal and active in supporting the introduction and implementation of a monetarist strategy emphasizing the paramount importance of eliminating inflation, reductions in public spending, balanced budgets and the abolition of external exchange controls. Much of this has been very much in accordance with City philosophy and good for City business. However, the argument of previous chapters suggests that, to say the least, it is debatable whether similar benefits will accrue to the economy as a whole and the manufacturing sector in particular.

More specifically, critics claim that the City institutions are not sufficiently geared to the requirements of British industry:

● Banks have been traditionally reluctant to offer the long-term finance that industry requires, preferring short-term lending to the government, personal and professional sectors.

● Institutional investors have generally used their funds in ways which offer safe short-term profitability rather than face the risks involved in the 'venture capital' on which new enterprises are likely to be particularly reliant.

UNLISTED SECURITIES MARKET

A major criticism of City institutions has been their failure to provide 'venture capital' for small businesses, new growth points and higher risk initiatives. Rather their fund managers have preferred property, foreign investment and 'blue chip' shares.

The odds are stacked further against such businesses by stock-market regulations which require a quoted company to sign a 'listing agreement', giving details of its financial structure and historical profits record. It is also obliged to sell at least 25 per cent of its shares to stock-market investors, and thus risk losing control to outsiders.

The Stock Exchange therefore instituted a new system in 1980 known as the Unlisted Securities Market, relaxing the obligations. Of over a hundred new small companies placing their shares on this new market, half have been in high-risk areas of electronics, bio-engineering, energy and minerals. The market has also drawn in the pension funds and other institutional investors, who invariably take up to three quarters of a new company's share offer.

- Major institutional shareholders in companies have not used their influence effectively in ensuring that they are managed as efficiently and enterprisingly as possible.
- Stock-market prices (which affect the ease or difficulty in raising fresh finance) in fact tend to reflect current views about the short-term profitability rather than the long-run prospects of enterprises.

The City *does* do a proper job, if that job is to maximize the immediate returns to the savers and shareholders who provide the huge sums of money on which its business is based. Whether these coincide with the needs of the economy as a whole and those savers whose future employment may be at risk is more doubtful. If they do not, then the answer must lie in a radical alteration of the criteria according to which the major financial institutions operate. This might only be achieved through the public control and ownership advocated by the left-wing critics of the City. Since this is not on the current political agenda, we shall have to see whether the market alternative is successful in reviving the ailing economy – and whether, since to some extent it recognizes its own shortcomings, the City can itself adjust in taking more active responsibility in improving Britain's economic performance.

CITY WITHOUT A COUNTRY?

Others have made much stronger criticisms of the City than those already indicated in this chapter. In particular they concentrate upon
- the international dimensions of its activities
- the short-term horizons of its views
- the costs to the domestic economy of these emphases.

Here is how some authors have developed this critique (all go on to advocate public ownership and control of the City institutions as the only solution):

. . . the City's international operations are central to the pursuit of its interests, and for two reasons: first, the institutions' and markets' functions of trading in foreign exchange and in lending and borrowing to and from foreign operators in foreign currencies are a major source of the City's profits; and, second, their influence over the exchange rate and . . . over interest rates gives the City power over the two prices – of foreign exchange and of credit – that affect the whole economy. If British sovereignty is being undermined by finance, it is not a plot from abroad – Gnomes of Zürich, or the IMF furthering US capital's hegemony – that is doing the tunnelling: it is the operations of the City of London pursuing its interests . . .

Jerry Coakley and Laurence Harris, *The City of Capital*, Blackwell, 1983.

Because of the overseas orientation of UK finance, our savings are therefore used against us. Industry is multinational, finance is international, but the workforce is *here*. What has emerged is a fundamental dislocation between UK residents as *savers*, and as *employees* . . . It is not surprising that, with the massive diversification of the City's assets and investments throughout the world, the financial institutions pursue only a short-term view of risk and return both for pension funds and British industry alike. Their dependence on what happens to production and pensions in Britain is substantially limited by the overseas role which has characterized the City as a financial centre. This has also endorsed an ideology of investment in Britain which emphasizes short-term return and the minimization of long-term risk. Major shareholdings have been acquired in British industry by pension funds and insurance companies, investing savings on our behalf. The large companies which these institutions concentrate on are also overseas oriented and are not dependent on what happens in the UK. The investments in the shares of firms, the operations of the firms themselves, and the poor returns which result, are a major challenge to the interests of people as employees *and* savers in the UK. The City has successfully separated these interests and put them in conflict. Union trustees on pension funds have been persuaded to accept this ideology of savings.

Richard Minns, *Take over the City*, Pluto Press, 1982.

16

Is Big Business Out of Control?

- *The largest multinational companies have turnover in excess of the national output of countries such as the Netherlands.*
- *Of the 100 largest economic powers in the world today, fifty-three are countries and forty-seven are multinational companies.*
- *Multinational corporations are estimated to control between a quarter and a third of total world output. Trade within multi-nationals themselves accounts for 30 per cent of all world trade.*

Are these figures merely pressure-group statistics, designed to alarm and shame you into some kind of concern? Why should you worry about the inevitability of such concentration of the world's production capacity? What's good for business must ultimately surely be good for the consumer?

But can we rest assured with such assumptions? When privately owned and independently managed enterprises challenge national governments for control and allocation of the world's resources, can we be sure that the outcome will be in the best interests of countries, consumers and employees?

This chapter looks at the growth of the large firm, and its impact domestically and internationally upon economies.

Despite the wide range of brand labels on the supermarket shelves, the chances are overwhelming that the next packet of washing powder that your family buys will have been manufactured by Lever Brothers (Unilever) or by Proctor and Gamble. Similarly, one of the world's giant oil corporations will be responsible for your next tank of petrol. And your car itself is more likely than ever to come from part of the world manufacturing system of Ford or General Motors.

Market dominance   Both the home markets and product markets world-wide are increasingly dominated by a small number of large companies. Typically, some two thirds to three quarters of total output of UK industries is accounted for by three or four major producers. In 1950 the top 100 companies in Britain were responsible for 20 per cent of manufacturing output. In 1970 their share was up to 50 per cent and by 1985 it represents nearly 70 per cent.

This is a far cry from the state of market forces guiding competition between a large number of firms that was described in the idealized picture of Chapter 11. And while only rarely does an actual monopoly (single producer) emerge, the typical market structure is now one of *oligopoly* – a small number of producers (or 'duopoly' if there are only two producers as in the case of detergents). Conventional competition working through the market mechanism to the benefit of consumers is not necessarily the result of such a situation.

Oligopoly

Oligopoly is characterized by interdependence and uncertainty. Thus if one firm cuts its price, it knows that because of its market size its decision is bound to affect its rivals. But what it does not know is just how they will react. Will they follow suit, matching its new price or cutting still further? Or cut by less, or hold to their old price? The outcome is 'indeterminate' – which is the economists' way of saying that they can't predict what will happen. All kinds of behaviour are possible, including:

● An open price war between the rivals – perhaps the least likely because all of them will be fearful of where it will end.

● Hidden price competition – through the distribution of gift coupons or money-winning vouchers or concealed rebates – so that rivals cannot be sure by how much prices are being reduced.

● Forms of non-price competition – through advertising, packaging, the provision of services like toilets in petrol stations, and other ways of increasing consumer loyalty to particular brands.

● Price leadership, whereby one of the firms regularly makes the running and the others customarily follow its lead.

● Collusion, with an informal, unwritten agreement enabling the oligopolists to act collectively as a monopolist in maintaining high prices and possibly erecting barriers to the entry of new competitors.

● Take-over or merger activity, designed to eliminate competition and strengthen market dominance.

Large firms are frequently in a position to reduce costs of production as a result of the 'economies of large scale'. But there is no guarantee that these will be passed on to consumers or that their preferences can be clearly signalled and bring about the required response from large enterprises engaged in complex oligopolistic strategies. In such circumstances, the consumer has to rely on the extent to which governments can regulate against the abuse of market dominance by firms and stimulate competition between them. This is now the responsibility in Britain of the Office of Fair Trading, the Monopolies Commission and the Restrictive Practices Court, which have had only limited success in identifying the problem areas and in ensuring that consumer interests are best served.

COMPETITION POLICY

Three UK agencies are charged with promoting competition.

THE OFFICE OF FAIR TRADING

Set up by the Fair Trading Act of 1973 to replace restrictive trade practices legislation and given the task of overseeing consumer affairs as well as competition policy.

Powers
- to initiate references to the Monopolies Commission;
- to give evidence on merger proposals;
- to carry out investigations into potential anti-competitive practice;
- to investigate practices of individual firms over a certain size which restrict, distort or prevent competition;
- to refer cartels or cases of resale price maintenance to the Restrictive Practices Court.

Limitations
- no power to refer mergers to Monopolies Commission;
- confusion over definition of anti-competitive practices, especially regarding mergers.

THE MONOPOLIES COMMISSION

Originally set up by 1948 Act, extended in 1965 to cover mergers and in 1980 to cover public bodies.

Powers
- to decide whether situations referred to it are 'in the public interest' or not;
- to consider mergers involving large companies or market shares;

Limitations
- 'public interest' vaguely defined;
- no powers of initiative, decision, or setting of precedents;
- can only consider mergers referred to it by government.

THE RESTRICTIVE PRACTICES COURT

Set up by 1956 Act, supplemented by further legislation in 1964, 1968, 1973 and 1976, deals with cartel practices such as price fixing.

Powers
- more specific criteria than Monopolies Commission;
- to outlaw cartels and resale price maintenance.

Market power

Three examples illustrate the powers that large firms can exercise if unchecked:

Case 1. In the seventies, as a result of investigations by the Monopolies Commission and by European Community agencies, the Swiss-based pharmaceutical company Hoffman La Roche was found to be making huge excess profits on its sales in certain countries, including the UK, of the popular tranquillizers Librium and Valium.

Case 2. The British Oxygen Company already has a near monopoly in supplying medical gases to the NHS. It has recently been revealed that it has now been given the right to examine and change the dispensing equipment in 850 hospitals – and that by phasing out an earlier model it is in effect inducing them to buy a new type of vaporizer at a time of shortage of funds which they might have chosen to spend on other priorities.

Case 3. The European Community is currently subjecting to critical scrutiny the methods used by the vast IBM Corporation to secure its market dominance, especially its refusal to divulge specifications which would permit competitors to make their own software compatible with IBM's computer systems.

Multi-nationals

It is clear from these examples that the possible exploitation of power by big business is no longer confined within national boundaries. Such power is greatly increased when exercised by a multinational company (MNC) operating on a global basis. Multinationals now dominate in many important areas of world production like oil, cars, tyres, chemicals and pharmaceuticals, food and drink, computers – and, increasingly, banking, finance and accounting.

Apart from its sheer size, the additional influence that a multinational can exert as compared with its large domestic counterpart stems from its ability to operate two key mechanisms:

● its *location policy* enables it to set up business wherever labour, government, taxation and other conditions are most favourable;

183

The Multinational Involvement

Of the 1,500 companies in the Department of Industry's 1975 survey:

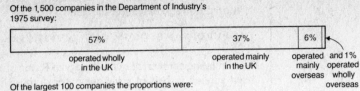

57%	37%	6%
operated wholly in the UK	operated mainly in the UK	operated mainly overseas

and 1% operated wholly overseas

Of the largest 100 companies the proportions were:

12%	61%	25%

2%

Of the largest 50 companies the proportions were:

8%	64%	26%

2%

And of the largest 20 companies:

15%	50%	30%	5%

- through *transfer pricing*, it can effectively concentrate its profits in products, plants and countries according to what it sees as its best advantage.

Since each of these makes possible major conflicts of interest between multinationals and the countries in which they function, they need explanation and analysis if we are to draw any conclusion about whether big business is indeed now out of control.

Location policy

The investment strategy of a multinational is normally extremely complex. Consider, for example, the problems currently facing Technifloss Inc., a household name for useless consumer gadgetry that clutters every home in the affluent western world, that is rapidly becoming a prestige symbol in the Third World, and has recently permeated even the Eastern bloc (with production under licence). Currently under discussion at the corporate head office in Kansas City is a proposal for a major expansion in world-wide production and sales of flossettes, its most popular product. The question before the board is where investment in new capacity should be located.

It is quickly agreed that it should not be in the United States itself. One of the most important considerations here is the high dollar exchange rate which would mean that exports would be inordinately expensive. Even to the extent that part of increased output will be sold in the home market, it will prove cheaper to produce flossettes elsewhere and import them back.

So what are the key factors that will determine the corporation's decision? Amongst the most important will be these:

- Where are the most rapidly growing markets? There is a clear advantage in producing close to the point of sale.
- The labour market. Production techniques will be capital-intensive, i.e. using a lot of sophisticated plant and relatively little labour – so cheapness of labour is important (particularly in the assembly process) but not the paramount consideration. More significant is that the labour force should be docile and disciplined, with trade union power well limited. Ideally, the firm will export its own senior management team or use local personnel trained in the US.
- Taxes should be avoided wherever possible. It is important for the corporation to 'protect profits' to the maximum extent. Which of the countries on the shortlist for location offers the most favourable tax climate?
- Investment grants and other concessions are offered by many countries in an attempt to attract multinational capital. Comparative benefits will require careful analysis and negotiation may lead to even more attractive terms being proposed.
- Political conditions in the 'host country' should be favourable to free enterprise, stable for the foreseeable future – and with a regime that is sensitive, not to say adjustable, to the corporation's needs.

It is not part of a multinational's remit to take into account the national interest of either its country of origin or that in which it decides

---

INCENTIVES TO MULTINATIONALS

It is not only developing countries of the Third World who vie for the attentions of multinational companies. In our own case, the UK has in recent years:

- offered the most generous taxation package of full free first-year depreciation on investment by manufacturers, allowing the whole cost of capital expenditure to be offset immediately against tax;
- succeeded in attracting Ford to Bridgend with a high ratio of government assistance which Ford gave the Spanish government a week to beat (transport costs across the Pyrenees ultimately counted against the equally generous Spanish);
- included in its official publicity the advantages of a high-spending high proportion of teenagers in its population, and of the unrestricted opportunities of waste disposal around its island shores.

to locate. Its decision will form part of its own global corporate strategy. (In the event, Technifloss Inc. opted to close part of its UK operation where regional inducements had now expired; to concentrate its main component manufacture in the Philippines because of its particularly sympathetic regime and the existence there of an 'exporting processing zone' into and out of which products are allowed duty-free; and to undertake the assembly processes in Spain – offering relatively cheap labour, good investment inducements and the future prospect of access to the EEC market.)

The case of the UK

The location policy of multinationals has certainly had a considerable impact in the case of the UK economy. In Chapter 15, we argued that foreign investment from the UK is not necessarily at the expense of home investment. But this argument is more obviously true of portfolio investment than it is of *direct* investment by British-based multinationals, which may clearly opt for overseas rather than home location for reasons similar to those that we have just been outlining. In particular, much 'portfolio' investment in foreign stocks and shares is made by the managers of the big financial institutions seeking the most lucrative outlets for their funds – who do not themselves have much, if any, control over the amount of capital re-equipment that is being undertaken by British industry and which might therefore be financed by them.

However, in the case of 'direct' investment abroad by British-based multinationals, there is a much clearer decision being made by a company to expand its operations overseas *rather* than in the UK. The dramatic collapse of manufacturing industry in the West Midlands provides a classic example of this process in recent times.

Thus, in ten major companies accounting for a large part of the West Midlands industrial base, the late seventies and early eighties saw:
- approximately one third of their workforce being made redundant;
- actual *disinvestment* on a substantial scale, i.e. a reduction rather than an increase in their capital assets (plant, machinery, etc.).

During the same period, between 1979 and 1982, the same ten companies:
- increased the value of their overseas production by 12.1 per cent per annum (compared with 1.7 per cent per annum in the UK);
- increased the share of overseas production in their total world output from 30 per cent to 41 per cent.

It is difficult to avoid the conclusion that overseas production and sales were to a considerable extent actually in place of British employment and exports.

Transfer pricing

It is not only through investment and location policies that multinational behaviour may conflict with the national interest and be at variance with a government's economic objectives. They are also in a position to manipulate their costs and internal pricing between different

186

Percentage of the Workforce in Great Britain: Ten Multinationals in the West Midlands
(The companies are GEC, GKN, Cadbury, Dunlop, Lucas, Tube Investments, IMI, Delta, Glynwed and BSR.)

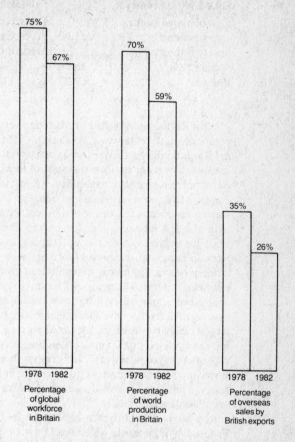

Source: *Jobs Crisis and The Multinationals: The Case of the West Midlands*, F. Gaffikin and A. Nickson, Birmingham Trade Union Resource Centre, 1984.

parts of the company to show high or low profits and losses in their various operations in ways that minimize tax liability and maximize other advantages. The mechanism by which they do so is transfer pricing. It is a process which can best be defined by a simple illustration.

Suppose that there are subsidiaries of a multinational, one producing component parts and operating in a low-tax country and the other performing the final processing and sale and based in a high-tax country.

In the company's accounts, the components are sold from country A to the subsidiary in country B. The accounts of the transactions involved, which are internal to the company, might look like this:

Subsidiary in country A		Subsidiary in country B	
Cost of manufacturing components	£1.00	Cost of components	£8.00
		Processing cost	£1.00
Sale to subsidiary in country B	£8.00	Marketing cost	£1.00
		Total cost	£10.00
Profit	£7.00	Sale price	£10.00
		Profit	£0.00

What has happened is that by charging a very high price (£8.00) for its components, the company makes a large profit in country A where taxes are low, and shows a zero profit in country B where taxes are high. Its ability to determine the internal values of each of the constituent parts of its output thus enables the multinational (or, for that matter, a domestic company with several plants) to boost or lower profits made at the various production stages and in different locations.

In the UK at least, transfer pricing along these lines would be regarded by the Inland Revenue as a clear case of tax evasion. But the internal nature of the process together with the sheer complexity of modern production makes it very difficult for the authorities to identify instances and prove them to be aimed at evasion.

However, there can be little doubt that the practice is widespread.

● Various studies have shown that at least twelve of the UK's twenty largest companies have paid no tax whatever during recent years. When it is remembered that for most of this time they were subject to a formal rate of corporation tax of 52 per cent on their profits, there is a clear suspicion that transfer pricing practices might have been a contributory factor in addition to shrewd accounting and the generosity of corporate tax allowances and reliefs.

● A study over a decade ago by the International Metalworkers' Federation of the world-wide Ford Motor Corporation found that Ford of Germany was the most productive and profitable unit of the Ford empire. But this appeared to be due, not to the quality of German management or the industriousness of German workers so much as the high exchange rate of the Deutschmark and the low transfer price attributed to component parts bought in from Dagenham (UK) and Bordeaux (France).

It is perhaps worth repeating that a large domestic company, without any international ramifications, is also often in a position to seriously affect the local economy where its plants are sited. It may be possible, for example, to justify closure in a certain area by reference to losses which are more the result of its internal accounting procedures than

WHY PAY MORE?

The following table, calculated by Kay and King in *The British Tax System* (3rd ed., OUP, 1983), shows how little tax liability is enjoyed by the UK's major companies.

COMPANY TAXATION IN THE UK

Payments of mainstream corporation tax, 1976–1982   (£m)

Company	1976–7 Profits	1976–7 Tax paid	1981–2 Profits	1981–2 Tax paid
Allied Lyons	63	nil	95	nil
Bass	69	17	126	25
BAT	374	2	684	nil
Bowater	78	nil	107	nil
British Leyland	71	nil	(333)	nil
BP	1784	nil	5932	145
Courtaulds	46	nil	5	nil
Distillers	91	7	172	36
Dunlop	74	nil	(3)	nil
Esso	69	nil	805	nil
Ford	122	nil	220	nil
GEC	207	41	476	144
Grand Metropolitan	57	nil	187	nil
GKN	70	nil	46	nil
ICI	540	12	524	nil
Imperial Group	130	9	102	nil
Marks & Spencer	84	29	178	62
P & O	31	nil	41	nil
Reed International	37	nil	72	nil
RTZ	279	nil	348	4
	4,276	117	9,784	416

Notes: Profits are those of the accounting year ending in 1976 or 1981: tax mainstream tax payable in 1977 or 1982.
Source: Own estimates.

failure of the plant itself. But because multinationals deal with different national economies, regulations, tax and government-assistance structures, industrial relations systems and trade union organizations, their power to play one off against another and to select the best mix for their overall strategy is correspondingly greater. Nor should the sheer size of MNCs be forgotten; nearly a hundred MNCs have turnovers exceeding the national outputs of most developing countries, while that of the largest MNCs is greater than the national product of several European Community states.

The fact that multinationals operate across national frontiers means that their decisions may have serious implications for individual countries' balance of payments and exchange rates. In maximizing their world-wide profitability, their balance between importing and exporting activities in any one country, and the shifting of their funds from one centre to another, are not likely to be much influenced by a single government's declared policy objectives.

Controlling MNCs

Attempts to control the global power of MNCs have not as yet been very promising. Governments and international trade union bodies have worked towards codes of agreement in dealing with multinationals by presenting them with a common front. But they have been beset by the difficulty that they represent different and often conflicting national and sectional interests. There have thus been problems of reaching agreement; failures to implement codes of practice and make them effective; and the MNCs themselves have resisted attempts at control. A recent example of this has been the massive and expensive lobbying campaign by MNCs upon the European Community, especially Members of the European Parliament, against the 'Vredeling Directive'. This set out to oblige MNCs to provide regular standard information to its workforce at each subsidiary. But it has already been watered down considerably, and is being talked down still further by our own Department of Trade and Industry.

The corporate strategies of MNCs are determined as a world-wide basis for global implementation over a lengthy time period. They will be constructed by head office boards whose loyalties are to the corporations themselves and their overall profitability rather than to governments. National governments have difficulty enough in regulating the behaviour of their own domestic large enterprises. 'Leaving things to the market' is an even more dangerous game where many of the players are multinational companies. Democratically elected governments may increasingly find their economic sovereignty circumscribed by the power of these new industrial giants responsible only to themselves.

17

What Should be Done about the Unions?

These are the aims of trade unions as described by the TUC in its 1965 evidence to the Donovan Royal Commission on Trade Unions and Employers' Associations:
- *improved terms of employment;*
- *improved physical working environment;*
- *full employment and national prosperity;*
- *security of employment and income;*
- *improved social security;*
- *'fair' shares in national income and wealth;*
- *industrial democracy;*
- *a voice in government;*
- *improved public and social services;*
- *public control and planning of industry.*

How does the list strike you? Do unions appear to be over-demanding, biting off more than they can chew?

Are some of the items perhaps not proper or appropriate aims of unions, as opposed to a political party? Or are they all perfectly acceptable and reasonable, and therefore a sad record of many of the things unions have as yet failed to achieve?

This chapter looks at trade unions in post-war Britain: their power, their weaknesses, their achievements and the criticisms and legislation mounted against them.

Concentration of output in relatively few giant enterprises, and the rapid development of multinational companies, have made big business very powerful indeed. Decisions made by large firms can have profound consequences for whole communities, the working lives of millions of people, the success or failure of national economic policies.

And yet these are not matters that are regularly drawn to our attention in the newspapers or that fill our television screens. There, it is the ogre of organized *labour* rather than capital that provides the major industrial stories day after day, week after week – partly at least (and

Trade Union Membership

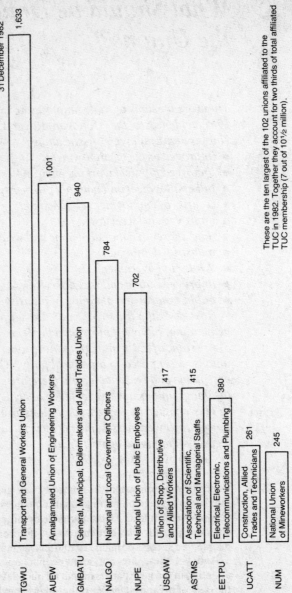

Membership in thousands,
31 December 1982

TGWU	Transport and General Workers Union — 1,633
AUEW	Amalgamated Union of Engineering Workers — 1,001
GMBATU	General, Municipal, Boilermakers and Allied Trades Union — 940
NALGO	National and Local Government Officers — 784
NUPE	National Union of Public Employees — 702
USDAW	Union of Shop, Distributive and Allied Workers — 417
ASTMS	Association of Scientific, Technical and Managerial Staffs — 415
EETPU	Electrical, Electronic, Telecommunications and Plumbing — 380
UCATT	Construction, Allied Trades and Technicians — 261
NUM	National Union of Mineworkers — 245

These are the ten largest of the 102 unions affiliated to the TUC in 1982. Together they account for two thirds of total affiliated TUC membership (7 out of 10½ million).

Source: TUC Statistical Statement 1983.

there are many other reasons) because the effects of trade union activity are so much more immediate and visible to the general public.

According to opinion polls, a majority of people – including trade union members themselves – see unions as too powerful, unrepresentative and undemocratic. There seems to be general support for moves to limit the freedom of unions to implement closed shops, to mount picketing and strike action, and to run their internal affairs in their own ways.

Certainly, the unions continue to have an unenviably bad image. The following are just some of the views that many people hold about trade unions, and which the media, recent governments (and the trade unions themselves) have done little to discourage:

● They are greedy, seeking extortionate pay rises for less or easier work.

● They are responsible for outdated restrictive practices, 'Luddite' in their approach to new technology and improved working methods.

● They are fighting yesterday's battles, outdated in the context of today's more enlightened and progressive employers and higher living standards.

● They are 'strike-happy', ready to hold the economy to ransom and inconvenience the general public in pursuing their own narrow aims.

● Their leaders and activists are out of touch with their general members but able to bully and manipulate them because of their dubiously democratic organizations.

● They have become too political in outlook, challenging democratically elected governments on matters of policy rather than confining themselves to protecting and advancing their members' interests.

● They are unrepresentative of changing employment patterns, with an emphasis upon full-time, male manufacturing and manual workers (all currently in decline) as against part-time, female, non-manual and service occupations (all increasing); and they are confined to representing the interests of those in work rather than the growing numbers of unemployed.

Moreover, unions have been blamed by economists and politicians for a number of our economic problems. Sometimes their activities have been regarded as contributory factors only but in other cases they have been cast as the main villains of the piece. Thus balance of payments difficulties have been partly ascribed to reluctance of foreigners to place export orders for fear that the orders might not be met on time because of industrial disputes or the goods might be overpriced as a result of labour practices common here but not amongst our competitors. One element of Britain's relatively slow growth in the postwar period has similarly been put down to trade unions' ability to maintain overmanning in many industries, and their reluctance to accept the need for change. Above all, during the decades after 1945, it was the compatibil-

193

ity of full employment and price stability that was seen to be threatened by the power of unions to create cost inflationary pressures. More recently, the emphasis has shifted, and unions have been held responsible for growing unemployment.

These are extraordinarily comprehensive (if, at times, self-contradictory) catalogues of shortcomings as perceived by the public, and of problems for which the unions are blamed. It is hardly surprising that by the late seventies there was a widespread feeling that 'something must be done about the unions'.

What *would* be surprising is if there was no substance in any of these criticisms. But while they need to be taken very seriously, both by trade unionists and others, it is also important to separate reality from myth, misconception and prejudice in order to arrive at an accurate and balanced assessment of the trade union role.

OBSTACLES AND POISONS?

Sir Keith Joseph, then Secretary of State for Industry, articulated the case against the unions most strongly:

> The fifth obstacle that stands between a society and full employment and rising standards of living is politicized to a great extent by a Luddite trade union movement, which is indifferent, if not hostile, to the consumer on whom jobs depend; and which often – not always – obstructs competitiveness and higher productivity, defends overmanning, thus pricing firms and jobs out of existence or aborting them in advance.

Hansard, House of Commons, 21 May 1979.

> The existence of a politicized trade union movement is one of the six poisons responsible for Britain's ills. Such poisons wreck a country's prosperity and full employment. It is easy, or possible, to get some of the poisons out of the country's system, but tackling a political trade union movement, associated with Luddism, is a difficult thing to do. A politicized union movement is hostile to the interest of its members. I warn union leaders against encouraging their members to oppose the Government's policies. I think trade union members are beginning to realize that there is a real danger they can price themselves out of a job. I don't believe that trade unions will necessarily follow those leaders – and there may be a few – who attempt to lead them to defy reality.

BBC radio interview, 30 July 1979.

(Sir Keith's other five 'obstacles' or 'poisons', were excessive government spending, high direct taxation, egalitarianism, excessive nationalization and an anti-enterprise culture.)

Just *how* powerful are trade unions? How representative? Have they exercised their power irresponsibly? And what are their economic consequences? To even begin to answer these questions, we need to recall the reasons why unions came into being, and to look at the ways in which they organize and behave.

Why unions?   Trade unions came about as a result of workers in a particular category of employment seeking to combine together in a collective organization which could match an individual employer's far greater power – to hire, fire, pay and treat employees at will. Since those early days, the strength of capital has enormously increased, and although today employers in industrialized countries are far more regulated by law about employment and working conditions, the need for the 'countervailing power' of *organized* labour must surely remain unchallenged. Recent events suggest widespread public disquiet at any threat to the *right* to belong to a trade union, and suggestions that trade unions are becoming redundant in a modern world would seem misplaced. What does seem likely is that unions will have great difficulty in sustaining their organization in face of rapidly changing work structures. Originally, they were groupings based on crafts or skills. Later these were supplemented by industrial categories of workers, and later still by general 'open' unions. But the future possibility of work becoming more dispersed and fragmented – fewer people working in vast industrial complexes and more in smaller production enterprises, part-time jobs and work based in the home – will pose considerable problems for unions in retaining their membership and control.

Trade union methods   The *methods* adopted by trade unions to further the interest of their members have always included a political element in their pressure for the introduction of sympathetic and supportive legislation to protect their pay and conditions. But their principal means of achieving their aims has been through collective bargaining with employers. This has come to mean the somewhat ritualistic annual wage round, beginning with widely different claims and offers, talks and breakdowns of talks across the table, resumption of negotiations and a final agreed settlement.

To some extent these are paper battles, a charade in which both sides can more or less predict the final outcome. From a trade union standpoint, it is interesting that in the UK to a greater degree than elsewhere collective bargaining has been narrowly focused on pay and conditions. Generally excluded from the agenda have been matters that have exercised trade unions in some other countries – questions of employee involvement in decision-making about corporate strategy on location, investment, technological change, product development and marketing. This narrowness of approach is something we shall return to in a moment.

But from the point of view of the public, the narrowness of trade unions' attitudes manifests itself most obviously in those relatively few cases where negotiation is stalemated and a union resorts to industrial action. It is true that research shows shop stewards to be spending most of their time solving problems, defusing issues and avoiding disputes. And a recent Department of Employment Survey revealed that 98 per cent of workplaces were strike-free over a year. But it is the other 2 per cent of which there is general awareness – of strikes which, to make matters worse, so often seem to hurt consumers and other workers more than they do the employers.

Unrepresentative?

And how democratic are the procedures on which decisions to take industrial action are based? The unrepresentativeness of unions appears to be one of the main sources of recent public disenchantment. Thus it is argued that the closed shop coerces workers into union membership, and their own apathy then yields union representatives who are more 'political', left-wing and militant than the membership itself. But again evidence indicates that this is a problem as seen by others from the outside rather than by the members of a particular union. Research suggests that British workers expect their unions to be 'instrumental'. That is, so long as they deliver the goods, providing 'industrial insurance' of secure employment and enhanced pay and working conditions, the membership is indifferent to the more political dimensions of the leadership's attitudes and activities. The growth of white-collar union

Manual and White-collar Union Membership in Great Britain (millions)

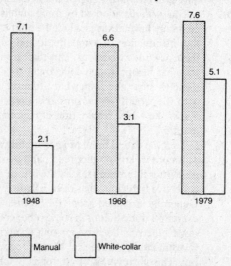

Source: R. Price and G. S. Bain, 'Union Growth in Britain, Retrospect and Prospect', *British Journal of Industrial Relations*, March 1983.

membership between 1968 and 1979 – where it might be expected that members would be rather more conservatively inclined – seems to reinforce this view.

Too much power?

By the early seventies, the key issue was whether unions had achieved a quite unwarrantable degree of *power* – to the point, indeed, at which the question was being asked: 'Is Britain governable?' Certainly, union strength had never been greater. By the sixties and seventies they were enjoying:

- a high and growing membership;
- the confidence that full employment would be sustained through demand-management policies regardless of their actions;
- supportive and sympathetic employment legislation.

ACTS OF SYMPATHY

Sympathetic legislation flowed from the Social Contract's early years in the mid-seventies:

- The Trade Union and Labour Relations Act (TULRA) of 1974 repealed most of the limitations placed upon trade unions by the previous Conservative government in its Industrial Relations Act of 1971, restoring to unions rights of organization and industrial action.
- The Employment Protection Act (EPA) of 1975 gave unions minimum standards upon which they could build through their collective bargaining, including recognition by employers, fair comparison of pay, maternity leave and provision of information by employers. It also set up the Advisory Conciliation and Arbitration Service, ACAS, whose function was to foster good industrial relations through collective bargaining and thus through the representation of workers by unions.
- Parallel legislation built up rights and opportunities for trade unions acting on behalf of workers with respect to equal pay and equal opportunities between men and women, racial equality at work, and health and safety.
- At the same time retirement pensions were significantly increased as a result of union lobbying, the capital transfer tax (gifts tax) replaced the old estate duty, and a wealth tax was proposed.
- An industrial strategy was pursued on a tripartite basis through the National Economic Development Office (NEDO) and its economic development committees and sector working parties at industry level.

Never before had they been in a position to press their demands so vigorously and with such impunity. Never before could they claim to be in a position to make or even break governments – as, in effect, they did with the Heath administration in 1974.

Powerful they certainly were. But even from their own point of view, it was a power that could be exercised only too little or too much to achieve their ends.

For unions have operated historically mainly at the level of the *industry*. There they have sought across-the-board agreements with federations of employers, to establish basic rates of pay and conditions. In the postwar period, this has been supplemented increasingly by the more informal bargaining by shop stewards at the level of the *workplace*.

But the truth is that neither the industry nor the workplace are the levels at which major decisions are made that affect workers' long-term interests. Questions of investment, location and the general allocation of resources are all mainly determined at the level of the *company* and the *state*. At neither have British unions been effectively organized, coordinated and active. Thus the exercise of their power has frequently resulted in maximum public irritation and inconvenience with minimum real effect.

Sectionalism   At the heart of the problem lies a basic characteristic of British trade union organization and behaviour – its sectionalism. That is to say, unions in the UK are there essentially to serve the interests of relatively narrow groups. There are a very much larger number of trade unions in this country than in most others. In each of them, it is the officials' job to defend and pursue their own members' interests in the way that they negotiate pay, conditions and working practices and the way they handle the consequences for their members of industrial, organizational and technological change. That is what they are paid to do – to look after their own, in just the same way that the concern of a private enterprise company is with the level and security of its profits rather than the success of industry in general or the national interest however defined.

But the rationality of trade union behaviour (and the same could be said of companies) is therefore very narrowly conceived:

● it can put a union in a position where its defence or furtherance of its own members' interests may be at the expense of the pay or jobs of other trade unionists – or even potential new members of its own;

● it can lead to an emphasis on short-term priorities of raising money wages and defending jobs when what really matters, it might be argued, is the value of *real* take-home pay and the 'social wage', and the development of more secure, competitive, lasting employment with modern production techniques and the latest technology.

These features of British trade unions can be largely explained by their essentially defensive outlook. It is the fact that the interests of labour are little represented in the key areas of industrial, economic and technological decision-making that leaves them primarily dealing with problems to which they can merely *react*.

This is not the situation everywhere. As we saw in Chapter 9, and similar illustrations can be found in other countries, the power of organized labour can be democratically and constructively channelled into political and economic decision-making, with positive benefits to the economy. In Austria there is the close collaboration of the Chamber of Labour in the Social Partnership. In Sweden, an active government manpower policy, including provisions for re-training, relocation of workers and generous welfare benefits, means that unions do not feel the need to resist change and defend existing jobs and working practices to the same extent as they do here.

In Britain, perhaps the two most obvious attempts at harnessing sectional interests to achieve wider goals have been:
● the National Economic Development Council;
● the so-called 'Social Contract' in the second half of the seventies.

Neddy

The NEDC (more popularly known as 'Neddy') was set up in 1962 as part of the attempt at the time to introduce 'indicative planning' along the lines that it was thought were being followed successfully in France. The essence of indicative planning is that by bringing together the various parties involved and forcing them to face common problems together, obstacles to faster growth could be more easily identified and removed – without recourse to the imposition of controls from above. Neddy thus consists of the Chancellor of the Exchequer as chairman and a membership made up of representatives from industry and the trade unions; over the years they have discussed a wide range of problem areas, often in a useful and constructive spirit. They have been supported by a full-time secretariat and some thirty 'little Neddies', or joint working parties dealing with specific industries or sectors of the economy.

Many valuable reports have been produced, and until recently, Neddy has continued to be one of the few institutional links between government, industry and the trade unions. But unlike the Austrian case, it has never been more than a talking shop. It has never had executive powers of its own; its deliberations can influence the moulding of government policy but, equally, they can be ignored at will.

The Social Contract

The Social Contract, on the other hand, offered a clear commitment by government to introduce sympathetic labour legislation, more involvement for unions in industrial planning and broad measures to redistribute income and wealth in return for trade union cooperation in the implementation of a continued prices and incomes policy. Remarkably successful to begin with, it ultimately foundered in the 1978–9 'winter of discontent'. The reasons for the failure of this ambitious initiative are complex, but among those relevant for our present purpose are:

● it was an agreement between government and organized labour rather than a truly consensual (or even tripartite) approach;
● partly as a result of this, government in the event was unprepared or unwilling to introduce the decidedly radical changes that it had offered as its part of the bargain.

Moreover, there was an unfortunate deterioration in the economic circumstances in which the Social Contract was to be administered. The post-oil recession coupled with mounting inflation and balance of payments difficulties caused government to react by deflationary cuts in public spending, partly because of pressure from the IMF and partly as a result of the growing influence of monetarist economic thinking.

Free collective bargaining?

The Social Contract was the last in the line of attempts to resolve the basic dilemma posed in the concept of 'free collective bargaining'. Trade union supporters of such freedom argue against incomes policy on two broad grounds. First, that an essentially unplanned economy is a jungle in which they are entitled to pursue self-interest along with everyone else; and second that restraint on pay rises for UK Ford car workers, for example, would do nothing to help nurses or other low-paid workers – but simply lead to more profit for Detroit. On the other hand, advocates of incomes policy claim that free collective bargaining benefits those with the greatest industrial muscle to the detriment of the others – the gains are limited, as one trade union leader put it, 'to the biggest snouts at the trough'.

New realism

Such niceties have no place in the 'new realism' that governments in the eighties have tried to create in the field of industrial relations. Legal limitations have been introduced aimed at curbing the power of the unions – particularly in regard to secondary picketing and the closed shop. Full employment, in which union membership and bargaining strength are likely to be maximized, have given way to mass unemployment. And at the same time, as we shall see in Chapter 19, there has been a powerful re-assertion of the 'right to manage' without detailed involvement of trade unions in decision-making.

It is far from clear, in the first place, that this new approach is *working*. Non-monetarists, as we have seen, dispute the basic contention that unemployment is caused by too high wages. Unemployment has anyway not prevented the income of those in work from rising faster than the current rate of inflation. And if the number of industrial disputes has diminished, their severity has increased and inevitably widened into attacks on a basic economic policy that is seen as fundamentally hostile to workers' interests.

And, secondly, it is not an obviously *desirable* solution to the problems of deeply entrenched 'them' and 'us' attitudes that so deeply beset postwar Britain. Many see it as an attempt to re-impose an old and socially divisive order rather than face up to the need for compromise and cooperation within a freshly worked out framework of institutions and aims.

REDUCING UNION POWER

In sharp contrast to the sympathetic employment legislation of the Social Contract in the mid-seventies, the government after 1979 set out on its path to 'bring the unions within the law' again. The key Acts were the Employment Acts of 1980 and 1982 and the Trades Union Act of 1984.

The legislation, amongst other things,

● curtails employee rights under previous legislation relating to, for example, unfair dismissal and maternity leave;

● limits rights to a 'closed shop' (whereby workers are effectively obliged to be union members as a condition of employment);

● limits rights to picketing and industrial action, especially 'sympathetic' or 'solidarity' support for other workers, and for 'political' as opposed to 'industrial' objectives;

● narrows the definition of a trade dispute to provide greater opportunities for employers to sue for damages resulting from industrial action;

● requires postal ballot elections for union executive elections, for closed shops, for strike action and for the 'political levy' (i.e. trade union donations to the Labour party).

Rights to trade union membership have subsequently been withdrawn from government employees at GCHQ Cheltenham, and suggestions have been made that key public service workers should not have the right to strike.

Sooner or later we may expect a new attempt to be made at formulating a joint policy on employment, incomes and prices. The likely impact of new technology coupled with renewed wage pressure in the event of any economic recovery will make the mechanism of a prices and incomes policy (or whatever else it might be labelled in the future) more *necessary* than ever before if an ever-widening gap between the haves and have-nots is to be avoided. It is just possible, having seen the alternative, that trade unions will be more *receptive* to the idea than ever before. And that on the basis of consensus and public support, within an expansionary context, it might even work.

18

Are You Happy in Your Work?

'I don't care one way or the other about job satisfaction as long as the money is good.'

'You spend a big part of your life at work so it ought to be satisfying.'

'Factory work will always be boring and repetitive – that's the only way to make it efficient.'

'The best way to give workers more satisfaction would be to reduce the length of the working week.'

These days whether you worry about the quality of working life will first of all depend on whether you have a secure job, a decent rate of pay and civilized hours of work. Such questions must appear a luxury to the millions on the dole. (There is after all a certain irony that Herzberg, the American advocate of job enrichment, should be paid several hundred dollars for an after-dinner speech about how money is no longer a prime incentive for working efficiency!)

But in an economy in which employment opportunities appear to be becoming scarcer, and in which technological change is leading to new working practices and relationships between workers and machinery, the quality of working life takes on a new significance.

This chapter considers the pressures likely to reduce job satisfaction, the arguments for giving the quality of working life a higher priority, and the overall relationships between work, income and leisure. What is the future of work? Do we live to work or work to live?

'Next to war, unemployment has been the most widespread, most insidious, and most corroding malady of our generation: it is the specific social disease of western civilization of our time.' That was the view expressed by *The Times* way back in 1943.

The conquest of unemployment during the next thirty years seemed, once and for all, to have removed the insecurity that had previously blighted so many millions of lives. An important freedom had been achieved – freedom from the fear of being thrown on to a human scrap heap.

In those circumstances, there was increased questioning of whether full employment should really be regarded as an *end* in itself. Given that the right to work had been established, should we not be more concerned with *how* people spent their working lives, with the nature of the work they had to do?

The past few centuries have seen vast increases in our level of material affluence. This has resulted from the process of economic growth – the ability to generate year after year ever higher output of goods and services. And at the very heart of economic growth is the increased application of a principle first laid down by Adam Smith, the *division of labour*.

Specialization

In modern language all this means is specialization – which, over the years, has been pushed to a more and more sophisticated degree. To begin with it was by product. Instead of everyone trying to produce all their own requirements, they instead concentrated on producing particular goods or services, and then exchanged their surpluses. Thus the cobbler, the baker, the candlestick maker produced not only for their own needs but for the rest of the community as well. Subsequently, jobs have become infinitely more subdivided into specialist processes, to the point where today most people spend their time at work engaged in only a tiny part of the business of production. In some cases, indeed, they may not even know what the final product is.

Gains from specialization

There are two main economic gains to be derived from specialization:
● workers become more efficient by repeating the same task time after time;
● once production is broken down into a series of simple stages, it opens up the possibility of mechanizing them.

However, as Adam Smith himself observed, 'the division of labour is limited by the extent of the market'. The cobbler, performing all the processes in shoemaking himself, was appropriate for the village market. But when using complex machinery, the output per worker is enormously increased. The cost of making a pair of shoes will be greatly reduced as huge quantities are produced – but that in turn depends on a large number being sold. In many industries, therefore, it is only the largest firms which have been able to push the division of labour to the point at which the maximum reduction in unit costs can be achieved.

As consumers, we have benefited from enormous increases in the standard of living. But as workers, specialization to such a degree has had two major drawbacks:

• a process of 'de-skilling', so that a great deal of work has been reduced to monotonously repetitive tasks that require little other than manual dexterity;
• the concentration of many workers into very large enterprises for which it is difficult for them to feel any concern, where they are remote from the making of decisions which affect their working lives, and in which they anyway have no personal stake.

The first of these, although not necessarily the second, is likely to be exacerbated by applications of 'new technology' which will not only further dehumanize manual operations but also extend de-skilling to service occupations and lower levels of management that have hitherto not been so much affected.

It is not really surprising that worker attitudes are frequently characterized by a sense of alienation, a lack of interest or pride in the job to be done and a resentment of management that sometimes boils over into open hostility.

Job
satisfaction

During the period of full employment, these were problems to which increasing attention was being drawn. Ways were discussed in which greater 'job satisfaction', 'enhancement' or 'fulfilment' might be achieved. Strangely, the initiative in such discussions more commonly came from management than the workers themselves. It was management that realized that size and the division of labour had developed to a

---

IF A JOB'S WORTH DOING . . .

It is the Scandinavian countries which have pioneered positive approaches towards the quality of working life. In Norway, for example, the following criteria have been worked out as desirable characteristics for jobs to meet human needs.

Jobs should include or involve:
• skill or knowledge worthy of community respect;
• a contribution to the utility of the product to the consumer;
• a contribution to the setting of standards (quality, quantity, timing, etc.);
• feedback and knowledge of results;
• the opportunity to learn and to go on learning;
• a desirable future;
• an optimum variety of tasks (high and low levels);
• some insight into production as a whole;
• familiarity with auxiliary and preparatory tasks.

You might find it interesting – and revealing – to consider just how many of these characteristics are associated with *your* job.

SECTION 12, THE NORWEGIAN WORKING ENVIRONMENT

The Scandinavian enthusiasm for a positive approach to work organization and job satisfaction is not confined to general exhortations or academic curiosity. The structure of Section 12 of the Norwegian Working Environment Act is a concrete illustration of a practical approach, from which we in the UK seem to be light-years away:

THE STRUCTURE OF SECTION 12 OF THE NORWEGIAN WORKING ENVIRONMENT ACT

What the section is about
Production methods, work organization,
working hours and payment systems
|
Aims
Avoid harmful effects on employees, make jobs as satisfying
and rewarding as possible
|
Key issues
Skills and freedom or self-determination for
all members of the workforce
|
Practical implications

Avoiding:	**Promoting:**
work paced by machinery or assembly lines whose speed the operator cannot control	variety
	social contact
monotonous, repetitive work	a meaningful relationship between tasks constituting a job
planning or control systems into which employees lack insight and in which they have no voice	insight into planning and control systems plus a voice in their design
certain combinations of work situation and payment system (particularly piece rates in dangerous work)	information to employees about production requirements and performance
	steady rates of work
	greater safety consciousness
working hours producing harmful physiological or psychosocial effects	better integration between work and other (e.g. family) roles

Source: Björn Gustavsen, 'A legislative approach to job reform in Norway', *International Labour Review*, Vol. 115, No. 3, May–June 1977.

point at which efficiency was being jeopardized rather than further increased.

The much-quoted experiments of the Swedish car firms, Volvo and Saab, were early signposts to other enterprises of possibilities in re-humanizing the workplace. The car industry was one in which, from the time of the early Ford T, had been based the 'economies of large-scale production' with assembly-line operations exploiting the division of labour as fully as possible. By the sixties, however, the 'dis-economies' involved were becoming increasingly apparent.

Volvo, in particular, was suffering acute problems with its labour force. Absenteeism was rife and labour turnover extraordinarily high. Indeed in Sweden (and many other European countries) it was becoming difficult to persuade indigenous workers to accept the conditions of the car industry at all – and the workforce was increasingly made up of 'guestworkers' imported from poorer nations.

In an attempt to solve these problems, Volvo accordingly built a new car plant at Kalmar which was based on quite different principles of operation:

● the workforce was split into groups of between fifteen and twenty-five;

● the work performed by each group represented an identifiable production stage, e.g. the installation of the electrical system;

● the division of the work between members of each working group was a matter that they decided between themselves;

● instead of the traditional assembly line, components were shunted by trolley into the groups' working bays as required.

The Kalmar plant was some 10 per cent more expensive to establish than a traditional factory. But by and large this, and the similar reorganization of work introduced by Saab, have proved successful and paid off.

Others have subsequently followed their example. In Britain, there exists in the Department of Employment a Work Research Unit which offers a consultative and advisory function for firms that recognize that 'The maximum return on . . . investment will not be realized unless the work system is designed *as a whole*. This means getting the *human aspects* of the system right – as well as the *technology*.' Clients using the Unit's services include Carreras Rothmans Ltd, Courage Breweries and the National Westminster Bank.

The impact of unemploy-ment   But will these small beginnings continue to be built upon with the return of mass unemployment, a situation in which there are millions who would be thankful for jobs of any kind, almost regardless of the quality of work involved? Or should perhaps the unemployment of today instead be seen as a move towards a new era, an age of leisure in which the application of new technology will finally release men and women from relentless drudgery? A liberation from tedious, dirty, dangerous, often meaningless toil, with sons and daughters no longer

FORCED TO BE FREE?

Amongst the many visits to Volvo was one organized for the United States Union of Automative Workers (UAW), which includes many women amongst its assembly-line workers. Far from being impressed with the group-production system, the visitors were horrified. They did not like the idea of spending time at work *thinking* about work. They preferred to think on the mindless assembly line about what they would be doing *after* work: who they would be going out with, where to, what clothes and make-up they would wear, etc.!

Moral: that *imposed* improvements in work organization, defined and implemented without consulting the workers themselves, do not necessarily represent an improvement. As Björn Gustavsen, Norwegian expert, has argued:

. . . Few working-environment problems – whatever their nature – will be solved unless the employees solve them themselves or at least take an active part in the solution process. Even technical issues concerning the working environment cannot easily be settled by experts themselves . . .

. . . Take job rotation: this can be a disagreeable burden for employees if it is forced upon them from above and organized in every detail by the foreman, for example. It is something very different if carried out on the basis of agreement between the workers concerned because they want to broaden their experience.

Björn Gustavsen, 'A legislative approach to job reform in Norway', *International Labour Review*, Vol. 115, No. 3, May–June, 1977.

having to follow their fathers and mothers into the mines and mills of an earlier industrial phase?

Certainly it is easy to find people who claim that redundancy was the best thing that ever happened to them and who now happily pursue their pigeon-fancying or gardening or whatever was their main interest into which their 'work' used to be an unwelcome intrusion. Millions fantasize every week about what they will tell the boss to do with his job when they finally win the pools. And many of the 'idle rich' have been without work for generations now – and have apparently thrived upon it.

However, it is one thing to opt out of paid work deliberately and quite another to be thrown involuntarily on to the dole because of a lack of job opportunities. Looking at the human implications of our current unemployment enables us to understand the present role of work in people's lives and the possible ways in which future advances in technology *could* enable that role to be redefined to the benefit of the great majority.

ALL THAT GLISTERS IS NOT GOLD

Bill Sirs, General Secretary of the Iron and Steel Trades Confederation (ISTC), Britain's major steel union, said that he wished he could have steelworkers who had accepted redundancy in the past with him when seeking to organize local resistance to closure plans: 'Only they can get across the real feelings of regret as the redundancy payments wither away.'

The myths of high redundancy payments and the benefits they bestow are qualified by such points as the following:

● The *average* redundancy payment at the beginning of 1981 was just over £1,000 from the state scheme, which might be doubled to just over £2,000 by company payments.

● The major uses made of redundancy payments according to detailed research of one closure was 46 per cent on 'nothing special'; 21 per cent on a purchase of or down-payment on durable consumer goods (TV, car, furniture, etc.); and 12 per cent 'not known'.

● Redundancy pay allows people to maintain their standard of living somewhere around its previous level only for a limited period, before the big crash comes. This may be after a couple of years or within only months, according to the size of the redundancy payment.

Source: 'Redundancy Pay: All That Glisters is Not Gold' (Discussion Paper no. 25), Trade Union Research Unit, May 1981.

Human costs of unemployment Status

For most people, unemployment represents:
● loss of social status;
● loss of activity;
● loss of social and political contact;
● loss of income.

For the bulk of those who have had jobs and lost them, there is a sense of failure and rejection. For the increasing number of young who have never had employment, this is compounded by frustration at the irrelevance of education and training for work that has failed to materialize. The loss of dignity in both cases is compounded by the attitudes of those lucky enough to have kept their jobs. Far from envying the unemployed as the vanguard of the newly liberated, or being grateful to them for taking the 'necessary medicine' that the economy has had to swallow, they more commonly castigate them with the stigma of scrounging dependence.

Activity　　There is no doubt that most of those made redundant or compulsorily retired feel lost without work. This may be surprising, given the extent to which those in jobs bemoan the nature of what they have to do. But it seems that most work is none the less preferred to no work. That is partly because unemployment generally means the loss of a structured occupation. Thus going back for a moment to the 'idle rich' or the 'happy redundant' it is generally the case that both lead active and structured lives. These may centre round their personal interests – whether they be the social round, hunting, fishing and shooting, cultivating an allotment or breeding budgerigars. Or time may be spent in more community oriented activities like sitting on committees, working with voluntary agencies or public service of one kind or another. The point is that it may not be *work* that is necessary for most people, but structured *activity*.

Social and political contact　　Part of that structure has traditionally come to be provided by the workplace itself. It offers a framework of friendships and enmities, relationships and problems, to which we have become accustomed and which we miss when it is removed. And the workplace is also the focus of much political activity. The unemployed consequently find themselves to that degree depoliticized, voiceless and unorganized.

Work and income　　But of course the main reason why people seek work is as a source of *income*, and the main deprivation that results from unemployment is usually a dramatic fall in income compared with those in work. We work partly in order to earn the wherewithal to enjoy not working – for leisure has come to mean spending money on the variety of goods and services offered by the rapidly growing 'leisure industry'. For most people, therefore, enforced idleness through unemployment is cruelly meaningless since it provides the opportunity to enjoy leisure while removing the means to do so.

The human implications of mass unemployment are profoundly disturbing. On moral as well as economic grounds, it is difficult to avoid the conclusion that a return to full employment must be re-asserted as a prime objective of policy.

Whether it can be achieved is, as we saw in Chapter 10, a matter for debate. If it does prove possible, then attention is bound to be refocused on those questions we looked at earlier – of how the nature of work can be changed to enhance the quality of people's working lives and contribute towards rather than stifle their potential for self-fulfilment. These questions will be asked in particular by the present generation of young recruits to the labour force for whom the traditional work ethos has already been weakened by the failure of society so far to offer them abundant work opportunities. For many of them, the doubts have been sown about whether regimented drudgery is any longer acceptable.

New technology　　And what if the alternative proves to be the case, that the application of new technology represents a permanent reduction in the demand for labour? If that means that the same or even increasing quantities of output can be produced with less human effort, then it offers a potentially very exciting prospect for extending an important area of economic choice – the way in which an individual divides his or her time between work, activity and leisure.

Freedom of worker choice

At the moment that choice is open only to those with a private income or who work in a handful of privileged professions. But in principle it should be possible, within certain limits, for everyone to decide for themselves about matters like:

● how many hours a day, days a week and weeks a year they work;
● the time of the day or the night that they work;
● the distribution and length of their working lives;
● the division of their time between what is now conventionally wage or salaried work, unpaid activity and straightforward leisure.

FREE TIME

In Germany . . . 20 per cent of all employees freely choose the hours at which they begin and end work. It's a matter of organization and self-organization. In the Beck stores in Munich, employing 700 people, everyone is able to choose the monthly amount of work that suits them best. Their choices are reviewed each month at staff meetings, where employees monitor the situation and allocate days on by reconciling the needs of the job with each individual's preference.

André Gorz, *Farewell to the Working Class*, Pluto Press, 1980, p. 139.

There could be scope for reduced working hours, flexible scheduling of work, arrangements for sabbatical leave periods and opportunities for education to be taken at any stage of a person's life. All could be possible within limits set by two conditions:

Minimum hours and income

● everyone capable of it being prepared to contribute over their working lives the minimum number of hours needed for the total work requirement of the economy;
● everyone in return being guaranteed a lifetime income set at a level determined by what the productive capacity of the economy makes feasible.

Such notions may seem far-fetched and remote from reality. But it is interesting, first, that they are much discussed by continental and Scandinavian (if not British) economists. And second, that what has just been outlined broadly describes the conditions of service enjoyed by most university lecturers in the UK!

The implications of generally extending such freedom of worker choice are certainly radical. They involve, in effect, a divorce of income from paid work, and a blurring of the distinction itself between work, activity and leisure. Such ideas are of relevance, not in offering a practical blueprint for the overnight transformation of the economic system – but in suggesting lines along which we must begin to think if the more likely outcome of a deeply divided society is to be avoided.

As yet, there is little sign that this is happening and the spectre continues to loom of a workforce split into increasingly de-skilled machine-minders and those denied even that opportunity of earning their living.

19

The Right to Manage?

Have you ever felt that you could run your place of work at least as well – if not better – than your boss does? In what ways would you try to run things differently? And why?

In practice there has been a distinct change in the style of British management in recent years, exemplified by Sir Michael Edwardes at BL and Ian MacGregor at BSC and NCB. Trade union representatives continually report that managers are getting away with all sorts of things which they wouldn't have dared to try on a decade ago.

● *Is it a good thing that managers are re-asserting their right to manage? And will the economy benefit?*

● *Or is it a temporary phenomenon, against the background of high unemployment and a legislative attack upon trade unions, which has little to do with improving the performance and competitiveness of British industry?*

Your answers to these questions will be influenced by how you see the nature of the right to manage. Does it derive from ownership; hierarchy and authority; skills and qualifications; or proven competence and performance? This chapter seeks to explore these different possibilities in order to assess the new managerial style: does it confront or evade the most fundamental questions of relationships at work?

'At the end of the day' (as such statements are now nearly always prefaced) 'management must reserve the right to manage.' The proposition is unexceptionable, even self-evident, if it means that enterprises should be run decisively to ensure the smoothest and most effective achievement of clearly defined goals. And it is a common criticism that this is not what has been happening – that the poor quality of management has been one of the factors inhibiting Britain's economic performance.

But in practice, of course, the proposition generally implies much more than this. It refers to the style and nature of management. It is an assertion of the need for strong management 'from the top'. It rests on the belief that if such management backs its hunches and overrides misgivings that might be expressed by unions or other bodies (including governments), then it will win and retain the allegiance of its workforce by dint of its own self-confidence and successful performance.

PRIORITIES OF MANAGEMENT

From the start everything we did in employee relations was tested against the broad strategy of regaining management control of the business, and many of the management-initiated problems – the factory closures, the implementation of working practices, the discontinuation of models, the modest pay offers – were simply a reflection of agreed plans and policies.

Sir Michael Edwardes, *Back from the Brink*, Collins, 1983.

As a result of this style of negotiations we had the extraordinary situation where the employees had imposed upon them a grade structure, grade rates, an incentive scheme and working practices which took away forty years of trade union advance in industrial democracy . . . My real criticism of the Edwardes era was that he put commercial success above human needs, but surely there has to be a balance? If not, modern industry is turning people into robots, and no one should complain if they revolt.

David Buckle, District Secretary TGWU, reviewing Sir Michael's book, in *New Socialist*, July/August 1983.

Concern for management?

This is in contrast to the postwar tendency to recognize that there are worker as well as shareholder interests within an enterprise and these need to be reconciled within a framework in which government, too, will have its say. The approach of postwar decades has therefore increasingly been – especially with regard to industrial relations – to accommodate these interests through procedures allowing for joint regulation, collective agreement, consultation and compromise. Indeed, as we shall see, the debate has sometimes embraced the notion of genuine power-sharing and the introduction of industrial democracy with widespread involvement in the decision-making process.

The new style

However, all this has given way in recent years in many areas of the economy to a quite different approach. Trade union power has been limited – both by legal constraints and a background of mass unemployment. Government has increasingly withdrawn from the industrial scene and left the stage to managers with an altogether more abrasive style, described, at its crudest, as 'if you grab 'em [employees] hard enough by the scruff of their necks, their hearts and minds will follow'. It is the style that has been adopted in some of our largest public as well as private enterprises – BSC, BL and now the coal industry. Its advocates can find evidence of its success in restoring profitability, the determined pruning of less viable operations, and avoidance of disputes by direct appeals to the workforce and by securing their support through performance rather than tortuous industrial-relations machinery.

Many observers would agree that there have been periods, like for example the seventies, when the balance of industrial power swung to organized labour, which exercised it in a narrowly sectional way often damaging to our economic performance. But two questions need to be considered before concluding that the swing back to tougher management has been justified by results:

● How long can the new style of management survive? So far it has been applied in conditions of recession, with high and rising unemployment, lower order books and more intensive competition than was previously the case. Whether it would work in an economic upturn, with the tactical advantages between capital and labour being more evenly distributed, is debatable.

● From an economic point of view, is this the approach that is likely to lead to the most efficient use of resources, or are important potential gains being forgone in a reversion to a clear-cut 'them' and 'us' division of responsibility?

More generally, these resolve themselves into the issue of whether the only alternatives are these adversarial extremes, in which unions abuse any conciliatory moves by management, or where management determines to keep workers firmly in their place. Is there really not a third possibility of genuine participation in the management process? What in fact do we mean by management anyway?

Hierarchical v. functional

● Management can simply be defined as *control* of an enterprise, of its objectives and operations, and monitoring of its progress. This essentially implies a *hierarchical* approach requiring a structure of authority through which control is to be exercised.

● Management can also be defined in terms of the organization of the production and marketing of the goods and services which form the enterprise's activity. This is a *functional* description of a process, which does not necessarily mean that it must be vested in a few specially appointed individuals. Rather its exercise is more obviously related to knowledge of particular situations and problems, abilities and attributes, and this may be spread widely amongst all those who constitute the workforce of the enterprise.

These are sharply contrasting views of the nature of management. The first points to the responsibility of specialist 'managers' to perform their role unilaterally as senior individual employees. The latter calls for the maximum involvement and participation of all employees – or their representatives – as a prerequisite for achieving maximum managerial efficiency.

*Manage-
ment by
involvement*

An interesting example of the second approach occurred when a UK firm was commissioning a new production assembly line from a US manufacturer. Instead of the company's technical department simply ordering the machine on the basis of its own specifications, a working party was set up consisting of production workers, maintenance craftsmen and supervisors on the existing line. Over a period of six months this working party came up with some 200 proposals for amendments, additions and improvements which were readily incorporated into the final order which went to the US supplier. This was therefore a highly productive diffusion of the management process. How many times might this example be multiplied across the British economy and with what consequences for the efficiency and quality of management?

It must be emphasized that proposals aimed at tapping latent managerial talent *throughout* an enterprise rather than relying on the selection of a hierarchical management body are not inherently 'left-wing' or even radical except in British terms. Examples abound elsewhere of a recognition of the need to break down the 'them' and 'us' distinction between

HOW CAN WE MANAGE?

Alternative management styles, which might be characterized as 'authoritarian' and 'participatory', were identified, derived and developed from presentations made at a Work Research Unit Conference in 1981. Together with the trade union responses likely to be elicited, they are reproduced below.

'AUTHORITARIAN'	'PARTICIPATORY'
● Management's sources of power are its prerogative and status	● A manager's authority is earned through competence
which requires	*entailing*
● autocratic management with many layers of authority	● flat organization charts and a participative style
because	*so that*
● the organization's objectives are paramount	● members' and society's goals count
and	*and*
● financial management is more important than human-resource management because without profits there is no enterprise.	● both financial performance *and* human-asset management can be measured and both contribute to the survival of the enterprise.

UNIONS	UNIONS
● A union's job is to improve the terms and conditions of employment of its members	● The union's job is not only to improve the terms and conditions of workers in real terms but to enhance the quality of working life in every respect
thus	*and*
● the 'adversarial' stance is the only suitable one for a union.	● it is appropriate for unions to encourage and take part in participation at many levels on many subjects as well as to bargain.
ATTITUDES AND BEHAVIOUR WHICH LEAD TO:	ATTITUDES AND BEHAVIOUR WHICH LEAD TO:
● organization, competitiveness and gamesmanship	● cooperative collaboration
with	*towards*
● alienation and combat.	● commitment and effectiveness.

Source: *Annual Report of the Tripartite Steering Group on Job Satisfaction to the Secretary of State for Employment*, 1981.

manager and worker in ways which are not only compatible with, but positively contribute towards, economic success.

Views elsewhere

● Countries such as Austria (as we saw in Chapter 9) and Sweden have provided for much greater institutional involvement of trade unions in their industrial, economic and political decision-making.

● In countries like Germany and Holland, there is wide provision for workers' representatives both on company boards and on works councils (the latter flourish in Belgium, France and Italy too).

● Japan encourages worker involvement in management, less through trade unions than through a strong sense of company identity and commitment, including regular discussion groups or 'quality circles' related to various parts of the productive process.

● The European Commission, hardly a part of the revolutionary vanguard, has this to say about the need for wider participation:

Employees are increasingly seen to have interests in the functioning of enterprises which can be as substantial as those of shareholders, and sometimes

FROM THE PEOPLE WHO BROUGHT YOU LOST MARKETS

Japanese working practices are often held up to ridicule in the UK; singing the company song is difficult to imagine as a way to start the working day at BL! Although there are distasteful aspects of the Japanese ruthlessness in industrial organization (textile workers needing to wear roller skates to operate their machinery effectively is an extreme example), there are many aspects of their approach which merit more sympathetic attention.

Amongst these observed at Toshiba in Plymouth are
- the drawing up and discussion of daily production schedules;
- the announcement of the day's visitors to assembled employees;
- the replacement of such status facilities of managers as personal secretaries and private offices with a secretarial pool and open-plan office accommodation;
- the introduction of a single, common dining-room;
- the opportunity of self-management through open discussion of company policy with employee representatives, including shop stewards.

more so. Employees not only derive their income from enterprises which employ them, but they devote a large proportion of their daily lives to the enterprise. Decisions taken by or in the enterprise can have a substantial effect on their economic circumstances, both immediately and in the longer term: the satisfaction which they derive from work; their health and physical condition; the time and energy which they can devote to their families and to activities other than work; and even their sense of dignity and autonomy as human beings. Accordingly, continuing consideration is being given to the problem of how and to what extent employees should be able to influence the decision of enterprises which employ them.

The enterprise . . . cannot escape this reorganization of the relationships between those who have the power to make decisions and those who must carry them out.*

Scope for improvement   This is not the thinking of Britain in the eighties. And yet the *need* for new directions in our approach to management would seem to be amply borne out by the evidence of past experience. For example, the fact that

* European Commission 5th Directive Green Paper, *Employee Participation and Company Structure*, Supplement 8/75, Brussels, 1975.

Britain's share of world trade slips most sharply when world trade is expanding *fastest* suggests that we have been making the wrong products for the wrong markets – essentially wrong management decisions. Then again, studies show that British subsidiaries abroad tend to perform worse than their local counterparts while subsidiaries of foreign companies in this country out-perform home producers.

Is it that British management, like so many other aspects of our society, remains essentially class-based? Certainly, foreign observers often express surprise at the extent to which British senior managers and directors owe their position less to technical or professional qualifications than to family connections. And the cult of the gifted amateur may still play its part. Although we put as high a proportion of our population through university education as do the Germans, we fall way behind in comparisons of technical education and training. It is perhaps no coincidence that an engineer is addressed formally in social terms in Germany, like a doctor or professor, but in the UK enjoys a lower status than, for example, an accountant.

On the other hand, Britain now leads the European league for spending on management education and training through its business schools and other institutions and courses. Are we teaching the wrong things, or not getting them across, or teaching the wrong people in the first place – or merely suffering a time-lag while the new breed of managers achieve positions of higher responsibility? (It has been found, for example, that senior personnel managers from one generation without formal training or qualifications are reluctant to appoint professionally qualified personnel managers below them from a subsequent generation.)

On the whole, there has been remarkably little interest shown in the UK in the possible gains from greater worker involvement. Resistance has been expressed, not only from employer bodies but also from trade unions, which are wedded to the principle of collective bargaining and which see greater participation as a possible blurring of the traditional battle lines. But during the 1970s, partly in response to EEC initiatives (the European Commission's Fifth Directive called for worker representatives on the boards of all companies above a certain size), the British government did set up a committee of enquiry to investigate the possible scope and the problems involved.

The case for industrial democracy

The final paragraph of the official Bullock Report on Industrial Democracy published in 1977 makes an interesting comparison with political democracy which gives pause for thought.

. . . just as in the nineteenth century the shifts to the middle and working classes made it essential to harness that power to the benefit of society, by extending the suffrage, now is the time to provide scope for the growing power and unused capacities of organized labour, by giving them representation on the boards of large enterprises.

The fears expressed in the nineteenth century in face of proposals to give more people the right to vote did not stop short of the subversion of the constitution and the dissolution of society. Once the franchise was extended, however, the fears were forgotten and the Reform Acts were seen as essential to the country's stability and prosperity. We believe that over a hundred years later an extension of industrial democracy can produce comparable benefits and that our descendants will look back with as much surprise to the controversy which surrounded it as we do to that which surrounded the extension of the political suffrage in the nineteenth century.*

X-efficiency

When economists make comparisons of the economic performance of enterprises in different countries, or of differences in the overall rates of economic growth, they naturally concentrate in the first place on factors like the size of plant, the amount of capital equipment per worker and the level of demand. When they have performed their statistical manipulations in sorting out the relative significance of these and other more or less 'quantifiable' considerations, they are always left with a substantial 'residual' – an element which is clearly important in explaining why one company or country is more efficient than another, but which can't be accounted for. This has been dubbed 'X-efficiency' and by definition we do not know what it consists of. We can therefore only speculate about how far the extent to which worker involvement in the management process has been achieved in other countries has contributed to their relatively greater success. It may, as the Bullock Report suggests, be considerable – and if so, it is a bonus that Britain, with its divisive industrial society, can ill afford to forgo.

* *Report on Industrial Democracy* (Cmnd 6706), HMSO, 1977.

20

Whose Economy is it Anyway?

*If wealth were to be evenly distributed by an Act of Parliament,
how many generations – or even just years – do you think it would
take for today's actual concentrations to re-assert themselves?*

*Your answer will no doubt reflect your attitude towards wealth
and ownership of assets:*

● *They represent fair rewards for initiative, entrepreneurship and
successful enterprise: without wealth we'd have far fewer jobs.*

● *They represent historical and arbitrary patterns of fortune,
quite unassociated with any specific economic contribution from
wealth-holders: if anything, they are a drain on the economy.*

*Whether unequal distribution of wealth attracts attention on the
basis of 'the politics of envy' is probably far less important than the
role of ownership in economic terms. This chapter considers the
strains placed upon the economy by such concentrations of
wealth, and assesses the merits of alternative approaches to ownership. Is it necessarily the case that 'those with the money know
best how to look after money'?*

As a possible candidate for inclusion in the *Guinness Book of Records*,
'freedom' must rank high as the concept about which the most millions
of words have been written and spoken. To this we have added our own
modest contribution, examining in earlier chapters the current emphasis
in economic policy on enhancing the freedom of consumer choice in a
freer market economy. There, we suggested that there was a danger that
such apparent increases in freedom might prove to be illusory – or very
unequally divided in our highly imperfect 'economic democracy'.

In the last two chapters we have argued that other aspects of economic
freedom are equally deserving of attention – freedom from unemployment, freedom to have a say about the quality as well as the quantity of
the work that we do, freedom to be involved in the making of economic
decisions that have profound effects on so much of our lives. These are
important matters, not only for grandiose reasons of achieving greater
human fulfilment, but simply as ways of making the economy work – of

getting to the heart of why it hasn't and why it won't function as we would like it to.

So why are these not burning issues of everyday debate? Why could the industrial-relations director of one of our major car manufacturers admit a few years ago that the company had no plans for increasing job satisfaction 'Because the lads don't care; they just want more money'? Why is there no groundswell of demands for more participation in decisions at the workplace and in the enterprise? Could it be that most people are just not concerned?

Workers and profits

The truth may be, as the Czech economist Dr Ota Sik put it (in *The Times*, 4 October 1972): 'Wage earners are interested only in increasing their wages. They have no direct interest in capital, the use of profits or decisions on investments.' And this may be as true in those communist countries where capital has been taken over by the state as in the industrial economies of the West. It certainly seems to hold good as much in our own nationalized industries as it does in the private sector.

But, of course, wage earners have a considerable *indirect* interest in profits. They are there to be wrangled over, as a sign of a company's ability to pay higher wages. Companies do their best to conceal or present them in as modest a fashion as possible, so that they can provide a good return for their shareholders and a source of funds for future investment. And unions strive to whittle down this 'capitalist income' and transfer as much of it as possible into the pockets of their members. The balance of power shifts between the two from time to time, but the battleground remains the same.

Why can't workers see that they have a more direct interest in the earnings on capital, since it provides the means for financing the new plant and equipment which is the basis of workers' future jobs and living standards? The answer is that within an individual enterprise the link is a tenuous one if it exists at all.

● The enterprise *may* plough back part of its profits in investment that clearly benefits its present or future workers.

● It may invest part of its profits overseas or in financial assets of one kind or another.

● The profits that it distributes as dividends may be re-invested by shareholders or they may be used for consumption.

The least likely possibility is that workers will themselves be shareholders in their own enterprise and therefore have any say in the way in which profits are deployed. The *ownership*, and even more so the *control* is highly concentrated in very few hands.

Distribution of wealth

We have already, in Chapter 12, described the extent of inequalities of *income*, their often arbitrary nature and the limited degree to which they seem either morally defensible or economically necessary. How-ever, the U K pattern is not markedly different from that found elsewhere.

YUGOSLAVIA

Yugoslavia provides an interesting example of a country whose constitutional, social and economic principles owe allegiance neither to East nor West.

● The constitution is built upon the notion of *social*, as opposed to private or state, ownership.

● Constitutional rights are therefore expressed only through the contribution of labour (which includes not only wages rewarding *current* labour, but a recognition of the role which *past* labour has made in promoting the means of investment and enterprise development).

● Labour is given a prominent role in determining the allocation of economic resources through the process of self-management.

Self-management means, *first*, that workers have an institutional framework (the Workers Council) for making management accountable to them; and, *second*, that workers themselves determine for their enterprise:

● how much is set aside for investment as opposed to wages;

● how much is devoted to *collective* provision (housing, welfare, etc.) as opposed to individual pay;

● what differentials should apply to rates of pay for different jobs.

But not only are inequalities in the ownership of *wealth* in Britain far greater than income differences; they also represent a more unequal distribution than is found in most similar countries.

In round terms, two thirds of all personal wealth is in the hands of the richest 10 per cent of our adult population. Half is owned by the richest 5 per cent, and a quarter is in the hands of the single richest person out of every hundred. Striking though these figures are, they still understate the full extent of wealth disparities in several ways.

● *Within* the richest 1 per cent there is a remarkable *further* concentration, for the richest one tenth of them account for half of the wealth in that category. In other words, 12½ per cent of all personal wealth is owned by the richest person in every thousand.

● Some 30,000 people have personal wealth amounting to 150 times what it would be if personal wealth were evenly distributed.

● Concentration of ownership of land and stocks and shares (giving most economic power and control over resources) is much greater than for other types of assets like houses.

● Although income from wealth (like dividends and rent) is taxable, as

ALL FOR ALL

The Diamond Commission* estimated that in 1973:
- total personal wealth was estimated at £164 billion;
- if equally distributed, this would imply an average holding of about £4,000 per head of the adult population;
- The average value of assets possessed by the richest one thousandth of the adult population (around 30,000 individuals) was £600,000, i.e. 150 times the average.

More recent calculations, for 1980, reinforce these observations:
- average personal wealth of the bottom 50 per cent was £411;
- If total personal wealth were equally distributed, it would provide a figure of £13,705 for all adults.
- Invested at 10 per cent, this would provide an income of more than £25 a week.

*Royal Commission on the Distribution of Income and Wealth (Chairman: Lord Diamond), Report No. 1: *Initial Report on The Standing Reference* (Cmnd 6171), HMSO, 1975.

is its transfer between individuals (capital transfer tax has replaced the old estate duty), the actual ownership of wealth does not incur a tax liability as receipt of income does.

Institutional wealth

It can be argued that these figures for *personal* holdings overstate the unequal distribution of wealth as they leave out the most important and fastest growing form of *institutional* shareholding – pension rights. Thus, in addition to personal assets, most people today have an entitlement to a future income through a pension fund and/or through insurance arrangements. In this way, although the vast majority of people do not themselves own stocks and shares, they benefit from indirect wealth ownership through pension funds, insurance companies and other 'institutional intermediaries', which now account for the bulk of shareholdings.

However, the effect of institutional wealth-holding in modifying the extremes of personal wealth is limited. In the first place, pension rights are often not transferable, nor can insurance policies be cashed in for their full value; they are not 'marketable' like stocks, shares or land actually owned by individuals. Second, they do not confer any *control* over the use of wealth – the pension-fund contributor or insurance-policy holder has virtually no say in how the funds are used. And third, institutional intermediaries may even add to personal wealth disparities

Drawing on a Pension: Distribution of Personal Wealth (1981)

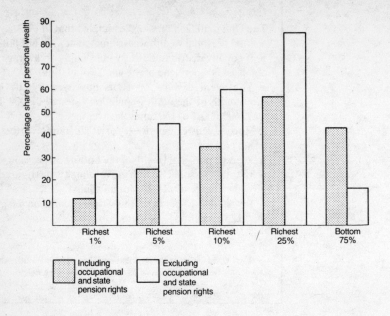

Source: *Social Trends* 14, Central Statistical Office, 1984.

– with, for example, the benefits conferred by 'top-hat' pension schemes being much greater than those enjoyed by the average non-manual employee, who in turn often gets a better deal than the manual worker, and so on, down to the part-time employee for whom no occupational pension provision may be made at all.

Significance of inequality

These, then, are the facts about the highly unequal distribution of wealth in the UK. What is their significance? We can ask whether such a distribution is a *fair* one – whether we find it acceptable within our general framework of moral and social values. And we can consider its technical economic consequences. As usual in economics, the two are very closely interrelated.

Equity

With regard to equity, it is clear that the ownership and control of land and capital, and the consequent returns, are much more concentrated than the third factor of production, labour. And yet the individual worker's stake and commitment in a particular enterprise or industry may be much greater than that of a shareholder, who has far greater freedom to switch from one type of investment to another. But, it may be argued, surely those who have by dint of their own efforts *accumulated* capital are entitled to higher returns as a result? Now certainly there are those who, starting from nothing, make their own fortunes. But the great bulk of personal wealth is transmitted from one generation to another through gift or inheritance. The process soon acquires a cumulative momentum. Wealth yields income, and the rich are thereby enabled to buy privileged education for their offspring and set them up

EXTREME EXAMPLES

The relative 'inefficiency' of collective bargaining on gross pay as the engine of raising living standards is revealed by the diagram.
● Gross pay increases are not matched by increased real net pay, but have to be met by employers, with consequences for inflation and competitiveness internationally.

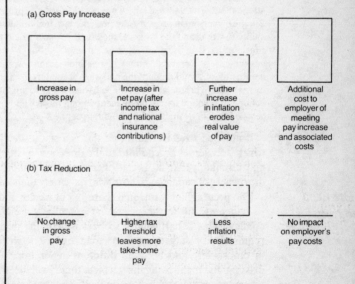

(a) Gross Pay Increase

| Increase in gross pay | Increase in net pay (after income tax and national insurance contributions) | Further increase in inflation erodes real value of pay | Additional cost to employer of meeting pay increase and associated costs |

(b) Tax Reduction

| No change in gross pay | Higher tax threshold leaves more take-home pay | Less inflation results | No impact on employer's pay costs |

● Tax reductions, by contrast, can provide the same or even greater improvements in real living standards without pressure on employers' pay costs, inflation and international competitiveness.

in professional or business enterprises where further wealth can be added to that passed on from the previous generation.

Economic viability

This is a dubious moral foundation on which to rest the case for extreme inequalities in wealth-holding. But can such a system be defended on the economic grounds that at least it works? Well, it certainly did so in the past, but there have been two major changes since the heyday of earlier capitalism:

● Then, as Keynes once put it, it was agreed that capitalists should take a large slice of the national cake, on condition that they did not eat it. The connection between wealth, profits and investment for the future was much clearer than it is today.

● Organized labour has grown powerful enough to question and challenge the way in which national income and wealth are shared out. The challenge has often been ineffectual but has led to economic behaviour that has reduced the efficiency of the system itself (through, for example, inflationary squabbles about the appropriate level of real wages).

Wealth and new technology

The application of new technology in coming decades is likely to accentuate the problem still further – as is vividly illustrated by Professor Meade's nightmare of an extreme scenario:

> Let us suppose that robots can produce everything, including manufacturing and replacing each other, and that they require an absolute minimum of labour to attend them. The wages of labour are transformed into profits earned on robots. But the ownership of property is at present much less equally distributed than the ability to work; and the profits earned on the robots would thus be more highly concentrated than the previous wage earnings. Although output per head might be immensely increased, either competition among workers for the smaller number of jobs would reduce the real wage absolutely to a very low level or else if by trade union or similar action the real wage was held up, there would be a large volume of involuntary unemployment among those who were not privileged to get the few jobs available at the fixed rate of pay.*

It must be stressed again that this is a simplistically extreme model which only serves as a pointer to the direction in which new technology may ultimately take us, i.e. an even more unequal distribution between the owners of capital and those who have only their labour to offer.

The need to transfer resources

The present highly unequal share-out of wealth and the possibility of its widening still further represent potentially great sources of future conflict. This is particularly so because coming decades are likely to require major shifts of resources to take place between different groups in our society and between different generations. The backdrop of existing inequalities against which these will be made makes their achievement that much more difficult. The three main transfers that will be needed are:

* James Meade, 'A new Keynesian approach to full employment', *Lloyds Bank Review*, October 1983, p. 11.

• *From consumption to investment.* Although it will not be sufficient in itself, there is no doubt that a substantial increase in investment will be necessary if the future prosperity of the economy is to be assured. Provided that we have economic growth, this need not involve actual cuts in consumption so much as holding back its rate of increase, to leave sufficient resources available for the restructuring of the economy.

HARSH CHOICES

The Public Expenditure Green Paper of 1984 concluded:

> Public expenditure, in Britain as in other countries, has risen over many years, both in real terms and as a share of national income. It is difficult to escape the conclusion that there is an inbuilt tendency for expenditure to rise; and an inbuilt resistance to expenditure reductions . . .
> . . . on one issue there can be no room for doubt: the government and Parliament must reach their judgement about what can be afforded, then contain individual programmes within that total.

The Next Ten Years: Public Expenditure and Taxation into the 1990s (Cmnd 9198), HMSO, 13 March 1984.

• *From the young to the old.* Demographic factors mean that for many years we shall have to cater for the wholly legitimate needs of a growing proportion of retired people – increasing claims in terms of pensions, health care and other social services. To do so on an adequate scale means that younger generations will have to forgo part of the increased living standards that would otherwise be possible.

• *From worker to worker.* The growth in real income of those benefiting from working with more capital-using technology will similarly have to be held back to provide incomes and activity for the remainder.

A market outcome

From a starting-point of wide inequalities in income and dramatically greater disparities in wealth, and through a mechanism of collective bargaining from which an increasing proportion of the population – the non-active young, unemployed and old – are excluded, it is difficult to envisage an outcome which is not sharply divisive and socially unacceptable.

Two well-tried forms of government intervention may have a further part to play:

Progressive taxation

• Progressive taxation on incomes of the kind to which we have become accustomed over the years until the recent reversal aimed at increased incentives. But, for the immediate future anyway, the problems of redistributive taxation will be made more difficult if the tax base itself declines because of the combined effect of higher unemployment, de-industrialization and the fall off in North Sea oil revenues.

Incomes policy

• Incomes policy – which will be difficult to introduce and implement except within a framework of expansionary policies and will even then encounter the problems of being based on the present inequitable distribution of income and wealth.

Radical alternatives

It is because of the predictable limitations of such methods that many thinkers of quite moderate political persuasion now believe that radical changes must be considered – either as alternatives to older methods or as the necessary preconditions for making them work.

Increasing attention is thus being paid to, for example, the encouragement of wider share ownership through institutions such as pension funds, unit trust and more widespread individual holdings. This indeed has even been incorporated in the current privatization strategy with massive advertising in the case of British Telecom aimed at attracting new small shareholders (with its critics arguing that this dispersion will leave the few *large* shareholders with even greater power). Then again, the size and potential power of pension funds offers a possible vehicle through which worker involvement in the process of capital accumulation and its uses could be greatly enhanced by a substantial extension of employee representation in the management of their own funds. And why should unions in their collective bargaining not, as a price of some restraint on the wage front, negotiate for a slice of any increased profits or for shares to be held in trust for the company's employees?

Another proposal, mooted in Scandinavian countries, is for a 'wage-earners' investment fund' into which each year a proportion of the total wage and/or profit bill would be paid – and used for investment according to commercial criteria modified by appropriate constraints, giving weight, for example, to domestic rather than foreign projects; workers would hold corresponding certificates which would then entitle them to dividends and capital gains associated with orthodox shareholdings. Such a scheme could bring about a very considerable relative redistribution of the ownership of capital within a matter of decades.

And last, but not least, there is the possibility of *absolute* redistribution of wealth – through capital levies, wealth taxes and effective estate duty. What might be particularly important here is that the proceeds should not simply be swallowed up in the general Exchequer to facilitate tax cuts but that annual earnings from the accumulated funds should be distributed throughout the population as a 'social dividend' which is therefore recognizable as each individual's earnings from the national wealth.

This is not the opportunity to discuss the various merits, problems and practicalities of any of these proposals in moving towards what Keynes called 'the accumulation of working-class wealth under working-class control'. But it seems likely that without serious debate on these issues, there will remain among a large section of the working population a deep sense of unfairness and injustice as a result of the extraordinary inequality in the distribution of wealth that exists today. On top of that is the practical consideration – that the sharp divide between capital and labour has lain at the heart of many of our past economic problems and will continue to frustrate attempts at solving our future difficulties. Both the equity and the efficiency aspects of this vitally important issue are summed up by Ota Sik when he writes: 'Only where man has an immediate economic interest in the future development of an enterprise, in investment, in the effectiveness of new capital equipment and so on, will he gradually begin to be master of his own conditions of production' (*The Times*, 4 October 1972).

If that sounds an inappropriately political note on which to conclude, the reader should be aware by now that very seldom is an issue simply 'a question of economics'.

Index

232

234

Discover more about our forthcoming books through Penguin's FREE newspaper...

Penguin
Quarterly

It's packed with:

- exciting features
- author interviews
- previews & reviews
- books from your favourite films & TV series
- exclusive competitions & much, much more...

READ MORE IN PENGUIN

In every corner of the world, on every subject under the sun, Penguin represents quality and variety – the very best in publishing today.

For complete information about books available from Penguin – including Puffins, Penguin Classics and Arkana – and how to order them, write to us at the appropriate address below. Please note that for copyright reasons the selection of books varies from country to country.

In the United Kingdom: Please write to *Dept. JC, Penguin Books Ltd, FREEPOST, West Drayton, Middlesex UB7 OBR*

If you have any difficulty in obtaining a title, please send your order with the correct money, plus ten per cent for postage and packaging, to *PO Box No. 11, West Drayton, Middlesex UB7 OBR*

In the United States: Please write to *Penguin USA Inc., 375 Hudson Street, New York, NY 10014*

In Canada: Please write to *Penguin Books Canada Ltd, 10 Alcorn Avenue, Suite 300, Toronto, Ontario M4V 3B2*

In Australia: Please write to *Penguin Books Australia Ltd, 487 Maroondah Highway, Ringwood, Victoria 3134*

In New Zealand: Please write to *Penguin Books (NZ) Ltd,182–190 Wairau Road, Private Bag, Takapuna, Auckland 9*

In India: Please write to *Penguin Books India Pvt Ltd, 706 Eros Apartments, 56 Nehru Place, New Delhi 110 019*

In the Netherlands: Please write to *Penguin Books Netherlands B.V., Keizersgracht 231 NL–1016 DV Amsterdam*

In Germany: Please write to *Penguin Books Deutschland GmbH, Friedrichstrasse 10–12, W–6000 Frankfurt/Main 1*

In Spain: Please write to *Penguin Books S. A., C. San Bernardo 117–6° E–28015 Madrid*

In Italy: Please write to *Penguin Italia s.r.l., Via Felice Casati 20, I–20124 Milano*

In France: Please write to *Penguin France S. A., 17 rue Lejeune, F–31000 Toulouse*

In Japan: Please write to *Penguin Books Japan, Ishikiribashi Building, 2–5–4, Suido, Tokyo 112*

In Greece: Please write to *Penguin Hellas Ltd, Dimocritou 3, GR–106 71 Athens*

In South Africa: Please write to *Longman Penguin Southern Africa (Pty) Ltd, Private Bag X08, Bertsham 2013*

10 × Economics

You need not be an economist to understand economics.

Peter Donaldson explains in terms that are lucid and easy for all to understand the monetarist policies of the early eighties and some of the possible alternatives that were available. He takes ten topics that dominated Britain's political scene – many of them are still very much on the agenda – and examines their significance, their effects and how they interact. Among them are unemployment, money and inflation, exchange rates, North Sea oil, de-industrialization and public spending. Taken together they trace the developments that have led to the current economics scene and the way forward into the nineties.

Economics of the Real World

Peter Donaldson describes here how a mixed economy is managed and (given the underlying market mechanisms) what can and what cannot be the subject of economic policy. More basically he argues that economics itself is strangely remote from the urgent problems of ordinary people and that policy-makers confuse ends and means. What matters, in his view, is not growth, but growth of what, for whom and at what cost; not full employment, but the nature of work; not just more wealth, but its more equitable distribution.

and

Worlds Apart